RAPID APPLICATION
DEVELOPMENT WITH
VISUAL BASIC 6

CONTENTS

McGraw-Hill

A Division of The McGraw·Hill Companies

1 2 3 4 5 6 7 8 9 0 AGM/AGM 9 0 4 3 2 1 0 9

P/N 135421-2
PART OF 0-07-135422-0

*The sponsoring editor for this book was Regina Brooks, the editing supervisor
was Scott Amerman, and the production supervisor was Clare Stanley. It was
set in Century Schoolbook by Priscilla Beer of McGraw-Hill's desktop composi-
tion unit in cooperation with Spring Point Publishing Services.*

Printed and bound by Quebecor/Martinsburg.

Rapid Application Development with Visual Basic 6

David McMahon

McGraw-Hill

New York   San Francisco   Washington, D.C.   Auckland
Bogotá   Caracas   Lisbon   London   Madrid   Mexico City
Milan   Montreal   New Delhi   San Juan   Singapore   Sydney
Tokyo   Toronto

Contents

Contents

Contents

Contents

Contents

PREFACE

With the introduction of many visual programming tools, rapid application development (RAD) has become the method of choice in the past five years for software development. Since the early 1990s, Visual Basic has been at the forefront of the technology. As Visual Basic has matured, it has become a software development tool that can be used to meet almost any business need. Gone are the days when Basic meant a cheap, second-rate language for people who didn't know how to program. With each new release, Visual Basic becomes a more respectable and powerful tool.

The ease and power that a tool like Visual Basic provides to the developer creates its own set of problems. It is here that we enter the world of RAD. This book attempts to address the issues of software development with Visual Basic, but in a larger context. We will not only see the usual how-to explanations about VB but also look at the product in the larger picture.

In Part 1 of the book, we examine issues involved in the software development life cycle, such as an introduction to the issues that programmers may face when they are working with a visual tool like VB. In Chapter 2, we will take a brief look at the Visual Basic IDE and introduce some of the new features found in version 6.0. In Chapter 3, we will take a look at other issues developers will face in the development life cycle, such as requirements gathering, user documentation, and issues involved in scheduling and team software development.

Part 2 explores designing with VB software. This section begins with an introductory discussion of networks and the three-tiered model of software development in Chapter 4. In Chapter 5, we will explore the Visual Basic language. The reader is assumed to have at least some previous exposure to Visual Basic, so the review will not go into detail on every feature. However, it is hoped that this chapter will provide a ready reference that should cover every aspect of the Basic language we will come across in this book. Also tackled in this chapter are some common mistakes and good programming practices to use with VB. In Chapter 6, we again take a step back to look at the use of VB in the larger context. Examined are such issues as commenting code and setting up language standards. Why are we taking the time to explore such concerns here? Because VB is not used in a vacuum, and any software development usually involves working with others and/or sharing one's source code. This interaction always brings up issues of readability and standards.

In Chapter 7, user interface design is investigated. In this chapter we are not so much interested in how-to issues such as adding a button to a form and putting some code behind it; instead, we will be looking at designing VB screens with the end user in mind. This means developing professional-looking and user-friendly forms.

Chapter 8 is a two-part chapter. We begin by considering object-oriented software design from a theoretical perspective. After the terminology and some abstract examples are introduced, we will explore how to put this type of programming into practice with VB.

Part 3 of the book explores implementation. Chapters 9 and 10 focus on the use of VB for database development, which is how VB got so popular in the first place. For those who haven't had in-depth experience in designing database software, we will explore the basics of database design and plain-file handling with VB. Of course, we will also spend some time examining the new database-handling components and features available in VB 6.0. Chapter 11 investigates the coming together of object-oriented software and database programming.

In Chapter 12 we will look at some of the advanced features of VB, like multithreading and creating ActiveX servers. We will see how to create a dynamic link library and an ActiveX control with concrete examples. The chapter ends with a discussion of ActiveX documents and creating a simple web browser.

Finally, the book closes out in Part 4 with a consideration of the issues involved in reviewing, testing, and distributing software. In Chapter 13, debugging VB projects and error handling are discussed. Included in the discussion is how to create a VB Add-In that will insert error handlers into the forms and modules of a VB project.

Many issues in software development a programmer would rather not explore, such as testing, user documentation, and distribution. But these considerations, covered in Chapters 14 and 15, are as important as the algorithms and forms that are a part of any project, and that is what this book is attempting to address—looking at software development as a whole.

DAVID MCMAHON

PART 1

Development Life Cycle

CHAPTER 1

An Introduction to RAD with Visual Basic

Introduction to Rapid Application Development

In the old days, and it really wasn't that long ago, a program either had no user interface or the developer put great effort into building one. Applications were often just a command-line prompt, where the user entered input data and waited for a response. Programs were not very intuitive, and certainly they were not user friendly.

Developing any kind of significant user interface as recently as a few years ago was nothing less than a major headache. Often doing something as simple as placing a button on a screen could involve long lines of code and hard work just to get the button to appear in the right place. Since there was no visual design environment, you had to compile your project and see where the button appeared. If it didn't look right, that meant opening up the text editor, changing your code, recompiling, and testing the program again to see how everything looked. All this work and you're not even talking about solving a useful problem yet—which is after all what software is supposed to do.

With the advent of the Windows operating system, we have seen nothing short of a revolution in the way applications are developed. Programming tools such as Visual Basic have taken away the work required to build a user interface. By designing the interface visually, in much the same way you would with a "what you see is what you get" word processor or graphics program, user interfaces can be designed quickly and with ease. Long gone are the headaches of the past; now you can place the button exactly where you want it to appear and concentrate on the code behind it. The ability to build an interface visually and use event-driven programming to place code behind objects has allowed the development of software to proceed at a faster pace than ever before. The ability to quickly build an application using a tool such as Visual Basic has become known as *rapid application development*, or RAD.

The Costs versus Benefits of RAD

As with anything in life, this ability to build an application quickly can have its downside. Often the first casualty with RAD is careful planning. In the past, when you had to code up everything and your program followed a neat series of steps from start to finish, coding required hours of careful design on paper before you actually sat down to write your program (in theory at least). With a RAD tool such as Visual Basic, a developer can turn on the computer and rush a program out the door, without paying special attention to those design issues. Just draw a few buttons and controls on a form, and it *looks* like you've got a pretty sophisticated application. In a sense, RAD has made software development too easy, and if there are any problems with RAD they usually stem from this fact. Let's consider some of the weaknesses of RAD:

- Since it's easy to build the user interface, an interface can be designed carelessly and without putting much thought into it. This can result in an unprofessional appearance and make the program a difficult, frustrating experience for the end user.

- The ease with which forms and controls can be put on screen may make it seem like your program is so intuitive that everyone will know how to use it immediately. This can lead to inadequate effort being put into online help and user documentation, again leaving the end user feeling frustrated. Online help and user documentation can also suffer because the RAD tool makes programming seem "fun," so who wants to spend time on boring issues like a help system?

- The wide choice of tools and components can make a programmer go overboard when putting together the user interface, adding too many controls and too many choices for the user.

- The ability to get a program out the door quickly can lead to sloppy coding, which can include avoiding the use of comments and of coding standards. RAD tools tempt the programmer to think he or she can just turn the computer on and whip out a program, which can lead to problems later on.

- RAD tools make it too easy to declare variables. What I mean by this is watch out for global variables. While there are times when you may need them, don't use them unless they are strictly necessary. When you've got a project with, say, 40 forms, tracking down problems associated with a global variable can be a big problem.

- A program can be released without adequate testing. A couple of runs in the design environment and "click here to compile"—and a program full of errors is out the door. Because the user interface is complete and "nice" looking, it may give the programmer the illusion that he has a solid working piece of code.

Before we get too down on RAD and dust off the old C compiler, let's think back to those old Pascal, COBOL, and FORTRAN days in the computer science or MIS lab, when long hours into the early morning were spent slowly stepping through the code. I'm sure no programmer wants to return to the days when building a dialog box was in itself a major project. Let's consider some of the benefits of using a RAD environment:

- RAD promotes good design of a user-friendly interface, as long as careful planning and industry standards are followed.

- RAD allows you to build your user interface quickly and easily so the bulk of your time can be spent using the computer for what it's supposed to do—solve problems.

- Since it's easy to build a user interface, you can give the user all the features that she needs, keeping the customer happy. This will require effective communication with the customer.

- A RAD tool will help you quickly test and debug your projects, leading to more fail-safe code development.

- RAD tools are easy to learn, which allows you to bring colleagues up to speed quickly on a new development environment and keep training costs down.

When you compare the good with the bad—and especially when you think back to the days of designing a user interface for a DOS program or with early versions of Windows—the advantages of RAD are clear.

Avoiding the Pitfalls of RAD

With a bit of careful planning and by avoiding the temptation to "whip out" a program, you can use a RAD tool to build successful, robust applications. But by sticking to a few good rules, you can ensure that RAD will help you deliver user-friendly, solid Windows applications quickly. Here are some suggestions:

- *Stick to effective problem analysis*: Visual Basic can tempt you to simply turn your computer on and draw up a program. You can avoid the problems this can cause by carefully designing your program before ever loading up Visual Basic. This can include determining what forms the project will contain and what data will be going in and out of the application and carefully planning your program logic on paper before you code it up. Taking these steps will save you from a lot of headaches later on.

- *Don't implement applications too quickly*: Again, a RAD tool like Visual Basic can allow the programmer to build an application in a flash, and that usually means that it contains poor logic, lots of global variables, and a poorly thought out user interface. Programmers can avoid these problems by avoiding the temptation to simply load up Visual Basic and start designing forms. Before beginning a new project, put in some time thinking about the project. Ask questions, such as who will use this program? In what way can I make the user interface intuitive? Will my code be readable by another programmer who needs to add a new feature six months from now? Also, spend time thoroughly testing and debugging your code to ensure that it will run smoothly when the user gets a hold of it.

■ Stick to good coding standards: Make sure that your code is readable by other programmers. This includes careful commenting, avoiding the use of too many global or public variables, and using naming standards for objects and variables. This will save you headaches later on. We'll take up the issue of coding standards in some detail in Chapter 6.

Picking the Right Tool for the Job

These days there are several RAD tools on the market. While virtually all Windows development is easier than it used to be, the different tools available range a great deal in power and ease of use. Your choice of development environment will depend on your level of expertise, what you need out of the application, and who the target audience will be. Let's consider a few of these tools.

Visual Basic Now that Visual Basic has a native code compiler and offers the ability to develop ActiveX controls and DLLs, it is a good choice for just about any type of Windows application development. Visual Basic is particularly strong when it comes to file processing and the development of a database front end. Some of the strengths of Visual Basic can be summarized as follows:

■ Visual Basic is probably the easiest RAD tool to use. The environment makes it very easy to build a user interface, and the Basic language is easy for just about any programmer to pick up.

■ Visual Basic is very strong for building database applications, especially those that use Microsoft Access databases.

■ Visual Basic now has a native code compiler, which allows you to build applications with much better performance. In the past, the inability to produce a real compiled program was the biggest knock against Visual Basic.

■ Visual Basic is more object oriented than in the past; you can now create and use classes and ActiveX controls.

■ Visual Basic gives you a wide array of choices in application types. This includes the ability to create dynamic link libraries (DLLs), ActiveX controls, and Web-based DHTML applications, among other types.

■ With the ability to create add-ins, the development environment of Visual Basic is extensible.

While Visual Basic is a strong choice for most applications, if you are doing a lot of number crunching you may consider using Visual C++ (see below).

Microsoft Access

If you are only going to be developing database applications that use Microsoft Access databases, especially for in-house use, you may consider using Microsoft Access. While not really a RAD tool, Access has a complete development environment that you can use to build forms and even write Visual Basic code. The advantages and disadvantages of Access can be summarized as follows:

■ Access is good to use if you are only going to develop Microsoft Access database applications.

■ Access may be a good choice if you are developing in-house applications for users who have Access on their machines.

■ Access cannot build a native compiled application; as a result, applications developed with Access are probably slower than compiled Visual Basic applications.

■ Access is not as flexible as Visual Basic.

Visual C++

Visual C++ is a good choice when you are building scientific and engineering applications. This is because it still has a large speed advantage over Visual Basic when performing these types of tasks. One drawback is that designing a user interface with Visual C++ is not as easy, and you have to know the C/C++ language to use it (not as trivial as learning Basic). Some developers may find that they can use Visual Basic to design their user interface while using Visual C++ to do any resource-intensive numerical processing in a dynamic link library. The advantages and disadvantages of Visual C++ can be summarized as follows:

- Even with native code compilation, for some applications Visual C++ will still provide a hefty speed advantage over Visual Basic.
- Visual C++ has more multithreading ability than Visual Basic, which still remains rather limited in this area.
- Visual C++ is based on a strongly object-oriented language.
- Visual C++ is a good tool for "low-level" programming tasks, such as building hardware drivers.
- Designing a user interface with Visual C++ can be more difficult and time consuming.
- If you don't already know the language, C/C++ has a much longer learning curve than Visual Basic.

A Brief History of Visual Basic

Visual Basic uses a derivation of the Basic programming language that was developed several years ago primarily as an instructional tool. That early form of the language was not thought highly of and was well known for using GOTO statements and other "spaghetti code" methods. While easy to use, the language found itself relegated to freshman-level MIS courses that prepared students for using COBOL.

That all changed when Microsoft introduced Visual Basic in 1991. An early version of Visual Basic could be used to develop DOS programs, and it showed programmers what was possible by allowing them to draw their windows and dialog boxes on screen, something that was unheard of to the average programmer at that time. Windows was catching on fast, however, so the days of Visual Basic for DOS were short lived. While version 1.0 of Visual Basic was limited by today's standards, the revolutionary nature of the product caused Bill Gates to remark that it was "awesome."

By the time of the third release, Visual Basic was gaining fast in popularity. Not only had Visual Basic made Windows programming a great deal easier, but the advent of VBX controls (the forerunner of OCX and today's ActiveX controls) allowed the extension of the language so that developers could produce professional applications while using ready-made objects such as grids, graphing tools, and more. Version 4.0 was released about the time Windows 95 hit the market and for the first time allowed VB developers to write 32-bit code. By this time, the language used had been extended so much that comparisons to the old Basic language no longer applied.

Version 5.0 of Visual Basic was a major step forward. Finally, Visual Basic had the long-sought-after ability to produce native compiled code. Visual Basic was also beefed up in a lot of areas, with special attention paid to strengthening its ActiveX technologies. Now developers could build ActiveX controls, documents, and dynamic link libraries.

In some ways, VB's inheritance of the Basic language has unfairly colored "real programmers'" perceptions of Visual Basic. However, Visual Basic has come a long way from the numbered lines and GOTO spaghetti code of yesteryear. The Basic language found in VB 6 is a much more robust and powerful event-driven language, complete with an object-oriented approach, that can be used to develop just about any type of Windows application.

Software Life-Cycle Models

A software life-cycle model is a method for studying, planning, and analyzing the development process, from product conception to actual release. A typical software model will have discrete steps, such as design or testing. Of course, these models are idealizations; nobody develops code in a neat fashion like that in the real world. However, using a software life-cycle model can be very helpful for keeping the coding process organized. This is especially important in a RAD environment because the model can help you stick to a carefully planned and organized method of software development, rather than just "jumping in" to the code.

Waterfall (Linear)

In a waterfall or linear software development model (shown in Fig. 1-1) the development of a project moves through neatly defined sequential steps. Like a flow chart, each step is listed in an orderly fashion where it is assumed that the previous step is completed before one moves on. A drawback to the waterfall model is that we all know this type of progress is unrealistic. The cold, hard truth is that in a real software development environment, the different phases of design overlap; each step will require repeated input from other design steps, and you will

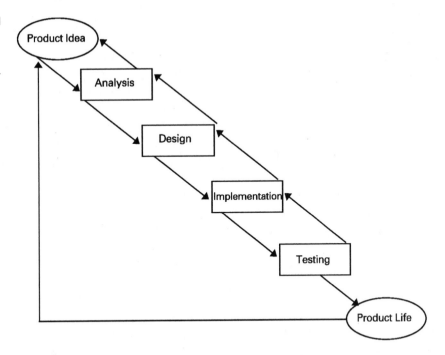

Figure 1-1
Waterfall life-cycle
model.

probably visit each step more than once. The waterfall model can be used to divide the software life cycle into phases like the following:

- Product idea
- Software analysis
- Design
- Implementation
- Testing
- Product life

Despite the shortcomings of the waterfall model, it can be a good starting point for keeping your coding efficient and organized. Just be aware that you will probably never follow such a neat sequence of steps when designing real software.

Cyclic Waterfall or Spiral

The cyclic waterfall or spiral model is a derivation of the linear waterfall model. This model attempts to come to terms with the reality that each phase of the development process will require multiple iterations.

The spiral model was developed at TRW in 1988. Besides allowing for multiple iterations through each phase in the development process, the key idea in this model is that an examination of risk and analysis is performed at each phase. This type of software model is preferred for programmers using object-oriented development. Due to its cyclical nature, it provides designers and managers with an opportunity to "loop" through the spiral at each level of abstraction, repeating the same sequence of steps from design to software maintenance. This approach resembles the real world better than the linear waterfall model. As a product is developed, it's more likely that new features will be thought of or designs reconsidered at many phases during the lifetime of the software.

Brute Force

In short, "brute force" is simply turning the computer on and coding up the program. Actually, this really isn't a life-cycle model. This is the kind of software development that college professors in freshman computer science classes warn their students about. Unfortunately, with a RAD environment the temptation to engage in brute-force software development is strong. Since this kind of programming lends itself to errors and poor planning, it should be avoided.

Hybrids

We've only scratched the surface of software life-cycle models here. Since none of them is perfect, you're likely to find a hybrid of one or more models useful. Let's consider two possible model hybrids.

Linear Waterfall with Multiple Iterations   In real life, there probably aren't many software products that move along so smoothly that someone doesn't think about a design change or a redefinition of the software requirements along the way. While the linear waterfall model offers a neat and organized view of the software development process, this is its biggest weakness. For this reason, a slight twist to the linear model can be thought of that allows each step or phase to be influenced by later phases. This means being able to go back at any point in the development cycle and revisit earlier phases.

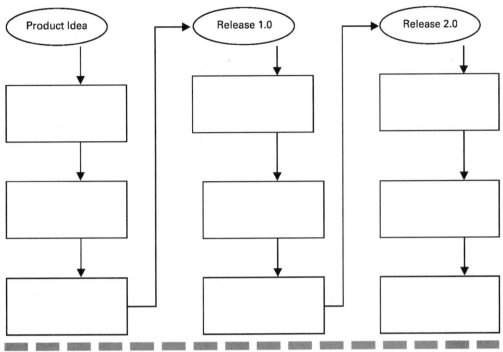

Figure 1-2 The incremental model.

Incremental In an incremental model (shown in Fig. 1-2) a software product is built up with successive iterations or releases. At each iteration or release, more complexity or functionality is added. Since each step adds a limited amount of functionality, this provides for effective testing and feedback from users. In between releases, a linear waterfall model can be used. As you can note by looking at products released in the software market, that is, version 1.0, version 1.3, version 2.3, this type of model is popular among computer circles.

Example Programs

Throughout the book, we will illustrate the capabilities and uses of Visual Basic with sample projects. In Chapter 8, we will take up the topic of object-oriented design, and we will use a bank simulation program to illustrate some of the object-oriented capabilities of Visual Basic. Let's consider what goes on in a bank. First, you have many different classifications of people who work at the bank, not to mention the customers. Each customer may have one or more accounts, which can themselves be classified into different types, such as checking, savings, or checking and savings. We will also need to track the different transactions that go on during the course of a banking day, such as deposits, withdrawals, and the cashing of checks.

As a first step, we can think of how the different elements in the bank simulation can be modeled as objects. This might include the following:

- *Person:* A person can be a bank teller, a manager, or a customer.

- *Accounts:* Accounts can be checking, savings, or checking and savings. Each of these will also be able to be classified into subtypes.

- *Transactions:* Here we will think about the activities that the customers will perform each day. This might mean opening a new account, making a deposit, or cashing a check.

In Chapter 8, we'll think about how to build the bank simulation program by using classes to represent the different objects we have listed here.

In Chapter 10, we'll explore the database-handling capabilities of Visual Basic, paying special attention to the new ADO and OLE DB technologies. We'll build an application that uses structured query language (SQL) to filter the records seen by the user. We'll also build an application that runs a vending-machine business, using the new ADO technology.

In Chapter 12, we will build two applications. First, we'll see how to build a statistics library by creating an in-process ActiveX component. We'll also create an ActiveX control, which will allow the user to set an alarm.

In Chapter 13, we will see how to use Visual Basic to create an add-in. An add-in is an extension of the Visual Basic development environment. When you get down in the trenches, you'll find that an add-in is an in-process component. We'll find out how to use Visual Basic to create an add-in that inserts error-handling code into a Visual Basic project.

CHAPTER 2

Overview of the Visual Basic Environment

Introduction

When you open Visual Basic, you open an *integrated development environment*, or IDE, where you can develop, test, debug, and compile several different types of applications. In the past, a programmer had to open a text editor to write the code, save the file, and then exit the text editor to command-line compile the project. Then the application would be tested on its own, outside of the code editor or compiler. When errors or bugs were located, the process would begin again, opening the source code in the text editor, saving the file, and then command-line compiling the program all over again.

With an integrated development environment like Visual Basic, this old back-and-forth method of building an application has faded into the past. Visual Basic provides all of the tools you'll need to complete a project in a single environment. This means you can design your user interface, write the code behind it, test it, debug it, and compile it without ever leaving Visual Basic. This is why this type of development tool is known as *integrated*. This environment makes the programming process much less painful and speeds development times.

Creating a New Project

When you launch Visual Basic, the first item you'll see is the New Project dialog box shown in Fig. 2-1. At the top of the window you'll see three tabs: New, Existing, and Recent. The New tab allows you to start a new project by choosing among the following types:

- *Standard EXE*: This is a standard Windows application. If you select this option, Visual Basic will load a single *form*, or window, with which you can start to build your project.

- *ActiveX EXE*: This is an executable that can behave as an ActiveX server. The objects that are part of an ActiveX server can be used by other applications. An ActiveX EXE is known as an *out-of-process server* because it runs in its own process, or address space, separate from the client application that uses its objects.

- *ActiveX DLL*: Like an ActiveX EXE, an ActiveX DLL can act as an ActiveX server. However, a DLL, or dynamic link library, is known as an *in-process server* because it runs in the same process as the client application that uses its objects.

Figure 2-1
New Project dialog
box.

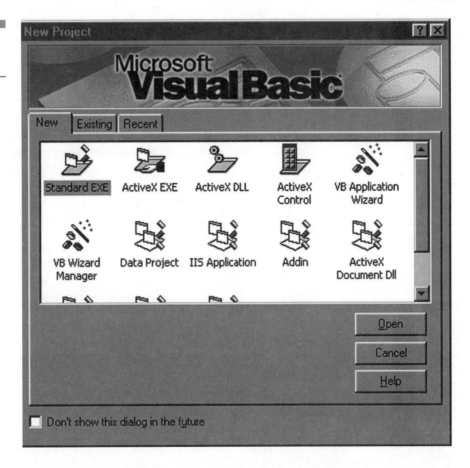

- *ActiveX control*: This option allows you to create your own ActiveX control.

- *Data project*: This type loads a project for use with database programming. This is a standard EXE project with a data environment and form loaded.

- *IIS application*: This is an Internet information server. This type of application will run on a web server running IIS 3/4.

- *Add-in*: An add-in can be used to extend the functionality of the Visual Basic development environment. You can create your own add-ins by selecting this option.

- *ActiveX document DLL*: An ActiveX document is a document object that can be placed in other applications such as Microsoft Internet Explorer or MS Word. When you create an ActiveX document DLL it will run as an in-process server.

- *ActiveX document EXE*: This is an ActiveX document project that is an EXE or out-of-process server.

- *DHTML application*: This type of project can be used to build a Web-based application. A DHTML project has a DHTML page designer for building web pages.

- *VB Pro edition controls*: VB Pro edition controls starts an application with the Professional edition controls loaded. Some of the useful Pro edition controls include MSFlexGrid, the common dialog control, tab strip, toolbar, status bar, progress bar, tree view, list view, image list, slider, image combo, date picker, month view, data list, data combo, and the ADO data control. If you have the Enterprise edition of VB, this option will be labeled *VB Enterprise Edition* controls.

- *VB application wizard*: The application wizard (shown in Fig. 2-2) will help you build the framework of your project, by single-stepping through several design choices. For example, it will ask you if you want to build a multiple document, single document, or Explorer-style

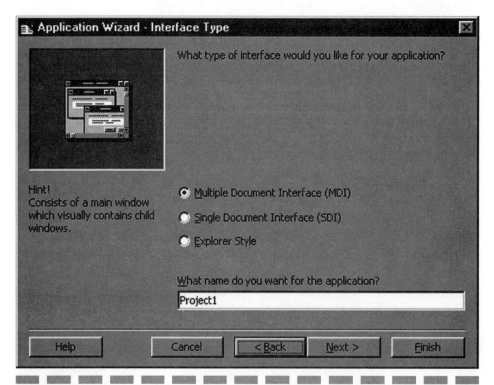

Figure 2-2   The Visual Basic application wizard.

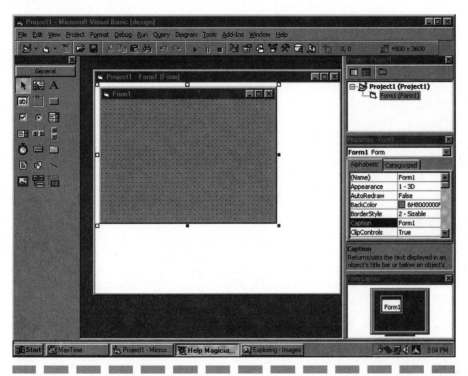

Figure 2-3   The Visual Basic IDE.

interface. Depending on the choices you make, the wizard will build the forms and add menus and controls as required.

■ *VB wizard manager*: Allows you to create "wizards," which are software interfaces that guide the user through a series of steps. The wizard manager will aid you in building the steps; you then put the code behind them to accomplish the tasks you need.

To create a new project, simply select the desired project type and click the OK button. To open previously saved projects, you can look under the Existing and Recent tabs. Once a project is opened, the Visual Basic integrated development (IDE) environment will look something like that pictured in Fig. 2-3. Let's explore each of the major elements of that environment, starting on the left.

The Toolbox

The ability to easily create a "what you see is what you get" user interface at design time has made Visual Basic a very popular programming tool. At the core of this approach to Windows programming you'll find the custom control. In Visual Basic, controls come in two varieties, built-in or *standard* controls and *ActiveX* controls. A standard Visual Basic control will become part of your EXE file when you compile your project, while an ActiveX control must be distributed with your project as an .ocx file. In either case, a control provides encapsulated functionality of an object that can be reused many times, so you don't have to reinvent the wheel. For example, you can use the *MonthView* control to include a calendar in your application without having to code up a calendar yourself.

The toolbox (shown in Fig. 2-4) is where you'll find standard Visual Basic controls along with any ActiveX controls and insertable objects

Figure 2-4
The Visual Basic toolbox.

that have been added to the project. To add an object from the toolbox to a form, you can use one of two methods:

- Double-click your mouse on the desired toolbox icon. The control will then be placed in the middle of the form that is currently selected.

- Select the desired control or object from the toolbox by left-clicking once on the toolbox icon. Then, while holding down your left mouse button, "draw" the object on your form. When you release the mouse button, the control will appear on your form.

When you start a Visual Basic project, the toolbox will be loaded with the standard Visual Basic controls. You can add other controls to your project by selecting *Components* from the Project pull-down menu. Visual Basic loads with the following standard controls in the toolbox:

- *Pointer*: The pointer is represented by an arrow icon in the upper left corner of the toolbox. The pointer is not actually a control but is instead used to manipulate the controls already placed on the forms in your project. If you want to move or resize a selected control, select the pointer from the toolbox and then use your mouse.

- *Picture box*: A picture box is a control that can be used to display picture files. Valid image formats include bitmap, .gif, .jpg, metafiles, and icons. You can also use the graphics methods to draw inside a picture box.

- *Label*: A label control can be used to display static text.

- *Text box*: A text box can be used to receive alphanumeric input from the user.

- *Frame*: A frame control acts as a container for other controls. You can display a group of controls inside a frame, such as a list of choices represented by check boxes or option buttons.

- *Command button*: The command button is that ubiquitous control found throughout Windows. This is a button the user clicks to execute a command.

- *Check box*: A check box provides the user with a choice that can be checked on or off.

- *Option button*: An option button, like a check box, allows the user to make an on or off selection. However, option buttons are selected exclusively and as such are used in groups where only one choice is allowed.

- *Combo box:* A combo box allows the user to select from a set of choices available in a drop-down list.

- *List box*: A list box displays a list of items. A list box can be set to allow the user to choose only one item or can be set for multiple selection.

- *HScrollBar*: The HscrollBar control is a horizontal scrollbar. The position of the scrollbar can be read and used to set other properties or to cause some action when a specified value is reached.

- *VScrollBar*: The VscrollBar control is a vertical scrollbar. It can be used like a horizontal scrollbar.

- *Timer*: A timer is a control that is not visible during run time. You can set a time limit in its interval property, and the timer will basically act as an alarm clock and fire a timer event. You can use the timer event to perform some specified action.

- *Drive list box*: A drive list box is a combo box that will display the disk drives on your computer.

- *DirListBox*: DirListBox is a list box that displays a list of directories on the computer. It can be used in conjunction with a drive list box.

- *FileListBox*: This is a list box that displays a list of files. It can be used in conjunction with a drive list box and DirListBox to provide the user with a means to navigate the files on her computer.

- *Shape*: This control can be used to draw various shapes on your form, such as a circle.

- *Line*: This control can be used to draw a line on your form.

- *Image*: An image control can display images in one of the following formats: bitmap (.bmp), icon (.ico), or Windows metafile (.wmf).

- *Data control*: A data control can be used to connect with a database, such as a Microsoft Access table.

- *OLE*: OLE is an acronym that stands for *object linking and embedding*. This control can be used to link or embed objects from other applications in your project, such as an Excel spreadsheet.

Forms

The forms in your project are displayed in a design window located in the center of the screen. Each window will have a caption that lists the project name and the form name. This is where you design and add controls to each form. To open a form for design, select the desired form in the Project Explorer (see below) and choose the View Object button, or double-click on the form's name. Visual Basic will then open the form in its own window where you can edit the design.

Code Windows

Code windows are displayed in the middle of the screen. This is where you actually enter and edit your Visual Basic code. Code windows can be brought up by double-clicking on an object for which you wish to enter code, for example, a command button. You can also open a code window by selecting the View Code button of the Project Explorer.

The Project Explorer

The Project Explorer, shown in the upper right corner of Fig. 2-3, displays all of the files in your project. This will include items such as forms, standard code modules, and class modules. At the top of the window, you'll notice three buttons on the left side. These are as follows:

- *View Code*: Click here to open the code window for any object in your application.
- *View Object*: Click here to display the currently selected form or object in the Project Explorer.
- *Toggle Folders*: This button will open or close the folders displayed in the Project Explorer.

You can open an object in the Project Explorer by selecting one of the View buttons or by simply double-clicking the object's name.

The Properties Window

The properties window, found directly beneath the Project Explorer, is where you can read and set the properties of any object in your project, such as a form, class, or ActiveX control. The properties of an object are defined as the characteristics that each object has, such as background color, width, caption, or border style. You can select from *Alphabetic* to view the properties in alphabetical order or select *Categorized* to view properties grouped by category, such as *Position* or *Font*.

The Form Layout Window

Directly beneath the Properties window you'll see the Form Layout window. The Form Layout window allows you to define the startup location where the form will appear at run time. You can use the mouse pointer to visually manipulate the position where you want the form to appear.

The Project Properties Dialog

By selecting *Properties* from the Project pull-down menu, you can open the Project Properties dialog shown in Fig. 2-5. The Project Properties dialog is divided into five tabs that allow you to change several important settings for your project. In this section, we'll explore some of the important settings on the General, Make, and Compile tabs. The

Figure 2-5
The Project Properties dialog.

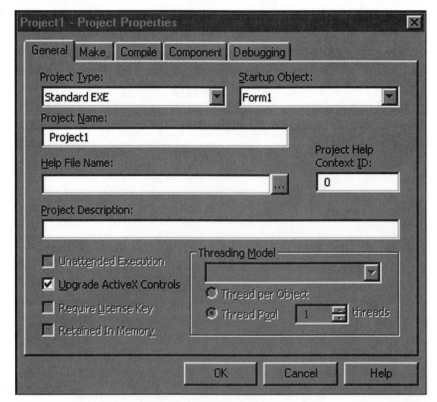

Component and Debugging tabs relate to the creation of ActiveX server and component projects, which will be the subject of Chapter 12.

The General Tab

At this stage, there are only a few items on the General tab that we are concerned with. These are as follows:

- *Project Type*: This is a drop-down list you can use to specify the type of project. Options include standard EXE, ActiveX EXE, ActiveX DLL, and ActiveX control.

- *Startup Object*: The startup object is the first component in your project to execute. The startup object can be a form or Sub Main. By default, if you open a standard EXE, the startup object will be a form. This form will be the first object displayed by Visual Basic when the application loads. If you select Sub Main as the startup object, you must add a Sub procedure called Main to a standard module in your project.

- *Project Name*: This is a name to identify your project. This is important when developing ActiveX projects since the project name will appear in the Object Browser.

- *Help File Name*: Use this setting to specify a help file to associate with the project. When the user presses the F1 key, that help file will load.

- *Upgrade ActiveX Controls*: If you select this option, Visual Basic will upgrade all ActiveX controls used by the project when you load it.

We'll discuss settings available with the threading model in Chapter 12.

The Make Tab

The Make tab allows you to set certain attributes that will be associated with your project's EXE file when it is compiled. Settings here include the following:

- *Version Number*: Here you can specify the major, minor, and revision release numbers of the application. If you select the Auto Increment checkbox, Visual Basic will automatically increase the revision number every time the Make Project command is executed for this project.

However, it will only change the smallest revision number. The major and minor values must be set manually.

- *Application*: The application title is the name of the application that the user will see when dialogs such as message boxes are displayed. You can also specify the icon that the application will use.

- *Version Information*: Here you can specify certain information about the project, such as company name and copyright information. Specify which item you want to set by selecting it from the Type list, and type in the information in the Value input box.

- *Command-Line Arguments*: You can test command-line arguments while running your project inside Visual Basic by entering them here.

- *Conditional Compilation Arguments*: Constant declarations used in conditional compilation can be entered here. A programmer can use conditional compilation directives to tell the compiler to include or exclude a block of code, based on the value of a constant that is known as a *conditional compiler constant*.

EXAMPLE: SETTING CONDITIONAL COMPILER ARGUMENTS FROM THE MAKE TAB

Conditional compiler constants can be helpful when debugging your project. You can also use conditional compiler constants to have multiple versions of a program in the same project. For example, by changing the value of the constant, code fragments can be included during the debug phase of development and left out when the code is compiled for the end user. It's easy to set the value of compiler constants from the Make tab. This is done by specifying the constant's name and value in the *Conditional Compilation Arguments* input box. For example, we could use the following constant to tell our program we are in debug mode:

```
DebugMode = 1
```

You can add more than one conditional compiler constant in the Make tab by separating the constants with a colon:

```
DebugMode = 1: LoadBinary=0
```

In code, you can test the value of conditional compiler constants with #If statements. In our example, we could test if we were in debug mode with a statement like this:

```
#If DebugMode Then
```

```
        'add debug testing code here
#Else
        'code to be used when not in debug mode goes here
#End If
```

Conditionally compiled code will not actually become part of the executable. It simply tells the compiler which code to use. In our example, if DebugMode is set to false, the code under the #Else clause will be included in the executable, while the #If section will be ignored. Using #ElseIf or #Else clauses is optional.

The Compile Tab

When you click on the Compile tab, you'll see several options that can be used to impact the performance and size of your project when it's compiled into an executable (see Fig. 2-6). The first item to notice is that you have two options, *Compile to P-Code* and *Compile to Native Code*.

Figure 2-6
The Compile tab.

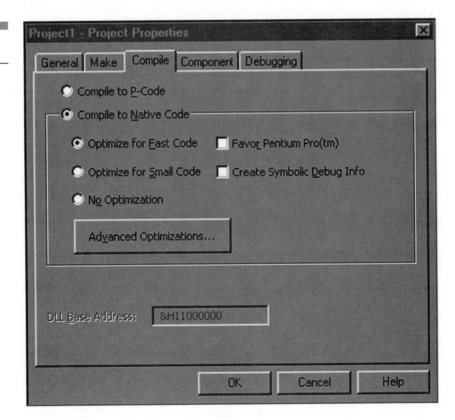

If you select *Compile to P-Code*, the other options on the Compile tab are disabled. This option will cause Visual Basic to compile your project to what is known as *pseudocode*. A pseudocode program is translated by Visual Basic into native code at run time. If a Visual Basic interpreter is present on the machine, a P-Code program can run on different types of processors, such as Intel, Alpha, or Motorola. The translation step takes time, however, and this means that P-Code programs run slower. If your project will only be running on Intel x86 machines, there is no compelling reason to use P-Code. Use native code compilation and take advantage of the speed boost.

When compiled to native code, the executable is written in the native instructions of the processor. If the program will not be used on different families of processors, this is the option you should use. A program that is native code compiled will outperform a P-Code program, especially if you are doing a great deal of numeric processing. I have seen numerical processing that takes up to an hour in P-Code be reduced to a few minutes by native compilation. If you compile to native code, you will have several options available. They are discussed in the following sections.

Optimize for Fast Code   By selecting *Optimize for Fast Code*, you will maximize the speed of the compiled EXE or DLL file. This option will increase the performance of your application but may result in a larger file size. In today's world, even on a desktop machine hard drive space is easy to come by, so you will probably want to optimize for speed.

Optimize for Small Code   If you select *Optimize for Small Code*, Visual Basic will try to keep the EXE or DLL file as small as possible. This may result in a compromise in performance. If you run into a situation where small executable size is a deciding factor, select this option. An example where this may be important might be an executable that runs over the Internet. By selecting small code size, you can improve download times.

No Optimization   If you select this option, Visual Basic will not try to optimize for speed or size.

Favor Pentium Pro   Selecting this option will cause Visual Basic to compile the executable to take advantage of capabilities only available on Pentium Pro processors. This type of executable will still run on other machines, but it won't perform as well. As a result, select this option only if you know the program will run mainly on Pentium Pro machines.

Create Symbolic Debug Info Use this option if you want to debug your executable with a CodeView style debugger, such as Visual C++. Selecting this option will cause Visual Basic to embed symbolic debug information into the application and create a .pdb file, increasing the size of your application.

DLL Base Address If your project is an ActiveX DLL, you can specify the base address where the DLL will load in memory. DLL base addresses must be between &H1000000 and &H80000000 (or 16,777,216 to 2,147,483,648 in decimal). Visual Basic will set the base address to 0X10000000 by default. During execution, memory space can fill up, and the operating system will have to find a new base address, which can increase the time required for the DLL to load. By specifying a custom base address you can avoid this problem.

Advanced Optimizations There are several advanced compiler settings that can be accessed by selecting the *Advanced Optimizations* button. Generally, you will not need to change these settings, but they can be modified if performance is at a premium. Care should be taken when selecting these options because they can lead to unanticipated side effects in your program.

Assume No Aliasing Visual Basic assigns a code to all variables that reference the same memory locations, for example, a global variable and the local version of that global. This code is called an *alias*. If you select the *Assume No Aliasing* option, the compiler will leave unchanged variables not directly modified within the local scope. This can result in a speed boost because Visual Basic will be able to optimize loop constructs and use registers to store variables. This can result in conflicts with global variables, however, so you should be careful when selecting this option.

Remove Array Bounds Checks Visual Basic will generate a trappable error if your code attempts to access an array element with an index that is outside the bounds of the array. If you select this option, Visual Basic will not verify that an index is within those limits. This may result in a small performance boost. However, since this can result in the program accessing incorrect memory locations, this option should be selected with care.

Remove Integer Overflow Checks When handling whole numbers, the default behavior of Visual Basic is to make sure that your code does not assign a value that is out of range. For example, a variable of type Byte can hold values between 0 and 255. If you attempt to assign 900 to this variable, Visual Basic will generate an overflow error. This testing adds a small amount of overhead to your project, and you can obtain a gain in performance by selecting the *Remove Integer Overflow Checks* option. However, if you do so, this can result in unpredictable behavior from your program. For example, a value that is out of range may appear to be a negative number to the computer. Since there is no overflow check, the program will go right along processing the data with the incorrect value.

Remove Floating-Point Error Checks   Selecting this option is similar to removing integer overflow checks, but it impacts variables of type Single and type double. This will also turn off important data checking such as division by zero. Again, you may obtain a small performance boost by selecting this option, but this could result in unpredictable errors.

Allow Unrounded Floating-Point Operations   The default behavior of Visual Basic is to round floating-point values to the correct precision during comparison operations. You can gain a small performance boost by selecting this option, which will allow Visual Basic to speed the comparison of floating-point values. However, since no rounding will be performed, you may end up with an incorrect comparison operation.

Remove Safe Pentium FDIV Checks   You may recall that when Intel first released the Pentium, the processor had a bug that caused errors in some floating-point calculations. By default, Visual Basic will check for this error. If you select this option, you can turn off this checking procedure, and you may gain a small performance boost.

Project References and Components

The References dialog can be opened by selecting *References* from the Project pull-down menu (see Fig. 2-7). This dialog will show a listing of object references that are available to your project. By setting a reference, you gain access to another application's objects, such as the Microsoft Word object library. You will then be able to program these objects in code, just like you can with built-in VB objects. You set a refer-

Figure 2-7
The References
dialog.

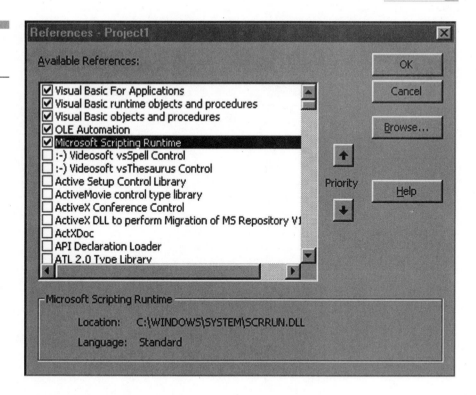

ence in your application by simply checking the appropriate boxes in the Available References list.

If a required reference is not shown in the list, you can click the *Browse...* button to search for it. Object references are stored in *type library* files, which have .olb, .tlb, or .dll file extensions. Be sure to only set references for the objects that you will actually use because a reference adds some overhead to a project.

If you want to use an ActiveX control in your project, you can set a reference to it by opening the Components dialog from the Project pulldown menu (see Fig. 2-8). The Components dialog has three tabs. The first tab, Controls, is where you'll find a listing of the ActiveX controls (with an .ocx file extension) that have been installed on your machine. On the second tab, you'll find Designers. An ActiveX designer object will provide you with a visual way to accomplish an otherwise difficult task. For example, you can select *Data Report* to easily build a database report. Designer objects can be files that have a .dll or .ocx file extension.

The final tab of the Components dialog box is the Insertable Objects tab. This is where you'll find objects such as a Microsoft Word document

Figure 2-8
The Components
dialog.

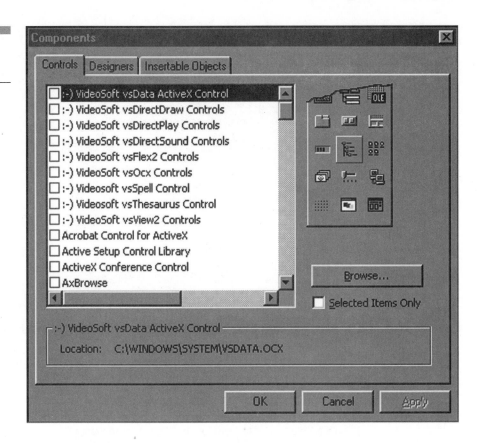

Figure 2-8
The Components
dialog.

that can be dropped into your project. Insertable objects generally work
by using automation, or as it was previously known, OLE Automation.

The Object Browser

Visual Basic is a language that works with *objects*. In fact, just about
everything used in Visual Basic can be thought of as an object. This
includes forms, standard code modules, intrinsic controls, the classes
you create and ActiveX controls, as well as references to ActiveX servers
like Microsoft Excel. Each object in turn has a set of *members*, which are
the properties, methods, and events of that object. To facilitate your use
of objects, Visual Basic has provided the *Object Browser* (see Fig. 2-9).
The Object Browser can be used to view all of the objects in your appli-

Figure 2-9
The Object Browser.

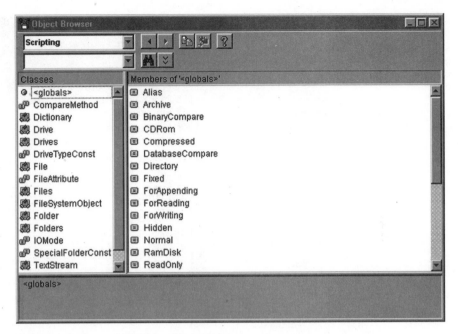

cation and to see the properties, methods, and events that each object has. You can open the *Object Browser...* by selecting *Object Browser* from the View menu or by pressing the F2 key.

The Object Browser uses a Windows Explorer-type interface to display the objects in your application. Viewing all of the objects together is quite cumbersome, so you'll probably want to examine one server component or library at a time. To select a particular server component to examine, click open the drop-down list marked *<All Libraries>* in the upper left corner. Once you've made a selection, the classes and modules of the object will be displayed in the left window pane. If you select a particular class, the methods, properties, and events of that class will be displayed in the right window pane. You can view the help file for the selected object (if available) by selecting the ? button in the upper portion of the window.

When you select a method, property, or event, a brief description will appear in the lower portion of the Object Browser. In Fig. 2-10, we have selected the *ReadAll* method of an object called *TextStream*, which belongs to the scripting library. Notice the bottom of the window, which informs us that this method reads a text stream into a string variable.

For objects that you've created, you can specify the help context ID

Figure 2-10
Examining a specific
method in the Object
Browser.

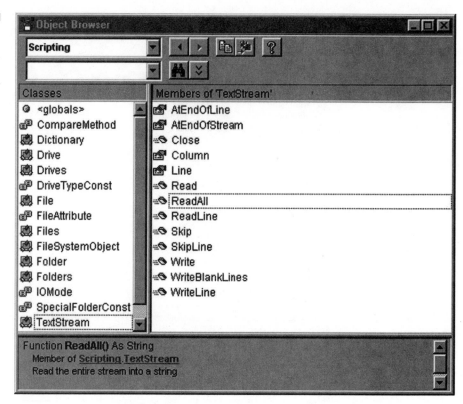

and description associated with that object in the Object Browser. This
is done by right-clicking on the object and selecting *Properties* (see Fig.
2-11). To specify the help file for the object, you need to specify a help file
for the project that it belongs to. You cannot set these properties for
objects that belong to other servers.

Figure 2-11
Properties of a mem-
ber in the Object
Browser.

The Procedure Attributes Dialog

The Procedure Attributes dialog, shown in Fig. 2-12, can be opened from the Tools pull-down menu when you have a code window open with the cursor located in a procedure. This dialog box applies to properties and methods of classes that you create in your ActiveX projects. The information entered here is what users will see in the Object Browser. This information includes the following:

- *Description*: Type the description that you want to appear at the bottom of the Object Browser when this property or method is selected.
- Project Help File: This will be the application's help file that you can set from the Project Properties dialog box.
- *Help Context ID*: If the help file for this project has topics organized by context ID, you can enter the ID for the procedure here.

Figure 2-12
The Procedure Attributes dialog, showing Advanced options.

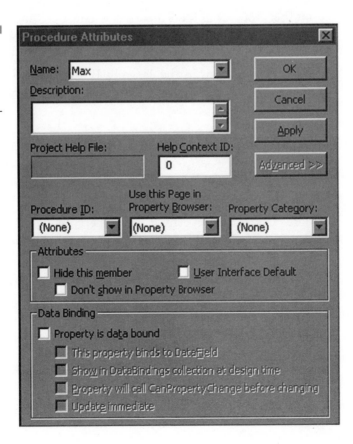

If you are developing an ActiveX control, the Advanced button provides access to several important settings. These include:

- *Procedure ID*: The Procedure ID field provides a way for you to create standard ActiveX properties. For example, many ActiveX controls have an About property that displays an About dialog box to the user. Your control can behave in this manner by adding a procedure that displays the About box and setting its Procedure ID field to *AboutBox*. Visual Basic will then automatically show the About box when the user clicks on this property. You can also specify a default property for your control by setting its procedure ID to *(Default)*.

- *Use this Page in the Property Browser*: In Visual Basic, there are several properties such as *Font* or *BackColor* that will display a property page or special dialog box to the user. You can click open the *Use this Page in the Property Browser* drop-down list and specify which property page to show the user when she edits the property during design time. For example, if you select *Standard Color*, when the user clicks on this property in the Properties window, a standard color dialog will open allowing her to select a color from the Windows palette.

- *Property Category*: This lets you specify which category the property belongs to as seen in the control's Properties window when the user selects the *Categorized* tab. Examples include Appearance, Behavior, Misc, or Position.

- *Attributes*: If you select *Hide this Member*, the property will be private to your control, which means the user will not be able to access the procedure directly. If you select *Don't show in Property Browser*, the property will not appear in the Properties window for the control.

- *Data Binding*: If this property will be data bound, you can specify that here. You can also specify if the property will appear at design time in the DataBindings collection and whether or not the property will call CanPropertyChange before changing its value. This allows you to create a data-bound field for a read-only database.

Add-Ins

Visual Basic comes with several add-ins that simplify development. An add-in is basically an extension to the Visual Basic environment. You can see all of the available add-ins by either clicking on the Add-ins menu or opening the Add-Ins Manager. The Add-Ins Manager can be opened by selecting Add-Ins Manager from the Add-Ins menu. There are several add-ins available; some of the more useful are as follows:

- *Visual Data Manager*: Lets you create and/or edit Microsoft Access databases. You do not need to have Access to use this tool

- *VB Property Page Wizard*: Aids you in building property pages for ActiveX controls

- *VB Data Form Wizard*: Helps you build a database form with a data control and bound controls

- *VB Class Builder Utility*: Assists you with defining your own classes for use in a VB application

- *Application Wizard*: Helps you create a standardized application, with a ready-built user interface

- *Visual Component Manager*: Enables software components to be managed and shared.

- *API Viewer*: Lets you view the procedure and type declarations for using the Windows API. You can copy and paste these declarations into your project.

The Options Dialog

The Options dialog, which can be used to change settings and the behavior of the VB development environment, is pictured in Fig. 2-13. The Options dialog has the following tabs:

- Editor
- Editor Format
- General
- Docking
- Environment
- Advanced

Some of the more important options are described below.

Auto Syntax Check. This option is found on the Editor tab. Selecting it will allow Visual Basic to check your language syntax while you type. This can be helpful in allowing you to catch syntax errors early.

Require Variable Declaration. This option is found on the Editor tab. Selecting this option is similar to typing *Option Explicit* in your code

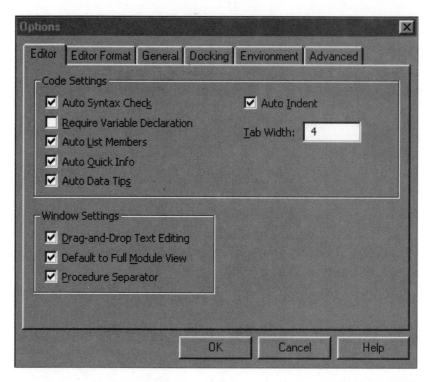

modules; it will force you to declare a variable before using it. While Visual Basic will let you use variables without declaring them, this is a sloppy practice and it should be avoided. As a result, it's a good idea to select this option.

Compile on Demand. This option is found on the General tab. Selecting this option will tell Visual Basic to compile just a few lines of code as needed when running in the development environment. If this option is not selected, Visual Basic will compile the entire project before entering run mode. Selecting *Compile on Demand* can improve loading times.

Background Compile. The Background Compile option, found on the General tab, can only be set if you select Compile on Demand and only affects the development environment. Background compile will tell Visual Basic to compile ahead in the background when you are not interacting with the application.

Break on All Errors. This option is found on the General tab. Selecting it will cause Visual Basic to enter break mode whenever an error occurs, even if an error handler is present in the offending routine. This can be helpful if you are tracking down an error during the debug process because Visual Basic will break on the line of code that is causing the error.

Break in Class Module.   With this object on the General tab, Visual Basic will break in the code of the class that caused the error. If an unhandled error occurs in a class, Visual Basic will break in the code that called that class. If you aren't using any classes, this will work like Break on Unhandled Errors, which is described next. If you are programming an ActiveX server, you should select this option. It will cause Visual Basic to break in the server rather than returning to the client application.

Break on Unhandled Errors.   With this object on the General tab, Visual Basic will allow any error handlers that you've included in your code to run. Visual Basic will enter break mode only when it encounters an unhandled error.

Save Changes.   This option is found on the Environment tab. If you select this option, Visual Basic will save any changes you made to your project whenever you enter run mode.

New Features in Visual Basic 6

Every new edition of Visual Basic seems to push the product to new heights, and version 6.0 is no exception. Microsoft has clearly recognized the increased role of the Internet and web page development, and as a result Visual Basic comes with an increased web capability. It also comes with new database technologies and control enhancements and an improved object-oriented approach. We review some of the new features in the following sections.

String Functions

Visual Basic has added several new string-handling functions in version 6.0. Visual Basic was already well suited to manipulating strings, and the new functions will increase that power even further. The following are some of the new string functions added to Visual Basic.

`Filter`   Based on a filter criterion, this function will filter an array of strings. The function returns a variant that only contains the data that you specified in the filter criterion. The syntax of the function is as follows:

```
Filter(strArray, filterpattern [ , include[ , compare]]
```

The following code shows an example that uses the `Filter` function:

```
Dim strMyArray(4) As String
Dim FilteredValue

strMyArray = Array("Hello", "Happy New Year", "GoodBye", "Aloha")
FilteredValue = Filter(strMyArray, "GoodBye")
```

When this code executes, the variable `FilteredValue` will contain the text string `GoodBye`.

Join   The `Join` function concatenates the strings contained in an array into a single string variable. The syntax of the `Join` function is as follows:

```
Join(arrayname [, delimiter])
```

The first parameter, `arrayname`, is a one-dimensional array of strings. The `delimiter` parameter is optional and can be used to specify a character to place between each array element when concatenated together. If no delimiter is specified, a single space is used. The following code shows how to use the `Join` function:

```
Dim strMyStrings(3) As String
Dim strMessage As String

strMyStrings(0) = "Hello"
strMyStrings(1) = "How"
strMyStrings(2) = "Are You?"

strMessage = Join(strMyStrings)
```

Format Functions

Version 6.0 of Visual Basic has four new format functions that can be used to convert a numeric expression into a formatted string. These functions are as follows:

- `FormatCurrency`: Converts a numeric expression into a string with currency format, using the currency symbol defined in the system control panel
- `FormatDateTime`: Returns a string in date/time format

- `FormatNumber`: Changes a numeric expression into a string
- `FormatPercent`: Transforms a numeric value into a string formatted as a percentage

The following example shows how to use the `FormatPercent` function:

```
Dim strPercentage As String
Dim sngValue As Single

sngValue = 0.754

strPercentage = FormatPercent(sngValue, 2)

MsgBox strPercentage
```

When this code executes, the message box will display the string `75.40%`.

MonthName   By passing an integer representing the month of the year, you can use the `MonthName` function to return the name of the month as a string. The syntax is as follows:

```
MonthName(monthnum [, abbr])
```

Where `monthnum` is a number from 1 to 12 representing the month. The `abbr` parameter is an optional Boolean parameter; if set to `True`, the returned string is an abbreviation. The following code shows how to use the `MonthName` function:

```
Dim strMonth As String

strMonth = MonthName(1)

MsgBox strMonth
```

Replace   This function can be used to perform a "find and replace"-type function. It will search a string for a specified substring and replace it with a value you specify. The syntax of this function is as follows:

```
Replace(str, find, replacewith, [, start [,count [,compare]]])
```

The `str` parameter is the string to search. `Find` is the substring you wish to replace. `Replacewith` is the replacement substring. The remaining parameters are optional. `Start` can be used to specify the character position where searching is to begin. `Count` can be used to specify the number of replacements to be made. If Count is omitted, all instances of the find string that are located will be replaced. Compare specifies the type of string comparison to use: vbUseCompareOption(-1), vbBinaryCompare(0), vbTextCompare(1), or vbDatabase Compare(2).

Split The Split function can be used to break a string down into a number of smaller strings. This function returns a variant and uses the following syntax:

```
Split(str [,delimiter[,count[,compare]]])
```

The str parameter is the string to be split up. Delimiter is an optional parameter that can be used to specify the delimiting string. If not specified, a space will be used. Count is an optional parameter that specifies how many strings to return. Compare is an optional parameter that will specify the type of comparison used. Available options are vbUseCompareOption(-1), vbBinaryCompare(0), vbTextCompare (1), or vbDatabaseCompare(2). The following code uses the Split function:

```
Dim x
Dim strMessage

 strMessage = "Hello You There"

 x = Split(strMessage)

 MsgBox x(0)
 MsgBox x(1)
 MsgBox x(2)
```

StrReverse The StrReverse function takes a single string parameter and reverses it. For example:

```
Dim strTest As String

strTest = "0123"

strTest = StrReverse(strTest)
```

When this code finishes executing, strTest will contain 3210.

WeekdayName By passing an integer representing the day of the week, WeekdayName will return a string containing the name of that weekday. The weekday can be specified by using one of the Visual Basic constants:

vbSunday(1), vbMonday(2), vbTuesday(3), vbWednesday(4), vbThursday(5), vbFriday(6), **and** vbSaturday(7). **The** syntax of the WeekdayName function is as follows:

```
WeekdayName(DayofWeek, [,abbr[,firstdayofweek]])
```

where DayofWeek and firstdayofweek are one of the Visual Basic constants just mentioned. The optional abbr parameter is type Boolean. If set to True, the returned string will be abbreviated. The following is an example of a call:

```
Dim strToday As String

strToday = WeekdayName(vbFriday)

MsgBox "The Weekend Starts on  " & strToday
```

Data Access

The ability to build database applications has always been the greatest strength of Visual Basic. As Visual Basic has matured, new methods and controls for data access have been introduced. In version 6.0, Microsoft introduces the ActiveX Data Object, or ADO. This includes a new data control as well as familiar objects such as a recordset. ADO provides an easier paradigm than previous incarnations of data objects, such as the Remote Data Object (RDO) and the Data Access Object (DAO). In version 6.0 of Visual Basic, RDO and DAO are provided for backward compatibility only. All new applications should use ADO.

Version 6.0 of Visual Basic also includes the new Data Environment Designer. You can use the Data Environment Designer by creating a Data Project. A Data Project includes a set of integrated tools such as connect objects, command objects, and data reports that can be used to build an ADO database application. The data report object works much like the report designer in Microsoft Access. We'll discuss the details of ADO and database development in Chapter 10.

CallByName

CallByName is a function that allows the properties or methods of an object to be accessed at run time by using a string variable. The syntax of CallByName is as follows:

```
CallByName(Object, MemberName, CallType, [argument list])
```

`Object` is a reference to a control that you wish to reference. `MemberName` is the name of the property or method you wish to access. This is a variable of type `String`, allowing you to set the property or method at run time based on the conditions under which the program is running. `CallType` is a constant that specifies the type of call being made. If you are setting a property, pass the constant `vbLet` for `CallType`. To read the value of a property, pass `vbGet`. If you are using `CallByName` to access a method of the control, pass `vbMethod`. The final parameter, which is optional and will depend on the method accessed, is the argument list that the method expects. As a simple example, we will use `CallByName` to set the text property of a text box control named `txtMessage`, and then add an item to a list box with the `AddItem` method:

```
Dim strPropertyName As String, strValue As String, strMethod As String

strPropertyName = "Text"
strValue = "Hello"

'set the text property of the txtMessage textbox control
CallByName  txtMessage, strPropertyName,  vbLet,  strValue

strMethod = "AddItem"
strValue = "John Smith"

'use the AddItem method of the lstClubMembers listbox to insert John
  Smith into the list
CallByName lstClubMembers, strMethod, vbMethod, strValue
```

File System Objects

The file system objects provide a new object-oriented way to access text files from Visual Basic. We'll explore the details of using file system objects in Chapter 10.

DHTML Applications

Visual Basic now provides you with the ability to build a dynamic HTML (DHTML) application. A DHTML application provides a way to combine the Internet Explorer 4.x DHTML object model with Visual Basic code. This is basically a web page on the client's machine that functions like a Visual Basic application. It can include DHTML pages along with code modules. We'll explore the development of DHTML applications in Chapter 12.

New Controls

Visual Basic has several new or enhanced controls in version 6.0. These include:

- *ADO Data Control*: This is a new data control that uses the new ADO technology to bind controls on a form to a database. This allows you to build a database application with little or no coding.
- *CoolBar*: CoolBar is a control that allows you to add a coolbar-type configurable toolbar like that in Internet Explorer.
- *DataChart, DataCombo, DataGrid and Data List*: These are OLE DB-aware versions of older data controls. They also support the new ADO data control.
- *Date Picker*: This is a drop-down calendar that provides an easy way to select dates and times.
- *Image Combo*: Image combo is a combo box that can include images in the list of choices.
- *Image List Control*: The image list control has been enhanced to support more file formats, including .cur, .gif, and .jpg.
- *MonthView*: MonthView provides a graphical representation of a calendar that you can drop into your forms. It allows the user to select dates.
- *MSHFlexGrid*: This is a new version of the FlexGrid control that can display a hierarchy of ADO recordsets. Each recordset is displayed as a band in the grid that can be formatted separately. Flexgrid controls only display information to the user; they cannot edit the data.

Building Lightweight Controls

Version 6.0 of Visual Basic now gives you the ability to create lightweight or windowless controls. A lightweight control does not have a windows handle, which means it is less resource intensive. This may be useful if your application or control will run in an environment such as the Internet, where download times favor smaller applications. We discuss the creation of controls with Visual Basic in Chapter 12.

CHAPTER 3

Requirements Gathering, Documentation, and Analysis

In this chapter we tackle some issues many programmers would rather not think about. This includes requirements gathering, documentation and technical support for the end user, and management issues such as estimating, scheduling, and staffing. While as a programmer you would rather "hack" away, the ability to provide good, efficient, and user-friendly code requires that we think about the larger picture.

Requirements Gathering

Requirements analysis involves identifying the needs that the software program is supposed to fulfill. Requirements analysis is a crucial step in the software development process. If not done properly, the entire development cycle is compromised. During the requirements-gathering phase, the following data need to be determined:

- The type of system that will be developed
- The skill level of the end user
- How data will be stored
- What tools will be used to develop the system

Thinking about these issues needs to done from the very beginning of a software project. This means that communication with the end user is important throughout the entire life cycle of the project. Effective communication ensures that the concept of the system is the same for the software team as for the end user. It also keeps the skill level of the customer in mind throughout the process. Failure to do so can lead to added costs later on, such as having to redesign the user interface.

Documentation

Documentation can take two forms. The first is documentation for the end user. Without adequate documentation, the best software product in the world will fall flat on its face. Documentation for the end user includes user's manuals and online help. These days it may also include a Web page. While we won't specifically address using Web-based documentation, the same principles described here will apply.

Documentation doesn't just include the end user. Don't forget that you'll need to document the code itself. This might be for other programmers or for members of the design team. In the technical world, communication often gets lost, despite the fact that it's as important as ever.

For the End User

Documentation for the end user is probably one of the most unpleasant aspects of the software design process, but it is also one of the most important. Without good software documentation, the user may feel frustrated and unhappy with the product. Good software documentation for the end user includes the following:

- A printed user's manual
- Online help
- Context-sensitive help

When a software project is finished and debugged, the tendency is to feel that it's all over. A software team probably would not rather think about it, but think about it we must.

Manuals   These days, some software companies are trying to keep costs down by skimping on the manual. However, this can actually damage your relationship with the customer. When a person buys a software product, he wants to feel like he's "getting something." We know that what he's buying is the bits and bytes on the CD-ROM or disk, but the customer needs to feel he is getting something "solid." A thick user's manual adds to this feeling.

Besides aesthetics, a user's manual can also reduce costs in the long run. By having a ready reference, users will feel less tempted to reach for the phone and call tech support. In practice, things don't always work this way; we all know that many users won't open the manual; they'll just call tech support anyway. Even so, by having a clear, concise manual you will give the majority of your users a ready source of information about your program and provide it with a professional appearance. Here are some suggestions for what elements or characteristics a good user's manual should have:

- Clear, concise step-by-step directions. Set off step-by-step tasks with bulleted text.
- Clearly identified menus, buttons, or commands; use bold or italic text.
- Plenty of screen captures and good illustrations.

- Arrows and pointers in your illustrations so the user can see important features quickly.

- An effort to avoid a condescending tone.

- No skipping obvious tasks; remember, the users of your program may not spend their lives on the computer.

- Nothing too technical. The inner workings of a software product should be invisible to the user.

- A "frequently asked questions" (FAQ) section where users can turn to address technical problems. Since several users will typically run into the same problems, addressing those situations in a central location can reduce tech support calls.

- Contact information such as phone number, web address, and e-mail address that is easy for the user to find in the manual—for those times when they do need direct help.

Online Help   Online help is just as important in documentation as the user's manual. Online help should mirror the manual if possible but may not necessarily be an exact copy. Don't skimp on online help. Again, this leads to frustrated customers who won't buy future products. There are several good online help tools available that make developing online help as simple as using a word processor. You should consider using HTML web-type help to keep up with current technology. When developing online help, use the same guidelines as you would when developing a user's manual. Be sure to use detailed explanations and a lot of screen captures and illustrations and don't leave anything out that you assume the end user should know. You can specify the help file for your application to use by setting the HelpFile property of the application object or using the General tab of the Project Properties dialog box.

Context-Sensitive Help   The goal of user interface design is to be "friendly." When designing help systems, the need to maintain a user-friendly approach is still there. This includes designing context-sensitive help. You can set context-sensitive help by setting the HelpContextID property of most controls. This property can be used to link a specific control or form to a specific topic in a help file. HelpContextID is type `Long`, and must correspond to the Context ID that you place in your help file. When the user has that form open, and presses F1, the help file will open on that topic.

Technical Design Documentation

Technical design documentation is a process that follows the software project throughout its lifetime. This includes commenting code, defining algorithms with flowcharts, communicating the structure of a project through diagrams, and maintaining scheduling and staffing requirements.

In-Code Documentation   In Chapter 6, we'll spend some time talking about commenting code. Commenting code is really documentation. It provides a record of the software development process and an accessible place to explain your code, and it keeps communication among the software team members at a high level.

Documentation as a Living Process   Documentation is a living process because its lifetime follows the lifetime of the software project very closely. This starts at the very beginning. In Chapter 1, we discussed the various software life-cycle models. No matter what life-cycle model you choose, the first step involves defining the problem and planning the allocation of resources, among other things. This is where the documentation process begins. Documentation can include the following:

- Clear definitions of the problem at hand. In other words, what task will the software perform or what problem will it solve?
- Staffing and scheduling estimation
- Algorithm definitions
- Progress notes
- A record of customer requests for new features
- A record of changes made to the software

Analysis

In this section, we'll consider analysis issues that will come into play, not only in the planning process, but throughout the entire development cycle. The important first step is estimating the resources required to complete a project. This will impact and involve our second topic, scheduling. Finally, we'll talk about staffing requirements.

Estimating

When it comes to software design, estimating is a tricky business. When determining how long a project will take or how many people will be required to complete it, you're always talking about a large amount of uncertainty. The risk of uncertainty varies from project to project, but there are three main areas where this risk lies. The first is the complexity of the project. This is not a hard-and-fast rule; an experienced manager will have a good grasp of how the complexity of a project will impact development time. For example, developing software to run a spaceship is going to be more complicated than a desktop database program, but a manager with 20 years of experience at NASA will have a reasonable grasp of how long it should take, despite the increased complexity. In today's world, however, the uncertainty risk is higher with any task because of the rapid pace of technology change.

Another important factor that has been identified as a risk factor in estimation is the size of a project. A large software project has a larger number of interwoven parts. This makes the estimating process more difficult and therefore gives rise to more error. Even if a large project can be made highly modular, each module may in itself be complex, injecting its own risk of error into the overall estimation process.

The third factor that can be identified as a risk to getting a good estimate is project structure. This means the ability to break down a project into a hierarchical and modular structure that is well suited to the use of different development teams. If a project fits this model well and your business has the resources necessary to build the required software teams, then it will be easier to provide a more accurate estimate.

Estimating is a complex process. Like software design, estimating can be made more effective and accurate by breaking the process down into smaller pieces. Once this is done, each task can be compared to tasks done in the past. Previously done tasks can then be used to provide a baseline estimate.

A detailed discussion of estimating is beyond the scope of this book. Readers who want to learn more should consult *A Manager's Guide to Software Engineering* by Roger S. Pressman (McGraw-Hill, 1996), for more information.

Scheduling

If you asked a randomly selected computer programmer what feature all software products have in common, he might say that the typical software project never gets completed on time. As I'm sure you're aware, the development of software never seems to go according to schedule. The causes for this are many, but we can probably identify a few that are common to most projects:

- An unrealistic goal was set by management. It's more likely that the time required to write software will be underestimated, especially by those not directly involved in writing code.
- Unforeseen technical problems can arise. This might include difficulties with a new language or technology.
- Customer demands or rethinking the software design requires continually retooling the code.
- Bad communication among staff members or from management. If it's not clear what management wants done, software may have to be redesigned after considerable effort has already been put in.
- New ideas don't pan out. Sometimes a new technology or idea might look good until it's actually placed in the code. When the decision is made to backtrack, the result is lost time.

Many scheduling problems can be resolved with careful planning. While we can never totally eliminate these problems, we can minimize them by taking the appropriate steps. Let's think about some of the ways we can do so.

Identifying Critical Tasks   In any given software project some tasks will play a greater role in determining whether or not the project can be completed on time. Some tasks may be peripheral or simply easy to complete, so you know they won't cause any bottlenecks. In contrast, a critical task will be one such that the time required to complete it will determine the length of the entire software development cycle. This means that it is important to lay out which tasks are critical and then follow those tasks more closely.

Make a Careful Match between Staff and Technologies   Time can be wasted by including a long learning curve in the development of a software product. For example, let's say your team has a product out that is running a bit slow according to the customers. Everyone on the team is a Visual Basic programmer, but the management decides to increase the speed of the project by moving some of the code to a dynamic link library written in C++. After three months, no progress has been made. The reason? The programmers assigned to complete the task, who assured you it would be no problem, have been busy learning C++ instead of attending to the task at hand. This kind of conflict can be avoided by making sure that everyone is comfortable with the technologies used before code development begins. This applies whether it's a new language, an ActiveX control, or the development of an Internet app. Management has to be thorough when considering this problem; programmers probably don't want to admit they don't know how to do something.

Communication among the Software Team Members   Bad communication among members of the software team can result in missed deadlines. While this seems obvious, it is often overlooked in the software world. That is because programming can be a loosely defined, independent activity. Programmers don't want someone peering over their shoulders as they work, and often management wants programmers to be independent and take the initiative. If this mode of operation is taken too far, communication can break down. A programmer might leave a kickoff meeting feeling clear about what the software requirements are, and then two months later it turns out she is totally off course. The result?: lost development time and a late project. It's important to keep in touch with the members of the software team to make sure that everyone is doing what he's supposed to and that scheduled deadlines are being met.

Meeting Customer Demands or Inside Suggestions   If customers demand a new feature but require that the product still meet scheduling deadlines, you obviously can't just dismiss them out of hand. Keeping the customer happy is the number-one goal, so if customer demands exceed your capacity to meet schedules you may want to consider adding staff to solve a problem. The increased cost can be offset by increasing the unit price or by spreading the cost out over many product sales. Compare this to the damage done by missing scheduled deadlines: unhappy customers, reduced market impact, and a bad reputation. The question of balance, however, rears its ugly head here. If you are selling to multiple clients, you simply can't add a new feature every time a customer requests one or someone in the company has a bright idea. Weigh each new feature against how many customers have requested it and how it will impact the existing software, and ask yourself how innovative that bright new idea really is.

Staffing

When working on a computer, it's easy to forget the human element in the design process. However, staffing for a new software project is one of the most important tasks that will be done in the development life cycle. Staffing will involve not only determining how many people will be required to complete a project but also evaluating each individual.

Evaluating the individual will involve a consideration of the following factors:

- *Knowledge*: This is a straightforward analysis of what tools each member of the team needs to know. This might include computer languages, familiarity with ActiveX controls, DHTML, database access, or the ability to write a DLL, to name a few examples. Knowledge can be outweighed by experience. If a software engineer has a great deal of experience, she will pick up new tools quickly, while a software engineer who knows a lot of tools but has little experience can be a liability without proper guidance.

- *Experience level*: Knowledge is one thing, but putting it into practice to solve a difficult problem may not be so easy without experience. The key is to build a software team with an experienced leader, especially if it is a critical task. Once an experienced leader is in place to provide guidance, the rest of the team may be easier to assemble.

- *Performance level*: Not all employees will perform at the same level or with the same intensity. Knowing how fast or effectively a member of the software team can work is an important factor in any requirements analysis. It is generally thought that the most productive employees will be three times more productive than average. As a result, knowing who the top performers are can be of great importance when delegating speed- or mission-critical tasks.

- *Personality characteristics*: The personality characteristics of each staff member can have a big impact on the success of the team. It's important to consider personality characteristics when putting a team together and when allocating tasks. There are several skills and characteristics to evaluate. Some questions to ask include: Does the employee have good communications skills? Is the employee a team player, or a loner? Can the person adapt well to change? Is he or she optimistic?

Putting together the right software team can be a complicated process. Once it has been done, the next issue to face is keeping the software team motivated. Some important issues here include:

- *Communication*: We discussed this earlier, but this is an important issue, so I'm listing it again as a factor to keep in mind when thinking about motivating the software team. If a programmer isn't clear about his responsibilities, this will create tension. It doesn't hurt to regularly meet with each team member to see how things are progressing.

■ *Burnout*: Everyone gets burned out from time to time, and if schedules are too tight or the pressure is too high, the risk of burnout increases. Paradoxically, programmers can burn out in a laid-back environment as well. This is because programmers tend to be driven people who like a challenge. In a relaxed or laid-back environment they will get bored. But even in a relaxed environment if everyone is putting in 12 hours per day for weeks on end, they'll start to question if it's worth it. The trick, of course, is to develop an environment with a middle-of-the road intensity level. Keep it challenging, but realize that employees have lives outside of work.

■ *Avoid jargon and too many diagrams*: We've spent some time talking about software models and analysis. In the real world, this approach is important, but it must be kept in perspective. Programmers tend to be practical people, and if they are overwhelmed by too many flow-charts and diagrams they won't take it seriously.

■ *Clearly define roles*: Make sure each member of the team knows his or her role. Roles should also be flexible to allow interaction and to enable members to effectively fill in if an important team member cannot complete the project.

■ *Keep meetings focused*: If there's one thing that wastes time in a business, it's endless meetings. It's important to keep the intended purpose of a meeting in focus. Meetings can often deteriorate to such an extent that by the end of two hours of discussion the original problem has been completely neglected. So you've wasted time, and you still have an unsolved problem on your hands. In short, stay on track in software meetings.

■ *Provide a helpful atmosphere*: The development environment should be one in which members of the team are encouraged to ask for help if necessary. Developers should be encouraged to ask questions or ask for help without being made to feel incompetent.

In summary, putting together a software team that has just the right mix is not an easy task. However, you can build effective software teams by keeping balance in mind. This means balancing experience and performance level as well as balancing personality characteristics to keep things running smoothly.

Designing VB Software

CHAPTER 4

Systems Architecture versus Software Architecture

Systems Architecture: The Big Picture

Chances are you will have to face the issues entailed in developing client/server software sometime during your programming life. This means that you will have to take the structure of the network into account when designing your software. Software should be designed in a flexible way so it can be used on a system of any size, from a single laptop to a large enterprise.

This means that you will have to break your software down into components. With this flexible design, an application can be scaled to work in a larger environment simply by distributing the components among different server computers. Since the Windows environment is built on, you should be able to design your application and have it run on a single desktop or in a client/server environment without much, if any, modification. This is done by building your application in three distinct layers:

■ *The user interface (UI) layer*: This layer is used to present and accept data to/from the end user. This layer of the application will not do any data processing or perform any business logic. The underlying structure of the data is hidden from this layer.

■ *Business logic layer*: This middle layer will perform the application logic and interface with the data layer. The business logic layer can be implemented as a component that resides on an intermediate server. You implement the business logic by designing classes, which we will cover in Chapter 8.

■ *Database layer*: In an enterprise environment, this layer will typically reside on a server. The database layer doesn't interact with the UI layer.

By splitting an application into three separate layers that more or less correspond to the hardware configuration of a network, the application is flexible enough to be scaled and modified without much pain. Each layer interacts with another layer through an interface. For example, if the business logic changes, the middle layer component can be swapped out and replaced with a new design. Since the UI layer and the database layer interact with the business logic layer only through the interface, things will go on running as they did before.

The three-layered approach allows us to scale the application to different-sized organizations. If it's a single user, all three components can fit nicely on a single machine. In a moderately sized two-tiered-network, we can run two tiers on the client machine and have the server perform data services. In a large network, each tier will be on a different component of the network.

Developing software to run on the network means that you will have to have a general understanding of how a network functions. You will also need to know about communicating with server computers, which may have specialized services. An in-depth treatment of client/server architecture is beyond the scope of this book. However, in this chapter we hope to give a brief overview of the client/server structure to justify the need to build three-tiered applications with Visual Basic.

For a detailed treatment of the client/server architecture, see *Second Generation Client/Server Computing* by D. Travis Dewire (McGraw-Hill, 1997).

Networks

Computer networks began with large mainframes that did all the processing while users sat at what was known as a "dumb" terminal. The terminal did not store any data; it simply provided the user with access to the mainframe. As the cost of computing power has fallen, the trend has been toward more distributed designs. Early versions of distributed computing involved connecting together a relatively small group, say a single department. Files and devices such as printers were shared among the group. Thus, the concept of a local area network, or LAN, was born.

Client-Server Model

The idea of a client/server architecture is based on specialization. Certain computers, known as servers, are specialized to perform certain tasks. With applications software, this usually involved fulfilling data requests. When a request is made for data, the server returns the result of the request rather than the entire database file. Processing the data and presenting them to the user is done on the client machine. With the server machine handling data services, in a first-generation client/server environment the client takes care of the following:

- Presentation of data to the user
- Application and business logic
- Data logic

Second-generation client/server takes further advantage of the concept of distributed access by adding additional servers to the mix. By including multiple servers on the network, different servers can be specialized to provide solutions for different tasks. The client machine will still be involved in presentation services as before. However, in second-generation client/server, application logic and business rules can be moved to a server computer. Still another server handles data requests. This type of architecture is known as a multitiered client/server architecture. A server is no longer a machine that is set up to perform a wide variety of tasks. Instead, you have several servers, each of which is specialized and optimized for a single task. The network is now divided into three tiers:

- *User interface tier*—implemented on the client machine
- *Application logic and business rules*—implemented on a specialized server, sometimes known as the intermediate server
- *Database access*—implemented on yet another server

The client machine is typically a single-processor computer running a Windows NT workstation. This is connected through a LAN to a departmental or application server. An application server can be a single processor or multiprocessor machine and may handle up to 100 users. This machine is connected through a wide area network, or WAN, to an enterprise or data server.

A multitier architecture allows an organization to maintain specialized or dedicated servers. Servers can be optimized for one particular task. For example, a high-performance computer can be used for computation-intensive operations. The architecture can be expanded as other needs are identified. New servers can be added that provide functions, in the form of objects or components, that are accessible to every application on the network. The network can include a data warehouse server that functions as a dedicated data processing server.

Distributed Applications

Today's software applications are broken down into components. Many of these components are shared by several different applications. This is as true on your desktop as it is in a client/server environment. However, in a distributed or client/server environment, common components can be maintained on a server. Typically, components that are common to several applications can be executed on the server with the results sent back to clients as needed. A distributed application may need to know how to interact with the specialized services of a server computer.

A distributed application can be either one that has distributed data or distributed processing. In a multitier environment, an application can have both data and processing distributed. During the design phase, the application must be broken down into separate units, which can run independently. The first step involves defining the three tiers: user interface, business logic, and data processing. Each tier may be broken down and refined even further. The goal is to allow the organization to replace individual components without affecting the application as a whole.

General Scalability

Scalability depends on a modular architecture. This means the ability to upsize or downsize an individual component without changing the system as a whole. The system can adapt to resource demands. For example, we can increase disk capacity or replace a server by another with more power. Scalability also means that servers are specialized for a specific function such as data warehousing.

Layered Application Development

An application should be designed in a modular fashion. By dividing an application into several modular components, the robustness of the software is ensured. This is because we can modify each component without having any impact on the rest of the application. Each module interacts only through the interface it presents.

When building a modular application, each component is assigned a specific task to perform. All computing tasks can be classified into three general areas: user interface tasks, business logic tasks, and data processing tasks. This type of breakdown leads us to the multitiered development model promoted by Microsoft. Each tier of the application is responsible for performing one aspect of the overall software model. At this point, we can consider three types of n-tiered applications.

The first type of model is known as the one-tiered model. This is just an application running on a single PC. The data, business rules, and user interface are all implemented on the same machine. If data sharing is not a requirement, this is a desirable model since speed is optimized. No time is wasted going out to retrieve data. However, in today's world there aren't many useful applications that don't need to share data in some way. As a result, there aren't very many one-tiered applications.

The two-tiered model is based on the client/server concept. In this model, the user interface and business logic are in an application stored on each client machine. The data is stored on a server computer. The user sends requests to the server in the form of queries, which the server fulfills and returns to the client. The client application formats the data and presents it to the user, either in forms or in reports. The user can then manipulate the data, print reports, and so on. The business logic layer can also be placed on the server in this manner. No matter where the business logic layer is placed, a compromise has to be made. This is because if we place it on the client machine and modifications are made as business logic changes we have to redistribute the software to each client. If the business logic is placed on the server, downtime can result as the server is updated and database programming is changed.

Three-Tiered Development

The most recent incarnation of n-tiered development is the three-tiered model. This model has been developed primarily because of the rising popularity of the Internet. With a web server, data is processed and formatted before being presented to the client, which in this case is a web browser. This led to the idea of using a middle layer to implement data formatting before sending it to the client. The middle layer also functions to validate data before returning it to the server. This middle tier is known as the business services tier. The benefit of having the middle tier is that it can be changed as business logic changes. This simplifies updates because the client does not have to receive new front-end software, while the server-side database can remain unchanged.

Don't think that this model is restricted to use on the Internet. The three-tiered model is a flexible model that can be used in all software development, even on a single machine. The way each tier is distributed will depend on how large the business is in which the application is used. In any case, the three-tiered model can be used in application development in three phases. Each phase should be completed before moving to the next.

- *Define the object model*: In this phase, we define the objects that will be used in this program.

- *Build the database*: The design of a database is just as important as the other phases of software development. We will consider the design and programming of databases in Chapters 9 through 11.

- *User interface layer*: The user interface layer should be built in the last phase of development. This runs counter to the temptation fostered by Visual Basic. Programming in a RAD environment can tempt a developer into drawing forms and controls before doing anything else. By building the business logic layer and database layer first, we can ensure that the application is more robust.

UI Layer   The first tier is the user interface (UI) layer. This is the client application that the end user has access to. The client application is typically a standard EXE program. This layer will include the forms and ActiveX controls that provide the user with a means to manipulate the data. The UI layer will manipulate the data through the objects presented by the middle tier. With three-tiered development, the underlying structure of the database is invisible to the UI layer.

Business Logic Layer   The business logic layer is based on an object model. This will entail the development of classes to implement each object (see Chapter 8). The main purpose of the business logic layer is to encapsulate the data interface. This will permit us to hide the data access from the rest of the program. It will then be easier to modify each layer of the software without impacting the other layers.

The business logic layer is built on business objects. These objects are abstract representations of something in the real world. This can be a model of a person, an object, or a process. For example, we can model employees, customers, orders, or products.

Once each object is identified, we need to define the interface for the object. The interface of each object is the way that other objects and layers of the system can communicate with the object. The interface is independent of the underlying design of the object. This means that the "internals" of the object can be changed while maintaining the same interface. The program then goes on as before with the new version of the object. With the same interface, other objects or layers that communicate with this object through the interface can continue to do so without modification.

One way to build the middle tier is to create a dynamic link library (DLL). This is an ActiveX in-process server. The library can contain all of the classes used to define the objects in the application. The UI layer, or the application presented to the end user, can access the objects of the DLL. When a business object is changed, the DLL is modified, but the client application can continue to use it as before.

Data Layer   The database is the final piece of the three-tiered model. This layer is placed on a server computer. This is where the actual data processing takes place. Information from the data layer is passed to the objects in the business layer, or middle tier. There is no direct link between the client application and the data layer.

CHAPTER 5

General Coding Practices

A Quick Basic Review

In this chapter, we'll provide a quick and dirty review of the Visual Basic language. First, we'll tackle declaring variables and data types, including such important issues as variable scope and public and private variables. Next, we'll explore the control statements available in Visual Basic, as well as discuss programming objects. After a discussion of subroutines and functions, we'll close out the chapter by taking a look at using version control tools, such as Visual Source Safe, with your projects.

Declaring Variables

A variable is a named memory location that stores data. Most variables will store data of one specific type, such as a number or a text string (the `Variant` data type is an exception to this rule; see below). A variable declaration tells the compiler what name you want to assign to the variable and what type of data it will store. In Visual Basic, variables are declared by using a `Dim` statement. The syntax of a `Dim` statement is as follows:

```
Dim [shared] name As [New ] Type [, name As [New] Type]
```

where `Type` is an optional parameter that is either one of the standard basic data types, an object, or a user-defined type that you create with a *Type* statement (see Chapter 10, "Random Access Files"). If the data type is not specified, the variable will be of type `Variant`.

Rules for Variable Names

Variable names must begin with an alphabetic character and can be up to 255 characters in length. Variable names are limited to alphabetic, numeric, or underscore characters. They cannot contain spaces. For example, to declare a variable called `salary`, we could use a statement like this one:

```
Dim Salary As Integer
```

We could then assign this variable a value further down in our code:

```
Salary = 28,000
```

Unlike in C++, in Visual Basic you can't initialize variables when declaring them. So a statement such as

```
Dim x As Integer = 100
```

will cause a syntax error. However, while variables in C++ will contain garbage unless explicitly initialized, Visual Basic variables are initialized to zero for numeric variables and to blank, zero-length strings for string variables.

Type-Declaration Characters

In a holdover from older versions of Basic, variables can also be declared by using a *type-declaration character*. A type-declaration character is one of the following symbols:

- % Integer
- & Long
- ! Single
- # Double
- $ String

The data type of the variable is specified by appending the type-declaration character to the end of the variable name. While using type-declaration characters is legal, they should not be used because this type of variable declaration does not make for readable code. Type-declaration characters can also be used with implicit variable declaration (see the next section), which is a sloppy programming practice that should be avoided. To use a type-declaration character in a Dim statement, we could declare the variable like this:

```
Dim Salary%
```

When referring to the variable in code, you can continue to use the type-declaration character:

```
Salary% = 28,000
```

The type-declaration character can be left off the variable name once declared, and Visual Basic will know we are still referring to the same variable. Declaring the variable with a type-declaration character while specifying the data type is a syntax error. The statement

```
Dim y% As Integer
```

is not allowed. In general, to keep your code as readable as possible you should avoid using type-declaration characters. Instead, explicitly list each data type in your `Dim` statements.

Declaring Multiple Variables on a Single Line

To declare multiple variables on the same line, use a comma to separate the variable list. For example:

```
Dim Age As Byte, Salary As Long
```

The data type must be specified for each variable, or it will be considered to be of type `Variant`. Consider this declaration of four variables:

```
Dim Salary As Integer, TaxRate As Double, SSN, Name As String
```

In this case, since no data type was specified for the variable SSN, it will be of type `Variant`.

Declaring Constants

Visual Basic also allows the programmer to declare constants, which will maintain the same value throughout the lifetime of the program. This is done by using the `const` keyword. The syntax is similar to that used with the `Dim` statement:

```
Const name [As Type] = expression [ , name [As Type] = expression]
```

As with a `Dim` statement, specifying the data type is optional. Constant names follow the same rules as variable names. Multiple constants can be declared on the same line by separating them with commas. For example, we could declare a constant to hold the value of pi:

```
Const PI As Double = 3.1416
```

Once a constant is declared, it can be referred to almost like any variable, with the obvious exception that we can't assign a new value to it. Here we use PI to determine the circumference of a circle:

```
Const PI As Double = 3.1416
Dim Radius As Double, Circumference As Double
Radius = 14

Circumference = 2*PI*Radius
```

Option Explicit

While a Dim statement can be used to declare variables, with Visual Basic this is not strictly necessary. A variable can be "declared" by simply using it in code. This type of variable declaration is known as *implicit declaration*. You can specify a data type by using a type-declaration character or simply leave it off, in which case the variable will be of type Variant. For example, we could simply place the following lines of code into our program without using a Dim statement:

```
HourlyWage#  =  7.50
WeeklyPay = (HourlyWage#)*(40)
```

HourlyWage# is a variable of type Double because we ended the variable name with the Double type-declaration character #. Since WeeklyPay has no type-declaration character, it's considered a variant.

Besides being sloppy, implicit variable declaration can cause bugs that are difficult to track down. One problem that can arise from using implicitly declared variables is that later on in your code you might misspell a variable name, and Visual Basic will simply think this is a new variable. Let's say we wanted to use the WeeklyPay variable later in code, but we didn't spell it right:

```
TotalPay = 2 * WeklyPay
```

Visual Basic will think that WeklyPay is a new variable, so the result, TotalPay, will be zero. While this is the wrong answer, nothing illegal has been done here. As a result, the code will compile and run, and it may be extremely difficult to track down the problem.

From this discussion you've probably realized that it's better to declare all of your variables before using them. Fortunately, Visual Basic provides a method that can force you to do so, the `Option Explicit` keyword. By placing the single line

```
Option Explicit
```

at the beginning of each general declarations section of your forms and code modules, you can avoid the problems that can arise from implicit declaration. With `Option Explicit`, we would have to declare all of our variables. The code would look like this:

```
Dim HourlyWage As Double, WeeklyPay As Double, TotalPay As Double

HourlyWage = 7.5
WeeklyPay = HourlyWage*40
  .
  .
  .
TotalPay = 2 * WeklyPay
```

This time, when we attempt to run our code Visual Basic will enter break mode with the error *Variable Not Defined*, saving us endless hours of searching through the code line by line looking for the error.

Having VB Automatically Insert `Option Explicit`

Of course, when you're working on a rather large project you may forget to place `Option Explicit` at the beginning of every code window. Luckily for the sloppy programmer, Visual Basic provides a way to have this done automatically: by selecting *Require Variable Declaration* under *Code Settings* from the Editor tab of the Options dialog (see Fig. 5-1). Chances are Visual Basic is already set with this option, but if not it's a good idea to set it yourself. To do so, use these steps:

■ Select *Options* from the Tools pull-down menu.

■ On the Editor tab, check the *Require Variable Declaration* box.

If you select this option, Visual Basic will place the `Option Explicit` statement at the beginning of every general declarations section for all forms and modules you add to your projects.

Figure 5-1
The Options dialog.

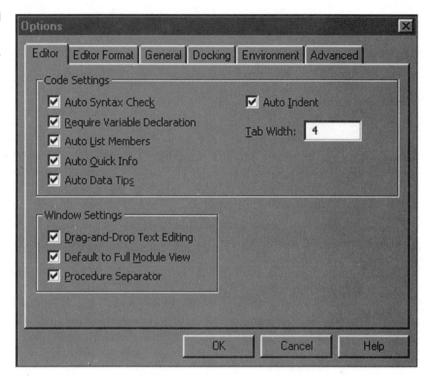

VB Data Types

The data type of a variable will determine what kinds of information it can store. Visual Basic provides several built-in types that vary in both size and the range of data they can hold. Good judgment is required when assigning data types; don't always assign the largest possible data type when memory could be conserved. In this section, we'll go over the basic data types. Later, we'll explore arrays and creating your own types.

Byte

Byte variables can be used to store numeric information in the range of zero to 255. With a storage size of only one byte, Byte variables are an efficient way to store data. Byte variables can also be used to store individual characters.

Integer

An `Integer` variable can store whole numbers in the range −32,768 to 32,767, with a storage size of two bytes.

Long

Like an `Integer`, a variable of type `Long` can store whole numbers but over a much larger range. A `Long` requires four bytes of storage and has a range of −2,147,483,648 to 2,147,483,647.

Single

The `Single` data type can be used to track floating-point values. A `Single` requires four bytes of storage and has a range of −3.402823E38 to −1.401298E-45 for negative values and 1.401298E-45 to 3.402823E38 for positive values.

Double

Type `Double` can also be used to store floating-point values. With eight bytes of storage, however, a `Double` has much greater precision and range than a `Single`. The range of a `Double` is −1.79769313486232E308 to −4.94065645841247E-324 for negative values and 4.94065645841247E-324 to 1.79769313486232E308 for positive values.

Currency

`Currency` can be used to track financial data. A `Currency` requires eight bytes of storage. Note that variables of type `Currency` maintain four digits of precision, not two. This is to ensure that there are no rounding errors. The storage size of type `Currency` is eight bytes, and the range is −922,337,203,685,477.5808 to 922,337,203,685,477.5807.

Decimal

A variable of type `Decimal` is a number scaled to a power of 10. Decimals can be whole numbers or have a fractional part. A whole number `Decimal` has a range of positive or negative 79,228,162,514,264,337,593,543,950,335. With a fractional part, decimal variables can have 28 decimal places and a range between positive and negative 7.9228162514264337593543950335.

Boolean

Boolean variables are used to store True/False values. A Boolean requires two bytes of storage. Numeric variables can be assigned to a Boolean variable, with zero becoming False and all other values being True.

Date

A `Date` variable can be used to represent dates from January 1, 100, to December 31, 9999. `Date` variables require eight bytes of storage space. The current date can be assigned to a `Date` variable by calling the `Now` function. Note that `Date` variables also contain time information. Time information stored in a `Date` variable includes hours, minutes, and seconds. These values can be obtained from a `Date` variable by calling the `DatePart` function. Visual Basic also provides the `DateDiff` and `DateAdd` functions, which are useful when manipulating dates.

String

To hold text information or numeric data that isn't normally manipulated (such as a social security number), you can declare a variable of type `String`. In Visual Basic, strings can either be variable length or fixed length. The size in bytes for a variable-length string is 10 bytes plus one byte for each character, and the range can vary from zero to two billion characters. To declare a variable-length string, you simply use a `Dim` statement with the data type specified to be `String`. A variable-length string can be assigned values that have different numbers of characters, as the following code illustrates:

```
Dim PetName As String

PetName = "Brandy"

PetName = "Jonathan Michael Jones the Third"
```

As you assign different-sized strings to the variable PetName, the size of the variable in bytes will change to reflect the number of characters it holds. Variable-length strings can hold an extremely large number of characters, so in practice you won't have to worry about how many bytes the data assigned to it will contain.

If you want to maintain the size of the string as a specific number of bytes, you can declare a fixed-length string. A fixed-length string can be from one to 65,400 characters. To declare a fixed-length string, you need to specify how many characters it will hold, as in the following example:

```
Dim StaffName As String * 20
```

A fixed-length string always contains the same number of characters, regardless of what values it is assigned at run time. If the variable is assigned a text string with fewer characters than allotted, the String variable will be padded with blanks. On the other hand, if you attempt to assign a text string that is larger than the number of characters allocated, the string will be truncated.

Variant

A Variant variable can hold any type of data. With numeric data, a Variant requires 16 bytes of storage and can hold any value up to the range of type Double. When storing strings, a Variant requires 22 bytes of overhead in addition to the length of the string. The range is the same as for a variable-length string. While a Variant provides flexibility, due to the extra memory overhead you should avoid using it. In a carefully designed program there is virtually no reason to use variables of type Variant.

Object

An Object variable requires 4 bytes of storage and includes any object reference in Visual Basic. Variables declared as type Object must use the Set statement when you assign a reference to them. We'll be discussing programming with objects in Chapter 8.

■■■■ ■■■■ Data Conversion Functions

A situation that often comes up in software development is the need to assign the value of one variable to another variable that is a different type. For example, you may need to convert a `String` variable that holds some numeric value into an `Integer`. In Visual Basic, this is something that will typically arise out of the need to retrieve information from the user, which is usually done with text boxes. Let's consider a program that asks the user to type in her age into a text box, and we need to store the data in an `Integer` variable. We could use the following code:

```
Dim UsersAge As Integer

UsersAge = txtAgeBox.Text
```

This code will work correctly since Visual Basic will do the data conversion for you. However, this is not a good programming practice, for two reasons. First, we can't be absolutely sure that the conversion will be done exactly as needed, and there is a chance of data loss. Second, it doesn't make for readable code. A better method is to use one of the built-in type conversion functions, each of which takes a single argument and returns the desired type you want to convert to. Conversion functions can be used to convert numbers to strings, strings to numbers, and strings to dates or for conversion among the different numeric types. There are ten type conversion functions:

■ `CBool` converts the argument to type `Boolean`.

■ `CByte` converts the argument to type `Byte`.

■ `CCur` converts the argument to type `Currency`.

■ `CDate` converts the argument to type `Date`.

■ `CDbl` converts the argument to type `Double`.

■ `CDec` converts the argument to type `Decimal`.

■ `CInt` converts the argument to type `Integer`.

■ `CLng` converts the argument to type `Long`.

■ `CSng` converts the argument to type `Single`.

■ `CVar` converts the argument to type `Variant`.

■ `CStr` converts the argument to type `String`.

To use a conversion function successfully, the argument must be within the range of the data type you are converting to. For example, to convert to a `String` to a `Byte` the string expression must be in the range of 0 to 255. If the argument is outside of the valid range, you'll get an overflow error.

Returning to the problem of reading in the user's age, we could explicitly convert the value from a `String` to an `Integer` with the `CInt` function:

```
Dim intUsersAge As Integer

intUsersAge = CInt(txtAgeBox..Text)
```

Variable Scope and Lifetime

Two important attributes that every variable in a program will have are *scope* and *lifetime*. The scope of a variable is the range throughout the program where the variable can be accessed. The scope of a variable is determined by where the variable is declared and whether it is declared as public or private. Generally, there are three types of scope in a Visual Basic program:

- *Global or public scope*: Access to a global or public variable is available throughout the entire program. In other words, every procedure in the project can reference and modify the variable. This is the widest type of scope a variable can have. Variables that have global scope are declared with either the `Global` keyword or the `Public` keyword. Note that a variable cannot be declared with the `Global` keyword if it is in a form module. Since the `Global` keyword is really provided for backward compatibility, however, it should not be used at all. Use the `Public` keyword to declare variables with global scope. If a public variable is declared in a form module, you must use `formname.variablename` syntax to reference it outside of that form.

- *Module-wide or private scope*: A variable with module-wide scope is available to all procedures within the form or module where the variable is declared. This type of variable is declared in the general declarations section of a form or module with the `Dim` or `Private` keyword.

- *Local scope*: Variables with local scope are those that are declared within a procedure. The variable is not known outside of the procedure in which it is declared. Local variables can only be declared with `Dim` or `Static` and can never be declared as `Public`. Once the procedure stops executing, the variable no longer exists, until the procedure is called again.

When defining the variables that will be used in your program, you should try to use the most restrictive scope possible. Global variables should only be used if strictly necessary. If you can think of a way to define a module-wide or local variable and then pass its value to other procedures, do that instead of defining a global variable. The overuse of global variables is a sloppy programming practice that makes code difficult to read and bugs hard to track down.

When two variables appear in a program with the same name, the variable with the most local scope has precedence. To see how this works, consider the following simple example in a form:

```
Option Explicit
Public x As Integer

Private Sub Command1_Click()

  MsgBox "Module Wide value of x is " & x
  x = x + 2
  DoubleIt
  MsgBox "New Value of Module Wide x = " & x

End Sub
Private Sub Form_Load()

  Dim x As Integer
  x = 36
  DoubleIt
  MsgBox "The Value of x is " & x

End Sub

Public Sub DoubleIt()
  x = 2 * x
End Sub
```

A public variable of type `Integer` called x is declared in the general declarations section of the form. This will make the variable available to other parts of the program as long as they reference the form where the variable is declared (i.e., *form1.x*). In the form load event, a local variable also of type `Integer`, and also called x, is declared. Local variable names have precedence, so any reference to x made within the form load event procedure will refer to the local copy. After assigning a value to x, we call the function `DoubleIt`:

```
Public Sub DoubleIt()
  x = 2 * x
End Sub
```

The code in `DoubleIt` refers to the form-wide variable, so it will have no impact on any reference to x inside the form load event. After program control returns from the `DoubleIt` procedure, the code in the form load event displays a message box containing the value of x. Again, since the form load event has its own variable called x, calling DoubleIt had no effect, and the message box will display *The Value of x is 36*.

In the Command1 click event procedure, we again call DoubleIt. This time, when we modify the value of x, since there is no local variable with the same name, we are referencing the form-wide variable. This time x is set to 2, DoubleIt is called, changing the value to 4, and the message box will display *New Value of Module Wide x = 4*.

Variable Lifetime

The second attribute that a variable has is known as *lifetime*. When a variable goes out of scope, the variable ceases to exist. In other words, its lifetime comes to an end. A local variable goes out of scope when the procedure in which it is declared ends. The next time the procedure is called the variables behave as if they had never been used before. This means that all previous data values will be lost. A module level or public variable, however, will continue to exist as long as the program is running. This means that those variables will maintain the values assigned to them. Consider the following code example:

```
Option Explicit

Public PI As Double

Sub Main()

 PI = 3.1416

End Sub

Public Function Circumference(NewValue As Double) As Double

   Dim Radius As Double

   Radius = NewValue

   Circumference = 2 * PI * Radius

End Function
```

In this case, the public variable PI will have a lifetime as long as the program is running. It is assigned the value 3.1416 in the Sub Main procedure at startup. If we don't modify the value anywhere else it will have this value throughout the lifetime of the program. The variable named Radius has local scope limited to the Circumference procedure. This means that its lifetime only lasts as long as the

Circumference procedure is executing. Once the procedure exits at the End Function statement, Radius goes out of existence. The next time the procedure is called memory is allocated for the local variables, and a new Radius variable comes into existence.

Static **Variables**

Local variables come to the end of their existence when the procedure in which they are declared exits. Most of the time this behavior is adequate for the problem at hand. However, there are situations when you will need the value of a local variable to persist between function calls. For example, you may want to count how many times a procedure is called. Visual Basic has provided the Static keyword for this purpose. The Static keyword will make a local variable retain its value between procedure calls, for the entire lifetime of the program. To declare a variable as Static, simply use the Static keyword in place of the Dim statement. The syntax of a declaration with the Static keyword is as follows:

Static name **As** Type

For example, consider a hypothetical program that keeps score in a basketball game. The following function is called every time a basket is made and returns a running count of the total number of points scored:

```
Function PointsScored(Shot As Integer) As Integer

  Static Points As Integer

  Points = Points + Shot

  PointsScored = Points

End Function
```

Recall that Visual Basic initializes numeric variables to 0, so the first time the function is called the Points variable is set to 0. Each time the function is called, the points scored with the current shot are added to the running total maintained by the static variable Points, which the function returns for use elsewhere in the program.

Visual Basic also allows you to specify that *all* of the local variables within a procedure are static. This can be done by using the Static keyword in the Function or Sub declaration. For example, returning to our basketball program, we could write a subroutine that uses static variables to track both the number of points scored and the number of free throws:

```
Public Static Sub PointsScored(Shot As Integer, ShotType As String,
TotalPoints As Integer, FreeThrows As Integer)

  Dim NumPoints As Integer, NumFreeThrows As Integer

  NumPoints = NumPoints + Shot

  If trim(ShotType) = "Free Throw" Then
    NumFreeThrows = NumFreeThrows + 1
  End If

  TotalPoints = NumPoints
  FreeThrows = NumFreeThrows

End Sub
```

In this case, since the procedure header contains the Static keyword, any variables declared within the procedure are statics and so retain their values throughout the lifetime of the program. You can specify that all the variables in a procedure be static from the Add Procedure dialog available on the Tools menu (see Fig. 5-2). If you check the *All Local Variables as Statics* box, the Static keyword will be placed in the procedure header by Visual Basic.

Public versus Private Variables

Visual Basic allows two other keywords to be used in the declaration of variables and constants. These are Public and Private. Using the Public keyword let's you declare a variable or constant that is available outside the form or module where it was declared. The Private keyword, however, let's you "hide" variables. A private variable is only available within the form or module where it has been declared. The Public and Private keywords can only be used in the general declarations section of a form, standard module, or class module. One restriction to note is that you cannot declare a Public constant in a form module. The syntax is similar to that used for the Dim statement:

[**Public**|**Private**] name **As** Type

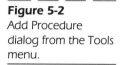

Figure 5-2
Add Procedure
dialog from the Tools
menu.

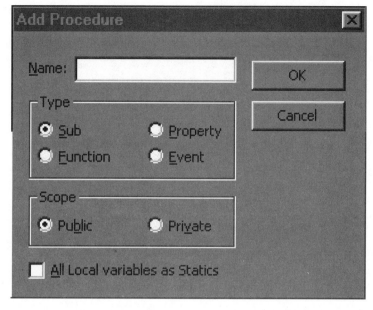

For example, in the general declarations section of a standard module we could declare a variable like the following:

```
Public Temperature As Byte
```

The `Temperature` variable is now accessible throughout the application, just like a global variable in past versions of Visual Basic. If we made the following declaration in the general declarations section of a form,

```
Private Dependents As Integer
```

the `Dependents` variable would only be accessible to code within that form. Any attempt to reference a private variable outside of the form or module where it has been declared will result in an error.

If you have declared public variables in different forms or modules with the same name you can use the name of the form or module in which it was declared to specify which variable you are talking about. The syntax is as follows:

```
[form name | module name].variablename
```

Let's consider the following example. Let's say that we had two public variables named `Temperature`. A form named `frmWeather` uses the `Temperature` variable to track today's temperature, while a standard module named `Averages` uses a `Temperature` variable to track the average temperature. We can use the following code to refer to each variable:

```
Dim TodaysTemp As Integer
Dim AvgTemp As Integer, Difference As Integer

TodaysTemp = frmWeather.Temperature
AvgTemp = Averages.Temperature

Difference = Abs(TodaysTemp - AvgTemp)
```

By using the form or module name with the public variable, Visual Basic is able to resolve which variable we are referring to. The `Public` and `Private` keywords can also be used when declaring constants, for example:

```
Public Const Pi As Double  = 3.1416
```

The constant `Pi` would then be available throughout the application.

Arrays

An array is a collection of elements that are all of the same data type. Each element of the array is identified by an index. In Visual Basic, an array is declared by specifying the array name, the upper and lower bounds of the array, and the data type of the array. For example, to declare an array with 100 elements of type integer we would use the following `Dim` statement:

```
Dim MyArray(1 to 100) As Integer
```

Visual Basic allows you to specify positive and negative array bounds. We could have declared the array like this:

```
Dim MyArray(-150 to -50) As Integer
```

By default, Visual Basic arrays start at index 1. The bounds of an array are type `Long`, which has a range of −2,147,483,648 to 2,147,483,647. You can declare arrays without specifying the lower bound, such as:

```
Dim MyArray(100) As Integer
```

in which case the lower bound is assumed by Visual Basic to be 1.

The `Option Base` Statement

Visual Basic provides the `Option Base` statement so that you can change the default lower bound of an array. `Option Base` can be used to set the lower bound to either 0 or 1. If you prefer to use arrays with C/C++-type bounds that start at 0, you can add the `Option Base` statement to the general declarations section of the module where the array is declared:

```
Option Base 0
```

Now an array declaration like this one

```
Dim MyArray(100) As Integer
```

declares an array that has elements indexed from 0 to 99.

Arrays of Type `Variant`

Since a `Variant` variable can contain anything, you can declare an array of type `Variant`, and in this case each element can contain any type of data. For example, we can mix numeric and string types:

```
Dim TestData(1 to 100) As Variant

TestData(1) = "This is a test string."
TestData(2) = 8.56
TestData(3) = 38
```

While this is permissible, this type of array declaration should be avoided because of the tremendous memory overhead it entails. Recall that a `Variant` requires several bytes of overhead in addition to the memory required to store the data. Put this in an array and you can add up wasted memory quickly.

Multidimensional Arrays and Arrays of Arrays

Just like other programming languages, Visual Basic allows you to use multidimensional arrays. For example, to declare a two-dimensional array, you could use the following `Dim` statement:

```
Dim TestScores(1 to 100, 1 to 5) As Integer
```

The elements of the array are accessed by specifying an index for each dimension. For example, to access the elements of the `TestScores` array, we could use nested `For` loops:

```
For k = 1 to 100
 For l = 1 to 5
   CurrentScore = TestScores(k,l)
 Next l
Next k
```

Visual Basic also allows you to use arrays that contain other arrays. The array that contains other arrays as elements must be of type `Variant`. For example:

```
Dim MyData(1 to 5) As Integer
Dim YourData(1 to 3) As Variant
Dim j As Integer, NewValue As Integer

For j = 1 To 5
 MyData(j) = j
Next

YourData(2) = MyData()

NewValue = YourData(2)(3)
```

The second element of the `YourData` array contains a copy of the `MyData` array. By referring to element (2)(3), the variable `NewValue` is assigned the value stored in the third element of the `MyData` array. Since this type of programming requires the use of a `Variant`, it should be avoided if possible.

Determining the Upper and Lower Bounds of an Array

Visual Basic has provided the `LBound` and `UBound` functions, which return the lower and upper bounds of an array, respectively. The return type of these functions is type `Long`. The syntax is as follows:

```
[LBound | UBound] (arrayname, [dimension])
```

These functions can come in handy when an array of unknown dimensions is passed into a procedure. Consider the following:

```
Public Sub SumElements(MyData() As Integer, Result As Long)
```

```
Dim lower As Long, upper As Long
Dim i As Integer

Result = 0
lower = LBound(MyData)
upper = UBound(MyData)

For i = lower To upper
 Result = Result + MyData(i)
Next

End Sub
```

In this case, the bounds of the one-dimensional array `MyData` are determined by calling the `LBound` and `UBound` functions. These functions can also be used with multidimensional arrays by specifying which array dimension you are interested in. Suppose we have a grid of data in x and y, represented by a two-dimensional array called *Voltages*. The bounds of the array can be determined with the following code:

```
Dim lowerx As Integer, upperx As Integer, lowery as Integer, uppery
  As integer

lowerx  = LBound(Voltages,1)
upperx = UBound(Voltages,1)
lowery = LBound(Voltages,2)
uppery = UBound(Voltages,2)
```

Now we have the information we need to loop through the array:

```
For k = lowerx to upperx
 For l = lowery to uppery
  MyData = Voltages(k,l)
   'code to manipulate data here
 Next l
Next k
```

Using `ReDim` and the `Preserve` Keyword

Visual Basic allows you to redimension the size of an array. To do this, you need to declare the array as a dynamic array. When declaring the array, rather than specifying the number of elements it will hold you simply place an empty set of parentheses. One set of parentheses is used regardless of the number of dimensions the array will hold. For example:

```
Dim TestScores() As Integer
```

Follow the array name with parentheses. Later, you can use the ReDim statement to specify the bounds of the array:

```
ReDim TestScores(1 to MaxStudents) As Integer
```

We can even change the array to be two-dimensional:

```
ReDim TestScores(1 to 10, 1 to Max) As Integer
```

This type of array declaration provides you with a flexible way to manage arrays. For example, you may not know how many students you will have for the TestScores array to track until run time. The ReDim statement allows you to declare the array and then resize it while the program runs using a variable. When you use a ReDim statement the contents of the array will be lost.

The Preserve keyword can be used in conjunction with the ReDim statement to preserve the data that already exists in the array. Say our program that uses the TestScores array is running, and we are required to add another test score beyond the current limits of the array. Of course, we don't want to erase the test scores that have already been input to the array. We can accomplish this by using the Preserve keyword:

```
ReDim Preserve TestScores(1 to MaxStudents + 1)
```

When using the Preserve keyword, in a multidimensional array, only the upper bound of the last array dimension can be resized.

Control Statements

Control statements are used to direct the flow of program logic. This may include using an If statement to test a condition, using a For Loop to fill an array, or using a Case statement to choose among a set of possible values. Without control statements a programming language would not be of much use.

If Statements

An If statement can be used to provide the conditional execution of a block of code. The top of the If statement is a logical condition that is tested. For example, we might ask questions like "Are there more than 100 customers?", "Is this employee an accountant?", or "Have we reached the end of this file?" The block of code in an If statement can be one or more lines of code, including more If statements. The syntax of an If statement in Visual Basic is as follows:

```
If condition Then
 Code Statements
End If
```

If condition is True, then Code Statements will be executed. If condition is False, program execution will pick up on the line following the End If statement. The code statements following an If do not need to be indented, but it makes your code more readable if they are. A good rule of thumb is to indent your code three or four spaces following an If statement. A simple If statement might be something like the following:

```
If JobType = 7 Then
  Wage = 8.50
  Shift = "Swing Shift"
End If
```

In this case, the Wage and Shift variables will only be assigned the values indicated if JobType is 7. If statements can be included in other If statements, as far down as you like. This is known as a nested If. The following example illustrates a nested If statement:

```
If JobType = 7 Then
 Shift = "Swing Shift"
 If Supervisor Then
   Wage = 10.00
 End If
End If
```

In this case, Wage is only assigned if the Boolean variable Supervisor evaluates to True. We can extend the If statement by using the Else keyword. The Else keyword allows us to include an alternate path of execution should the condition tested by the If statement prove to be False. For example, we can extend the previous code example to include workers other than supervisors by using an Else statement:

```
If JobType = 7 Then
   Shift = "Swing Shift"
   If Supervisor Then
     Wage = 10.00
```

```
     Else
        Wage = 8.50
     End If
End If
```

By using an `ElseIf` statement, we can further extend our logic to test for multiple cases. You can have as many `ElseIf` statements as you want, but the last statement must be an `Else` statement. The following code illustrates how this is done:

```
If Shift = "Swing Shift" Then

  If Position = "Supervisor" Then
     Wage = 10#
  ElseIf Position = "Floor Waxer" Then
     Wage = 8.5
  ElseIf Position = "Carpet Cleaner" Then
     Wage = 8#
  Else
     Wage = 7.6
  End If

EndIf
```

In this example, we test the value of the `Shift` variable to see if it is "Swing Shift." If so, the nested `If-ElseIf` statements inside will be executed. We use the `If` and `ElseIf` statements to test the value of the `Position` variable, and assign the appropriate wage. The `ElseIf` statements will only be evaluated in the case that the `If` statement is False. The final statement of the `If-ElseIf` block is an `Else` statement, which will handle all cases we haven't tested for explicitly. Remember that the last statement of an `If-ElseIf` block must be an `Else` statement. The code following the `Else` statement is only executed if all of the `ElseIf` statements evaluate to False.

Using Inline `If` Statements   For simple cases, you can use an inline `If` statement when you will only execute a single line of code when an `If` statement evaluates to True and there is no `Else` condition.

```
If rs.eof Then msgbox "Reached End of File."
```

The message box will only be displayed if the end-of-file (eof) property of the `recordset` variable is True. When using an inline `If` you can leave out the `End If` statement.

For Next Loops

A For loop can be used to repeat a block of statements a specified number of times. The syntax for a For loop is as follows:

```
For counter = start To finish [Step step]
  Code Block
  [Exit For]
Next [counter]
```

Counter is a variable, usually of type Integer, that is used to increment through the loop. The Step parameter specifies by how much to change the value of the counter each time through the loop. Step can be positive or negative, and if not specified counter will be incremented by one each time. The Next statement is used to specify the end of the For loop. It is not necessary to include the counter variable name here, but it makes for more readable code, especially if you have nested For loops.

For loops are ideal for stepping through arrays. Let's extend the previous example. First, we define a user-defined type called Employee and declare an array of Employees:

```
Option Explicit

Const MaxEmployees = 100

Type Employee
 Name As String
 Wage As Currency
 Shift As String
 Position As String
End Type

Private Employees(1 To MaxEmployees) As Employee
```

Now that we have 100 employees, it makes sense to test the shift and position of each employee and assign their wage in a For loop.

```
Private Sub cmdSetWages_Click()

Dim j As Integer

For j = 1 To MaxEmployees

If Employees(j).Shift = "Swing Shift" Then
  If Employees(j).Position = "Supervisor" Then
    Employees(j).Wage = 10#
  ElseIf Employees(j).Position = "Floor Waxer" Then
    Employees(j).Wage = 8.5
```

```
    Else
      Employees(j).Wage = 7.6
    End If
  End If

  Next j

End Sub
```

The `Integer` variable `j` acts as our loop counter. The loop counter is incremented by one at the bottom of the loop with each iteration. Like `If` statements, `For` loops can be nested; for example, we can use nested `For` loops to move through a two-dimensional array:

```
For k = 1 to 10
  For l = 1 to 20
    Sum = Sum + DataValues(k,l)
  Next l
Next k
```

For Each...Next Loops

Visual Basic also provides a different kind of `For` loop that can be used to iterate through objects. This is the `For Each...Next` loop. The syntax of a `For Each...Next` loop is as follows:

```
For Each Element In Group
  Statements
Next Element
```

`Element` is a variable of the type of object that you are iterating through. This can be any type of object in Visual Basic, such as a form or control. `Group` is a group of related items, or a collection. There are two collections that you might refer to in a `For Each...Next` loop. These are the `Forms` collection, which includes all forms currently loaded into memory by an application, and the `Controls` collection, which includes all controls on the current form.

To illustrate the use of a `For Each...Next` loop, consider the form pictured in Fig. 5-3. This simple program loads a list box with randomly generated numbers. The count, sum, and mean value for the numbers are displayed in three text boxes. In the upper left corner of the form, there is a check box that allows the user to select whether or not the form will display the statistics information. The code behind the `Click` event of the check box uses a `For Each...Next` loop to iterate through

Figure 5-3

For Each...Next
Loop.

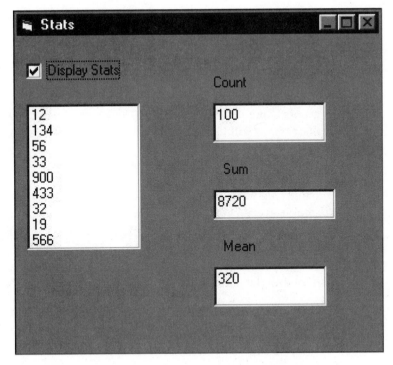

the controls and set the visible property based on whether the user specified that he or she wants the statistics displayed:

```
Private Sub Check1_Click()

 Dim ctlControl As Control

 For Each ctlControl In Controls

  If TypeOf ctlControl Is TextBox Or TypeOf ctlControl Is Label Then

    If Check1.Value Then
     ctlControl.Visible = True
    Else
     ctlControl.Visible = False
    End If

    End If

 Next ctlControl

End Sub
```

To use a For Each...Next loop, you need to declare a variable that is the same type of object as the collection you are looping through. This is done in the first line of the procedure, where we declare a variable of type `Control`, which can be used to iterate through the `Controls` collection of a form:

```
Dim ctlControl As Control
```

The next line of code is the `For  Each` statement, which specifies which collection we will loop through as well as the variable we will use to do it:

```
For Each ctlControl In Controls
```

Since we have specified the `Controls` collection, this loop will iterate through every control on the form. We can use the `TypeOf` function to test what type of control is currently referenced. On the sample form, the statistics information is displayed in three text boxes, which are identified by three label controls. If the current control is a text box or label, we can manipulate its visible property based on the user's selection:

```
If TypeOf ctlControl Is TextBox Or TypeOf ctlControl Is Label Then

    If Check1.Value Then
      ctlControl.Visible = True
    Else
      ctlControl.Visible = False
    End If

  End If

Next ctlControl
```

Using For Each...Next Loops with Arrays

A `For  Each...Next` loop can also be used to iterate through the elements of an array if the array is type `Variant`. For example, the following code loops through a `Variant` array and adds its elements to a list box:

```
Public Sub LoadData(MyArray())

 Dim Element As Variant

 For Each Element In MyArray

     lstData.AddItem(CStr(Element))

  Next Element

End Sub
```

The `Exit For` Statement

The `Exit For` statement can be used to exit a `For` loop before the iteration condition is reached. For example, suppose that we wanted to sum the elements of an array and stop the sum if we encountered an array element with the value 0:

```
For j = 1 to Max
 Temp = MyArrayData(j)
 If Temp = 0 Then
   Exit For
 Else
   Sum = Sum + Temp
 End If
Next j
```

The `Exit For` statement will cause program control to move to the first statement following `Next`.

`Do` **Loops**

A `Do` loop is another construct you can use to execute a block of code in an iterative fashion, much like a `For` loop. A `Do` loop is more powerful, however, in that you can use the loop to evaluate conditions to see if they are True or False or iterate through the code an indefinite number of times, as opposed to looping through the code a specified number of times as we did with a `For` loop. `Do` loops come in two basic varieties: testing the condition at the top of the loop and testing the condition at the bottom of the loop. The syntax of a `Do` loop that tests at the top of the loop is as follows:

```
Do [While|Until] expression

 Code block

Loop
```

If we test at the bottom of the loop, the syntax is:

```
Do
 Code block
Loop [While|Until] expression
```

A typical example of when a `Do` loop is useful is when reading in a file. We can test for the end-of-file condition each time through the loop

(for more information on file processing, see "Flat Files" in Chapter 10).
We can test for the end-of-file condition at the top of the loop:

```
Set myTextStream = myFileSystemObject("c:\Names.Dat")

Do while myTextStream.EndOfStream = False
 'code to read in file goes here
Loop
```

In this case, the Do loop will execute zero or more times. If the test
condition is met the first time we attempt to go into the loop the code
never gets executed. We can also place the test condition at the bottom
of the loop, in which case the loop will execute at least once:

```
Do
 'code to read in file goes here
Loop Until myTextStream.EndOfStream
```

This loop could also be written by using the While keyword:

```
Do
 'code to read in file goes here
Loop While myTextStream.EndOfStream = False
```

The things to remember about a Do loop are the following:

■ Do loops work well if you don't know how many times you need to go
through the loop.

■ If you need to execute the loop at least once, place your test condition
at the bottom of the loop.

Finally, if you need to exit the Do loop in the middle of the loop you
can do so with an Exit Do statement.

Select Case **Statements**

A Select Case statement is similar to an If-ElseIf-Else statement, in that it provides for conditional execution of a block of code. At
the top of a Select Case statement, a test expression is evaluated, and
its value is compared to a list of multiple choices or cases identified by
the keyword Case. Each case can include a single matching expression
or multiple matches, which are separated by commas. An optional Else
condition can be provided at the end of a Select Case statement to
account for the possibility that no match was found. The syntax of a

Select Case statement is as follows:

```
Select Case testexpression
  Case Value1
   [statements]
   [Case Value2]
   [statements]
.....
  [Case Else]
   [statements]
End Select
```

If you are testing multiple conditions with a large If-ElseIf-Else construct, a Select Case statement may be preferable. For example, consider a hypothetical tax program that calculates tax based on marital status. If marital status is coded as an integer stored in a variable called Mstatus, we can use the following Select Case statement to set the value of the tax:

```
Select Case Mstatus

  Case 0
    Tax = 1800
  Case 1
    Tax = 2100
  Case 2
    Tax = 2400
  Case Else
    Tax = 1400

End Select
```

The value of Mstatus is evaluated in the first line of the Select Case statement. Then this value is compared to each Case statement until a match is obtained. If none of the Case statements is executed the code following Case Else is executed, and Tax is assigned the value 1400.

Programming Objects: With...End With

Visual Basic provides the With...End With statement, which is useful when you need to manipulate a series of object properties. The syntax of a With...End With statement is as follows:

```
With object
 .property = value
 [.property = value]
End With
```

For example, let's say we wanted to change some properties of a text box control named *txtData* when the user clicks the *OK* button on a form. The standard way to do it would be like this:

```
Private Sub cmdOK_Click()
 txtData.text = "OK"
 txtData.BackColor = vbRed
 txtData.FontName = "Arial"
 txtData.FontBold = True
End Sub
```

Using a `With...End With` statement, the code would look like the following:

```
Private Sub cmdOK_Click()

 With txtData
  .Text = "OK"
  .BackColor = vbRed
  .FontName = "Arial"
  .FontBold = True
 End With

End Sub
```

`With...End With` statements can be nested inside one another. For example, we can use a nested `With...End` construct to manipulate the properties of a form and a command button on that form:

```
With frmEmployees
 .caption = "Record for " & strEmployeeName
 .StartUpPosition = 2      'load center screen
 With cmdPosition
  .caption = "Supervisor"
  .BackColor = vbRed
 End With
End With
```

When you are programming with objects, using a `With...End With` construct makes your code more readable and efficient.

Standard Program Modules

Visual Basic has three types of modules. These are known as form modules, class modules, and standard modules. Each type of module can be summarized as follows:

■ *Form module*: A form module has an *.frm* file extension and is basically a Window that allows the user to interact with your application. If you start a standard EXE project, it will have at least one form. A form contains any event procedures that are associated with the form and any controls placed on it, as well as any `Sub` or `Function` procedures, form-wide constants, and variables that you define.

■ *Standard module*: A standard module has a *.bas* file extension. Standard modules are used to declare `Public` variables, define program-wide or module-wide constants, and provide `Sub` and `Function` procedures that are used throughout the program.

■ *Class module*: A class module has a *.cls* file extension. Class modules are used to define your own classes and objects; we'll be talking more about class modules in Chapter 8.

In this section, we will consider the standard module, which is where you can place code that is used throughout the program. To add a standard module to your project, use these steps:

■ Select *Add Module* from the Project pull-down menu.

■ Select *Module* and click *Open*.

When you do this, Visual Basic will open a new code window. A standard module can contain the following:

■ `Global` or `Public` variables that can be accessed throughout the program

■ User-defined type definitions

■ DLL function declarations

■ Sub procedures and functions that you define

Using Functions and Subroutines

The main point of adding a standard module to your project is to add Sub procedures and functions that perform some common task that is needed throughout your program. By breaking down tasks into procedures you can make your code more modular and readable and avoid wasting memory. If a certain task needs to be repeated several times throughout your program it is more efficient to locate the code in one place, inside a procedure, than to duplicate the code several different places in your program. Then each time the task needs to be performed the code in the procedure is run, or "called." You can add a new function or subroutine to your project by completing the following steps:

- Select *Add Procedure* from the Tools menu.
- Type in a name for the procedure.
- Specify the type of the procedure. For now, we are only considering `Sub` or `Function` procedures. If the procedure will return a value, select *Function*; if it will not return a value, select *Sub*.
- Specify the scope of the procedure as *Public* or *Private*. If you select *Public*, the procedure will be available throughout the program. If you select *Private*, it can only be called by code in the current module.
- If you want the local variables in this procedure to be statics, select the *All Local Variables As Statics* check box.

When you select *OK*, Visual Basic will place the `Sub` or `Function` procedure in the code window.

Entering Code in a `Sub` or `Function` Procedure

When you close the Add Procedure dialog box by selecting OK, you will see the procedure heading in your code window. For example, if we created a public `Sub` procedure named `SumIt`, Visual Basic would display something like the following in the code window:

```
Public Sub SumIt()

End Sub
```

We place the code that we want this procedure to execute between these two lines. For starters, however, we need to add the parameter list. Let's say that the purpose of `SumIt` is to calculate the sum of the elements of an array of integers. We'll take as input the array called `MyData`, and a variable called `Result`, which is where we'll place the answer. `Result` should be type `Long` so it will be large enough to hold the sum. The subroutine will now look like this:

```
Public Sub SumIt(MyData() As Integer, Result As Long)

End Sub
```

We have made the array declaration without specifying its size so the user can pass an array containing any number of elements. The first thing we want to do is get the upper and lower bounds of the array; we can do so with the LBound and UBound functions:

```
Public Sub SumIt(MyData() As Integer, Result As Long)

 Dim lower As Long, upper As Long

 lower  = Lbound(MyData)
 upper = Ubound(MyData)

End Sub
```

We'll also need a variable for the array's index, and since we don't know that the Result variable hasn't already been assigned a value before the subroutine was called we need to initialize it to zero. The sum can be calculated by using a For loop. The routine will then look something like this:

```
Public Sub SumIt(MyData() As Integer, Result As Long)

 Dim lower As Long, upper As Long, I As Long

 lower = LBound(MyData)
 upper = UBound(MyData)

 Result = 0

 For I =  lower To upper
   Result = Result + MyData(I)
 Next

End Sub
```

Now we have a completed Sub procedure that will calculate the sum of an array's elements. In Chapter 13, we'll explore how to add error handling to your procedures.

Calling a Procedure and Passing Variables

There are two methods one can use when passing variables to a procedure:

- *Pass by value*: With pass by value, you are actually passing a copy of the variable. Changes made to the variable inside the procedure have no effect on that variable elsewhere in the program. Instead of passing the memory location of the variable, you are simply passing the value it holds. You can specify pass by value by using the `ByVal` keyword in your procedure header or by enclosing the variable in parentheses when you call the procedure.

■ *Pass by reference*: This is the default passing method in Visual Basic. When you use pass by reference, you are passing the actual memory address of the variable. If the variable gets modified inside the procedure, its value is changed everywhere. Since this is the default passing method, there is no required keyword to tell Visual Basic you are using pass by reference. However, for clarity, you can use the `ByRef` keyword in your procedure header.

The variables that are passed to a procedure are commonly known as a parameter list. The variables in a parameter list are delimited by commas. To call a `Sub` procedure, you can use one of two methods. The first method is to use the `Call` keyword, in which case the argument list needs to be enclosed in parentheses:

```
Call MySub(x,y,z)
```

If you omit the `Call` keyword, then don't enclose the parameter list in parentheses:

```
MySub x,y,z
```

To call a function, you need to use a variable to accept the return value. This is done by essentially treating the function as another variable or statement in code. For example, if we have a function that computes the average of two values, we could call it with the following code:

```
Dim Result As Double, a As Double, b As Double

a = 43
b = 23.4

Result = Average(a,b)

MsgBox "The Average Is " & CStr(Result)
```

If we were concerned about the contents of the two variables a and b, we could enclose them in parentheses to ensure that they are passed by value:

```
Dim Result As Double, a As Double, b As Double

a = 43
```

```
b = 23.4

Result = Average((a),(b))

MsgBox "The Average Is " & CStr(Result)
```

This way, even if the `Average` function modifies the variables in some way, when control returns from the function a will still be 43, and b will still be 23.4. Of course, we could specify that the variables be passed by value by inserting the `ByVal` keyword in the function header:

```
Public Function Average(ByVal One As Integer, ByVal Two As Integer) As
Double

 Average = (One + Two)/2

End Function
```

In this case, it isn't necessary to enclose the variables in parentheses when calling the function; the variables will automatically be passed by value. Also notice that the function header specifies what type of data it will return, which in this case is type `Double`.

Returning a Value with a `Function` Procedure

To return a value from a function, you assign the name of the function to the value that you want to return. You may have noticed that we did exactly that in the `Average` function shown in the previous section. As another example, we could rewrite the `SumIt` function so that instead of returning the value in the variable `Result` that the user passed, we have the function return the sum. The code would look like this:

```
Public Function SumIt(MyData() As Integer) As Long

 Dim lower As Long, upper As Long, I As Long
  Dim Result As Long

  lower = LBound(MyData)
  upper = UBound(MyData)

  Result = 0

  For I =  lower To upper
   Result = Result + MyData(I)
  Next

  SumIt = Result

End Function
```

Some Good Programming Practices to Follow

In this section we'll review some good programming practices that you should stick to when developing your Visual Basic projects. We've mentioned some of these issues already, and we'll be talking about some more of them in Chapter 6.

Avoid Global Variables

One of the flexible or perhaps unfortunate features of Visual Basic is the ability to declare global variables. There are two rules to keep in mind when thinking about using a global variable. First, don't use global variables, that is, if you can get by without them. Global variables can make code hard to follow and debug. If a program is full of globals, you might find yourself reading through the code in an event procedure or subroutine wondering where all the variables came from. That might mean searching through a large number of code modules to track down the declaration of the variable. Debugging a global variable can be difficult. Since all the code in the project can modify it, problems can be caused anywhere. If you have to declare a variable that needs to be accessed throughout the program, use the `Public` keyword to declare that variable rather than `Global`. `Global` is a holdover from older versions of Visual Basic and should not be used.

Use Standard Naming Conventions and Name Variables Clearly

In the next chapter we'll be talking about using naming conventions, which will convey the type of each variable. You should also give your variables meaningful names that reflect what kind of data they are tracking. For example, if you have a variable that tracks someone's age, don't call that variable `x` or `a`, call it `age`. By sticking to a consistent naming convention you can ensure that later on you or someone else can look at your code and immediately know what type of variable it is and what its function in the program is.

Don't Use Type-Declaration Characters

Type-declaration characters can be used to specify the type of a variable rather than having to explicitly write it out in a `Dim` statement. While they are permitted by Visual Basic, this is another sloppy programming practice that has its roots in the old Basic days. Type-declaration characters don't make for readable code and should be avoided.

Declare All of Your Variables: Use `Option Explicit`

Use `Option Explicit` in every module to force variable declaration. This will entail a lot of headaches since without it Visual Basic lets you implicitly declare variables. That means a misspelled variable name will go through the compiler without any warning and cause bugs in your program.

Place `Public` Variables and `Sub` Procedures in Standard Modules

While you can place public variables and procedures in a form module, it's better to use standard code modules for this. Keep everything in the form limited to variables, constants, and procedures used only by that form.

Indent Your Code

You should indent every code block by three or four spaces to make your code more readable. This includes code inside an `If` statement, `Do` loop, `For Next` loop, or in a procedure.

Comment Your Code

The importance of commenting your code can't be emphasized enough, and we'll be taking this issue up in the next chapter. It is especially important if you are programming professionally or developing large-scale projects. Don't forget, chances are you may have to go back and debug or modify the code months after you've looked at it last. Or if you're in a work environment, someone else may have to modify your code, and you won't be around to explain it to them. Commenting the code effectively will make this process run more smoothly because it will explain what each variable is doing, what algorithm you are doing, and so on. Don't assume that someone else will automatically know why you took some action in your code.

Break Code Down into Sub Procedures

If any task that's more than just a couple of lines gets repeated in a program, place that code in a Sub or Function procedure. This makes the code more readable and efficient. If it has to be modified later on, you can do so from one location rather than searching through the code to make the change everywhere it's used.

Always Specify Function Return Type

When you first create a Function procedure, no return type will be listed. For example, if we used the Add Procedure dialog box to create a function called MyFunc, Visual Basic will place the following into the code window:

```
Public Function MyFunc()

End Function
```

If we don't specify the return type, the function will be a variant. This is a sloppy programming practice. It is better to specify the data type that you expect the function to return, such as:

```
Public Function MyFunc() As Integer

End Function
```

If a Variable Doesn't Need to Be Modified in a Procedure, Use Pass by Value

There is no sense in risking the corruption of data when passing variables to procedures if it can be avoided. You can help ensure this won't happen by passing any variables that won't be modified by a procedure with the ByVal keyword. This brings us to another important point. While you can pass by value by enclosing a variable in parentheses, it's better to use the ByVal keyword if possible because this makes for more readable code. If you absolutely run into a situation where you can't use the ByVal keyword and you must still pass by value, be sure to comment your code, explaining why you're enclosing the variables in parentheses. There is one exception when you probably won't want to use call by value; that's if you're passing a large amount of data. That's because Visual Basic will have to make copies of everything before calling the procedure, which would take up a lot of time and waste memory.

Use Error Handling

In Chapter 13 we'll be discussing error handling. At this point, just keep in mind that every procedure should have an error handler in it. This includes every event procedure in a form or control as well as all Sub and Function procedures that you write.

Avoid the Use of Variants

Variants come with a lot of memory overhead. If you can't think of an explicit reason for using a variant, don't do so.

Plan Your Logic before You Start to Program

Visual Basic makes it easy to simply turn on your computer and go. While this might be tempting, you should plan out as many details of the program as you can beforehand on paper. This includes designing your user interface, designing any data storage or files, and working out problem-solving logic the program will use. While planning ahead may be tedious, the end result will be a more robust, bug-free program.

Common Mistakes and How to Avoid Them

In this section, we'll cover some of the common mistakes and provide suggestions on how to avoid them.

Converting a String That's Out of Range into a Numeric Data Type

Overflow will occur if you convert a string that represents a number into a data type for which that number is out of range. For example, recall that a byte can only hold numbers in the range 0 to 255. The following code will cause an overflow error:

```
Dim MyString As String
Dim MyVal As Byte

MyString = "45690"

MyVal = Cbyte(MyString)
```

You can get around this situation by testing the value that the string contains before assigning it. Strings can be converted into numbers by using the Val function. In our example, we can fix the code by using the Val function to make sure the range of type Byte is not exceeded:

```
Dim MyString As String
Dim MyVal As Byte

MyString = "45690"

If Val(MyString) > 0 And Val(MyString) <= 255 Then

  MyVal = Cbyte(MyString)

Else

  MsgBox "Error : String is outside valid range for byte " & MyString

End If
```

Declaring a Local Variable with the Same Name as a Global Variable

If you are using public or global variables, make sure that there are no naming conflicts inside your procedures. Visual Basic allows you to declare local variables that have the same name as a global variable; however, you should avoid this if possible. Consider a program that has a public variable named Temperature declared in standard code module. A form in the program also has a Temperature variable in a Click event. However, that is a local variable that is processed only in the

Click event. To avoid confusion, we can give it a slightly different name:

```
'standard code module
Public Temperature As Double

...

Private Sub cmdConvertTemp_Click()

  Dim Temperature As Double

  'suppose there are several lines of code here

  Temperature =  CDbl(txtTemp.Text)

  'code to process here
End Sub
```

This may cause confusion because in a large procedure, when you get down to the bottom and see the Temperature variable, you may forget that it was defined in the Click event procedure and think the global variable is being modified. We can avoid this problem by assigning a unique name to the local variable. For example:

```
Private Sub cmdConvertTemp_Click()
   Dim lTemperature As Double

   'suppose there are  several lines of code here
   lTemperature =  CDbl(txtTemp.Text)
   'code to process here

End Sub
```

"During Run Time, an Error Occurs and the Program Crashes"

This happens when you haven't put error handling into your routines. Every procedure in your projects should contain some kind of error-handling code. We will discuss error handling in Chapter 13.

Forgetting to Terminate If Statements, For Loops, or Do Loops

Make sure you terminate your If statements with End If, your For loops with Next statements, and a Do with a Loop statement. Failing to do so will cause a syntax error.

Misspelling a Variable Name

As we stated earlier, this mistake can cause unexpected results since Visual Basic allows implicit variable declaration. You can avoid this problem by using `Option Explicit`.

Overflow

An overflow error usually occurs when a variable is not large enough to hold the data that has been assigned to it. You can avoid this situation by either testing values to make sure they are in the allowed range before assigning them or by declaring your variables to be as large as possible. For example, declare a variable as a `Long` rather than an `Integer` if there is a reasonable possibility that the data will exceed 32,767.

Passing the Wrong Number of Parameters or Data Types to a Procedure

This one might sound obvious, but make sure you know what parameters a procedure expects and pass the correct data types. You can avoid this problem by turning on the auto syntax check. If you do this, Visual Basic will make sure that all procedure calls are correct.

Subscript Out of Range

This error will occur if you attempt to use an index that is outside of the bounds of an array. Be sure to carefully monitor an array index to make sure this doesn't happen. For example, you can use the `UBound` function to make sure the index doesn't go outside the limits of the array.

Using Keywords as Variable Names

It's a syntax error to use a keyword as a variable name. This will usually cause the syntax error *Expected: Identifier*. One way to help you identify these types of errors early is by checking the *Auto Syntax Check* box found on the Options dialog of the Tools menu.

Using Type-Declaration Characters in Function Names

Don't try to use a type-declaration character to specify the return type of a function; it isn't allowed. You can avoid this problem by avoiding the use of type-declaration characters in any situation.

Variable Not Defined

If you'll be using variables outside of a standard module where they're declared, be sure to use the `Public` keyword. Using a `Dim` statement makes those variables private to the module where they were declared.

When Calling a Function and It Doesn't Return a Value

Sometimes programmers might forget to assign the return value for a function. Consider the function `SumIt` that sums the elements of an array:

```
Public Function SumIt(MyData() As Integer) As Long
 Dim result As Long
 Dim start as long, finish as long
 Dim index as long

 start = LBound(MyData)
 finish = UBound(MyData)

For index = start To finish
 result = result + MyData(index)
Next

End Function
```

If we call the function, say with the line

```
SumValue = SumIt(MyArray)

MsgBox SumValue
```

the message box won't display anything. That's because we forgot to assign the return value for the function by setting its name equal to the `result` variable. To work properly, the function should look like this:

```
Public Function SumIt(MyData() As Integer) As Long
 Dim result As Long
 Dim start as long, finish as long
 Dim index as long

 start = LBound(MyData)
 finish = UBound(MyData)

For index = start To finish
 result = result + MyData(index)
Next

 SumIt = result 'assign return value for the function
End Function
```

When Calling a Sub Procedure, the Syntax Error *Expected: End of Statement* Occurs

This usually means that you are using the `Call` keyword but didn't enclose the variables in parentheses. For example, the line

```
Call MyProc a,b
```

will cause the error. It can be corrected by changing the line to:

```
Call MyProc(a,b)
```

Version Control

Overview: When and Why You'll Need It

Version control becomes an important issue if you work in an environment where teams of programmers will be working on the same project. Things can get pretty hairy if each programmer can simply modify the source code whenever he pleases. Consider a hypothetical company with two programmers, Susan and Bob. Susan might get a copy of the project and make some changes, then copy it back to the central storage location. However, while she is modifying the code, Bob gets a copy and is putting in his own changes. After Susan copies her changes over, Bob now copies his changes into the central directory, overwriting the changes Susan made. Of course, good communication can help prevent such mishaps, but in the real world good communication isn't always there, and these types of problems will occur. The way they can be prevented is by using a version control product, such as Microsoft Visual Source Safe.

Visual Source Safe

Visual Source Safe is a powerful product in its own right, and discussing all of its features is beyond the scope of this book. However, let's consider some of the main attributes of Source Safe to find out how it can protect code in a team developer or enterprise environment.

Source Safe can be loaded while running Visual Basic by selecting *Source Control* from the Tools menu. Once a project is loaded into Source Safe, to modify the source code of that project you have to "check out" the project or file. When a file is checked out, others can look at the latest version of the file and find out who checked it out, but they can't modify the source code themselves. In our little hypothetical example, if Susan had checked out the source code of her project, Bob would not have been able to modify the code until Susan "checked in" the project. This prevents the mishap that we described from occurring. Not only does Source Safe prevent such conflicts from arising, but when Bob goes to Source Safe in an attempt to open the source code, he will be able to see that Susan has the code checked out. In this way, Source Safe protects the source code from being changed by multiple developers at the same time, and it improves communication by allowing other developers to see who has the code.

Visual Source Safe also allows you to maintain a historical record as the code is checked back in. That way, every programmer can make a note of what he or she did to the code, and the date will be noted. This historical record is a valuable tool in any multideveloper environment.

Configuring Source Safe   To configure the way Visual Source Safe (VSS) works with Visual Basic, you need to open the Source Code Control Options dialog box. From the Tools menu in Visual Basic, select *Source Control*, and then choose the Options submenu. There are four basic options available:

- *Get latest checked-in versions of files when opening a VB project?*
- *Check in files when closing the VB project?*
- *Add files to source control when adding them to a VB project?*
- *Remove files from source control when deleting them from the VB project?*

You can select *Yes*, *No*, or *Ask* for each of these options. The best choice is to select *Ask* so you can determine how the project will work with VSS on a case-by-case basis. Source Safe comes with an Admin utility that allows you to set up user accounts and maintain databases. An administrator should be chosen to run the Admin utility. That person should set up an Admin account with a password to maintain security. Once this is done, the administrator can create a Visual Source Safe database. This is done by selecting *Create Database* from the Tools menu.

The administrator must set up an account for each of the developers who will be working on the projects stored in Source Safe. This is done by selecting *Add User* from the Users menu, where you can then set up the user name and a password. Once a user has been created, it can be changed by selecting *Edit User*. The user names and passwords of all users can be changed, with the exception of the Admin account.

Once Source Safe is configured with a database and user accounts, users can use the Visual Source Safe Explorer to check out, modify, and check in Visual Basic projects. To open Explorer, click on the Tools menu in Visual Basic and select *Source Safe*. Next, choose *Run Source Safe*. Once you log in, the Source Safe Explorer will open on your screen. Source Safe has two window panes that work in much the same way as the panes in Windows Explorer. The window pane on the left displays a list of projects as a series of file folders. By clicking open a folder you can see its contents in the right window pane. One or more files can be selected in the right window pane. You can click on *Select All* from the Edit pull-down menu to select every file. Source Safe also has a third pane at the bottom of the screen that will show the results of actions performed, such as checking out a set of files.

To check out one or more selected files, you can right-click on the selected files and choose *Check Out*. Visual Source Safe will then prompt you for the location on your computer where you want the files to be copied. Once a location is chosen, Source Safe will mark the files as checked out and copy them to your hard disk. You can then work on the project and make modifications without having to worry about another developer losing your changes.

When you are done working on the project, you can reverse the process by selecting *Check In* from the right-click pop-up menu. Source Safe will then prompt you to enter a note about what you did to the source files. This is where the historical record is built, so it's important to make detailed notes about what you did to the code. Once you click *OK*, Source Safe will copy the files from your computer into the Source Safe database and make the files available to other users. Note that once you check in a file the file remains on your computer, but will be marked as read-only.

Source Safe also provides an option called "Get Latest Version." If you need to examine changes that other users have made to the code or simply wish to include the latest version of some code in your own version of the project, you can choose this option. This will copy the files onto your computer, but it will not allow you to put any changes you make into the Source Safe database.

Finally, when you have Source Safe installed and configured, note that you can interact with it from inside Visual Basic. You can right-click on the file or files in the Visual Basic Project Explorer, and there will be menu options for checking in, checking out, or getting the latest versions of the files.

In summary, if you are developing in an enterprise or team environment, you should use like Source Safe. This will guard against the types of conflicts that can arise in an environment with multiple programmers as well as provide you with an accurate historical record of product development.

CHAPTER 6

Coding
Standards

Why Have Coding Standards?

Writing software is in many ways a subjective process. Every programmer is an individual, and that means each thinks in his or her own unique way. This fact will manifest itself in many different aspects of a software project. For one thing, some programmers will write neat and tidy code, with consistent indentation of blocks within If statements and Do loops, while others will just sit down and type, so absorbed in the problem at hand that they aren't giving a thought to how their code looks. Some programmers will give long, descriptive names to variables, while others will use short, cryptic names, and still others will use names with no meaning at all.

When designing a user interface, everyone will have different ideas of what looks good. One programmer may think the user interface is a trivial, unimportant aspect of the project and may not give any thought to how the end user feels about it. Another programmer may feel a bit too creative and produce a user interface with bright colors that are difficult to look at or arrange the controls in a completely nonstandard way that leaves the user confused.

When it comes to logic, everyone thinks differently, so unless you're doing something really simple like adding two and two, chances are multiple programmers will produce multiple solutions to a given problem. This can lead to many misunderstandings. Show your logic to another programmer, and he may not have a clue why you take the steps that you take.

All of these difficulties make it clear that in any organization with more than one programmer—or even with a single programmer who is not likely to be available for the next 50 years to explain what she did—coding standards are essential. When developing a large-scale project, you need to consider the likely possibility that another programmer will need to understand what you're doing, maybe sometime in the future when you're not there to explain it. With a visual design environment like Visual Basic, coding standards can impact two areas. First, they will promote the design of professional, user-friendly interfaces. Second, good coding standards will promote better communication among the design team and speed development. The other programmers in your team should be able to look at your code and easily figure out for themselves what it's doing.

Creating Coding Standards

Scope of Standards

When creating coding standards, it's important that you don't tie a programmer's hands too much. You want to make sure that code is understandable by all and follows some type of industry standard, but you don't want to stifle the creativity of the individual programmer. Coding standards will impact four general areas:

- User interface design
- Language standards and naming variables
- Commenting code
- Making code more readable

We'll spend some time discussing the design of a user interface in the next chapter. In this chapter, we'll be focusing on the other three issues.

Language Standards

In this section, we will consider some standards you may wish to adopt for use with the programming language itself. Next to user interface design, this is probably the trickiest aspect of creating coding standards because a programmer may think that you're stepping on his creativity. Let's consider a few examples of the types of language standards you might want to adopt. The following sections consist merely of suggestions so you can see the types of requirements you can include in your own coding standards. Some of these we mentioned in Chapter 5.

Using `Option Explicit` As we stated in the previous chapter, it's a good idea to explicitly declare all the variables in a project. A program that uses implicit variable declaration will be confusing to another programmer, especially if a variable suddenly appears out of nowhere in a large piece of code. So a good standard to follow is to require all programmers to use `Option Explicit` in every module.

Avoid Type-Declaration Characters Type-declaration characters don't make for readable code. If you bring a new programmer on staff and she hasn't used older versions of Visual Basic, she may not know what the following statement means:

```
Dim Salary%, Taxes#
```

Even if you're an old VB pro, you may not remember the meaning of these symbols off hand. Since a goal of coding standards is to improve the readability of code as well as communication between programmers, it makes sense to explicitly list the data types. In that case, our `Dim` statement would read:

```
Dim Salary As Integer, Taxes As Single
```

It's not really that much extra work to list the data types, and now we have code in which the intent is immediately obvious.

Declare All Local Variables at the Beginning of a Procedure
Sometimes, Visual Basic is too flexible. One area where this is true is in the ability to declare a variable wherever you feel like it. This unfortunate benefit of Visual Basic gives a programmer the opportunity to write sloppy code and encourages one to code "on the fly," without carefully planning out an algorithm beforehand. While the language doesn't require it, it's a good idea for your organization to require that programmers declare and initialize all variables at the beginning of a procedure, before starting the actual coding. Consider the following example:

```
Public Sub Stats(InputData() As Double, Average As Double, Min As
Double, Max As Double, Sum As Double)

  Min = 0 'initialization
  Max = 0

  Dim j As Integer

  Sum = 0

  For j = LBound(InputData) To UBound(InputData)
    Sum = Sum + InputData(j)
    If InputData(j) < Min Then
      Min = InputData(j)
    End If
    If InputData(j) > Max Then
      Max = InputData(j)
    End If
  Next

  Dim Count As Integer
  Count = UBound(InputData) - LBound(InputData) + 1
```

```
    Average = Sum/Count

End Sub
```

This subroutine will look better and be easier to read if we place all variable declarations at the beginning of the routine and follow this with any required initialization. The routine would then look like this:

```
Public Sub Stats(InputData() As Double, Average As Double,
  Min As Double, Max As Double, Sum As Double)

  Dim j As Integer   'loop counter
  Dim Count As Integer   'the number of array elements

  Min = 0 'initialization
  Max = 0
  Sum = 0

  For j = LBound(InputData) To UBound(InputData)
      Sum = Sum + InputData(j)
      If InputData(j) < Min Then
        Min = InputData(j)
      End If
      If InputData(j) > Max Then
        Max = InputData(j)
      End If
  Next

  Count = UBound(InputData) - LBound(InputData) + 1

  Average = Sum/Count

End Sub
```

This is a small, simple procedure. However, in the real world chances are you're going to write long complicated procedures. It makes more sense to have all variable declaration and initialization in one central location rather than having to jump around to find every variable in the procedure.

Avoid the Use of "Negative Logic"   By negative logic, I mean saying `If NOT Condition Then` rather than `If Condition Then`. In many cases, using `If NOT` is simply not as clear. There are times when you may want to use `If NOT`, such as testing for an end-of-file condition. In that case, you probably would say `If NOT End of File`. But in many other situations, using negative logic is not as clear. Consider the following `If-Else` statement:

```
If (Not(A > B)) Then
    A = A + 1
```

```
Else
    B = B + 1
End If
```

It's much better to write this as follows:

```
If A <= B Then
    A = A + 1
Else
    B = B + 1
End If
```

This makes for code that's easier to understand.

Don't Use Inline If Statements   By clearly delimiting If statements in an If-End If block, you make your code clear and easy to follow.

Use the Call Keyword When Invoking Sub Procedures   You may recall that Sub procedures can be invoked using the Call keyword, in which case the parameter list is enclosed in parentheses, or without the Call keyword, in which case the parameter list is simply comma delimited. Using the Call keyword more clearly conveys the fact that you're calling a subroutine.

Do Not Use the Global Keyword   The use of Global when declaring variables is outdated. Use the Public keyword instead. Your organization might even go further and forbid the use of any global variables.

When Programming Objects, Use the With...End With Construct
The With...End With construct lets the reader clearly see where an object is being modified in code. As a result, this method is preferable to using the object.property syntax, unless you're only modifying one or two properties.

When Facing a Multiple If-Else If, Try a Select Case Statement Instead   A Select Case statement is often preferable to using multiple If-Else If branches. Not only can a Select Case statement be more efficient, it simply looks better. For example:

```
If State = "TX" Then
    'code for Texas
Else If State = "AZ" Then
    'code for Arizona
Else If State = "NY" Then
    'code for New York
```

```
Else If State = "NJ" Then
  'code for New Jersey
Else If State = "FL" Then
  'code for Florida
Else
  'code for everyone else
End If
```

This could be handled better with a `Select Case` statement:

```
Select Case State
   Case "TX"
     'code for Texas
   Case "AZ"
     'code for Arizona
   Case "NY"
     'code for New York
   Case "NJ"
     'code for New Jersey
   Case "FL"
     'code for Florida
   Case Else
     'code for everyone else
End Select
```

By following a common set of language standards, you can help ensure that all the code in your organization is uniform and easy to follow.

Naming Conventions

Variable naming is one thing that many programmers tend to overlook. To save typing, they may use cryptic or even meaningless names. When other people look at your code, they'll have to ask themselves such questions as "What does H do? What kind of data is x storing?" In today's world of cheap memory and large hard drives, this kind of brevity is no longer necessary. Names should be clear and descriptive. There are two characteristics of a variable that a name should convey:

- The type of data the variable holds
- The function of that variable

In addition, some naming standards will include some means for specifying whether the variable is a public or private variable, a local variable, or what form or module the variable belongs to. However, while this information might be useful, it will lead to naming conventions that are too hard for programmers to follow. In the end, the programmer will become frustrated and you'll be back to cryptic, hard-to-understand names.

Hungarian Notation

Hungarian notation is a naming convention created by Charles Simonyi that is a favorite among programmers. Hungarian notation attaches a prefix to variable names to identify the type of variable or object being used. You can use Hungarian notation by following two simple rules:

- A prefix, usually the first three letters of a variable name, is lowercase and is used to indicate its data or object type.
- The rest of the variable name is a descriptive name that tells you what the variable does or stores.

By specifying the data type of the variable, you can help ensure that a programmer won't make avoidable errors such as assigning a value to that variable that's outside its range. Hungarian notation also makes code easier to read. If the name of the variable specifies its data type, you won't have to search for the variable declaration to see what it is. Let's consider an example of variable names that can be improved by the use of Hungarian notation:

```
Dim deps As Byte, AVG As Double, WG As Double, SSN As String
```

Using Hungarian notation, we would declare the variables like this:

```
Dim bDependents As Byte, dblAverage As Double, dblWage As Double,
    strSSN As String
```

The second declaration is much clearer. The data type of each variable is specified. There is no question as to what data each variable will track.

In Visual Basic, you should use Hungarian notation for the naming of variables and objects. For example, if you have a form with five text boxes, a list box, and two command buttons, it makes good sense to use Hungarian notation. This will allow you to identify the type of each object as well as what it does. To see how Hungarian notation is useful when naming objects, consider a program that copies the name, address, city, state, and zip code from five text boxes into five variables in the Click event of a command button labeled "OK":

```
'general declarations section
Option Explicit
```

```
Dim strName As String, strAddress As String, strCity As String,
  strState As String, strZip As String

Private Sub Command1_Click()
  strName =  text1.text
  strAddress = text2.text
  strCity = text3.text
  strState = text4.text
  strZip = text5.text

End Sub
```

You can see that it's not immediately obvious that each text box holds the data we assume it does. By using Hungarian notation, the command button's `Click` event will be more readable. We can start by naming the command button *cmdOK* to convey that this button executes code when the user clicks *OK*. A programmer reading the previous patch of code would have to go look at the form to see what `Command1` did. We can also give each of the text boxes a meaningful name. With these changes, the event procedure would look like this:

```
'general declarations section
Option Explicit

Dim strName As String, strAddress As String, strCity As String,
  strState As String, strZip As String

Private Sub cmdOK_Click()

  strName =  txtName.text
  strAddress = txtAddress.text
  strCity = txtCity.text
  strState = txtState.text
  strZip = txtZipCodet5.text

End Sub
```

This code leaves no doubt about which button was clicked, what type of controls we're accessing, and what kind of data each control contains. The following table provides some suggested abbreviations that can be used with Hungarian notation:

Data/Object Type	Abbreviation	Example
Byte	byt	bytNumChildren
Integer	int	intSalary
Long	lng	lngPopulation
Single	sng	sngVoltage

Data/Object Type	Abbreviation	Example
Double	dbl	dblAverage
String	str	strName
Currency	cur	curInvestment
Variant	vnt	vntEmployeeID
Object	obj	objWordDoc
Date/Time	dtm	dtmBirthDay
Boolean	bln	blnEndofFile
Command button	cmd	cmdClose
Combo box	cbo	cboFlavors
List box	lst	lstStudents
Menu	mnu	mnuFileOpen
Text box	txt	txtName
ADO data	ado	adoEmployees
Data control	dat	datControl
Form	frm	frmCustomers

Commenting Standards

Overview: The Importance of Commenting Code

The importance of clear and meaningful comments can't be emphasized enough. One thing we've talked about is the likelihood that another programmer will have to modify or debug code that you write. Even if this isn't the case, it's quite possible you'll have to modify your own code several months after you've written it. If the code you write is even of moderate complexity, chances are that without comments when you or someone else look at it later you will not understand what it's doing. Time will be wasted attempting to find out what the code means. By commenting the code effectively, you can save development and debugging time by making the intent of the code as clear as possible. Commenting extensively has no effect on the size or performance of your executables, so if you think a detailed comment is necessary don't hesitate to put it in. Comments in Visual Basic are denoted with an apostrophe.

Consider the following code:

```
For j = 1 to Num
 Mtot = Mtot + M(j)
 Mk = Mk + M(j) * X(j)
Next

K = Mk/Mtot
```

This code could be made a little clearer by inserting a few comments. Before we enter the loop, we add a comment to explain what the loop does and introduce the function of each variable. Inline comments in the loop explain what specific calculation is being performed. With comments, the code looks like the following:

```
'The following loop calculates the center of mass, which is
'given by the formula (Sum of each mass * position)/(total mass of all
  objects)
'M is an array of type Double that contains the mass of each object.
'X is an array of type Double that contains the position of each
  object.
'There are a total of Num Objects. Num can be at most 100.
'K will hold the center of mass for the objects.

For j = 1 to Num
 Mtot = Mtot + M(j)     'Mtot is the total mass
 Mk = Mk + M(j)*X(j)    'Mk is the sum of each mass multiplied by its
  position
Next

K = Mk/Mtot   'calculate the center of mass
```

You can see from this simple example how adding comments will make the code more readable. The following areas are good places to include comments:

- In the general declarations section of a form, include the form's purpose, the date of creation, and who created it.

- Procedure headers should tell you what the procedure does as well as describe the parameter list.

- Use inline comments when an operation is not immediately clear or elementary.

- Use comments when declaring variables and explaining the variable's purpose, data type, and lifetime.

- Use a detailed comment to explain any complicated algorithm. Don't assume that others will understand what you're doing.

■ Maintain a revision history for your project. By tracking who did what and when, it will be easy to keep things moving smoothly.

In the following sections, we'll explore some uses of comments in more detail.

Commenting Procedure Headers

Every procedure header should have a comment that provides a general description of the procedure. This includes event procedures as well as procedures in standard or class modules. The procedure comment should include the following information:

■ The purpose of the procedure

■ The author's name and the date when the procedure was first written

■ The names and data types of all variables passed into the procedure, and what each variable will do

■ The revision history for the procedure. When a modification is made, include your initials, the date, and a brief description of what was changed

The following example shows how a procedure header should be commented:

```
Public Sub Average(MyData() As Double, Average As Double, NumItems As
Integer)

' Procedure : Average
' Author : John Jones
' Date Created : 5/5/98
' Description:  Computes the average of the elements in an array of
  type Double.
'
' Parameter List:
' MyData : Array of type Double, the function finds the average of the
  elements in this 'array. The array is assumed to start at element 1.
' Average : Type Double. The average will be returned in this
  variable.
' NumItems : The number of elements in the array.
'
' Revision History:
' 6/2/98 : JJ  Changed NumItems from type Byte to type Integer.
' 8/1/98 : KL  Changed loop variable to type Long.
```

Notice that we've inserted blank lines to separate each section and make the comments more readable.

Inline Comments

Inline comments can be used to explain operations that aren't immediately clear, the purpose of a variable, or any limitations that the code may encounter. Inline comments can be placed at the end of a line of code by simply adding an apostrophe character. The following example illustrates the use of an inline comment:

```
Vol = 4/3*PI*R^3   'calculate the volume of the sphere
```

Revision History

When commenting code, one useful bit of information that should be tracked is the revision history for the project. Earlier in this chapter, we discussed keeping a revision history for each procedure. Some programmers may prefer to maintain a single revision history for the entire project. This can be done by including a standard module in your project whose only function is to store the revision history of the project. You can require that each programmer enter her name or initials, the date, and what she did every time the project is modified. With the revision history centrally located, it's easy to see who did what and when it was done, which can be especially important if bugs start creeping into a large project or if an unauthorized change was made. You may wish to include a central revision history along with a revision history for each procedure.

Code Construction Standards

Readability

When you've got multiple programmers working on a project, an important issue you will have to deal with is the readability of the code. By readability, we're simply talking about neatness, good spacing, and indentation, which basically make the code pleasant to look at. This sounds like a frivolous issue, but it's actually pretty important. You just have to consider the likelihood that either someone else will need to modify code you write or you'll have to fix up your code months later. Efficiency can be maintained at a higher level, not just by including comments and by following a set of adopted language standards, but by making the code easy to read and follow. In the following sections, we'll discuss three areas that impact the readability of code. These are indenting block structures, using white space, and using continuation with long lines of code.

Indenting Block Structures   If you took any freshman computer science courses in college, you were probably annoyed by the professor who deducted five points for not indenting your code. But the fact is, indented code is easier to read and clearly delimits what code is part of a block and what isn't. You should be able to look at a piece of code and almost see the logic flow. In the following piece of code, it's not immediately clear where one block begins and another ends:

```
If x > y Then
Max = x
Temp(j) = Temp(j) + 1
Else
Max = y
End If

Do
MyData(j) = MyData(j) + Total
Total = Total - 1
Loop While Total > Min
```

We can make this code more readable by indenting the blocks of code in each control structure by three or four spaces:

```
If x > y Then
   Max = x
   Temp(j) = Temp(j) + 1
Else
   Max = y
End If

Do
   MyData(j) = MyData(j) + Total
   Total = Total - 1
Loop While Total > Min
```

Using White Space   Spacing can be helpful in making code more readable as well. This can include placing spaces between operators and equal signs and including blank lines to separate logical blocks. Visual Basic will automatically add white spaces around equal signs and operators.

Using Continuation with Long Lines of Code   Long lines of code should be extended to the next line. This can be done in Visual Basic by using the underscore (_) character. Simply add a space followed by an underscore character, then you can continue your code on the next line. For example:

```
intMyData  = MyArray(LoopCounter) + 2 * dblAverage +
   SumElements - Total  _
              + 2 * Temperature - x + 4 * DataArray(LoopCounter + 1)
```

The whole mess on the right of the equal sign will be considered to be one line of code by Visual Basic, and will be assigned to the variable intMyData. By extending this to two lines, you can see the entire line in the code window without having to scroll back and forth.

Enforcing Coding Standards

Once you've decided on a set of coding standards for your organization, you've got to enforce them. This can be a difficult road to follow. I've seen plenty of resentment by programmers when coding standards are imposed. The trick is to enforce the standards without putting programmers on the spot or infringing on their creativity. Many organizations use code reviews to enforce standards. We'll discuss how a code review works next and then address the issue of balance in coding standards.

Code Reviews

A code review is a process in which a team lead, or perhaps the entire software team, reviews new code to make sure that it fits the standard. One way to run a code review is to have a supervisor check the code when it is close to completion to see how closely it meets the standard. Shortcomings can be pointed out to the programmer to give him a chance to fix up the code. This may include noting bad variable names, the failure to indent block structures, or the use of global variables. Once the programmer has had a chance to fix the errors, copies of the code can be distributed to the entire team for review. Then, in a group meeting members of the team can bring up issues that they see in the code.

If a code review involves the entire team, it can be hard on the programmer who wrote it as well as a waste of time and resources. A better approach is to have a supervisor do the code review one on one. This way, the programmer won't be embarrassed in a room full of people or feel undue pressure over every If statement, variable name, or comment she inserts. I've seen programmers dreading code reviews; it lowers morale, disrupts productivity, and often creates an environment in which resources are wasted counting spaces or complaining about variable names. If you stick to one-on-one code reviews with a supervisor or manager who is skilled at constructive criticism, these problems can be avoided.

Coding Up to Standard

The best defense is a good offense, so it's a good idea to have your standards clearly laid out beforehand. Standards should not be too "tight;" they should be easy to follow and not place too large of a burden on the programmers. Language standards should be kept to a minimum. Variable naming and comments are important standards to enforce, and it's a good idea to make sure programmers indent blocks of code and don't use long lines of code.

Balancing and Enforcing Standards without Constraining Developers

Earlier in the chapter we stated that you don't want to step on a programmer's creativity. This means that, in general, coding standards should not involve forcing programmers to use a particular method of logic unless failing to do so causes some undue problem such as slowing performance or giving an unexpected answer. Programmers should be free to use their own thought processes to solve problems, as long as they comment thoroughly so someone else can clearly see how the code works.

When it comes to issues such as indenting blocks of code, don't take that too far. I've actually worked in places where they sit down and count the spaces. This is a complete waste of time and energy and leaves everyone on edge. Instead of concentrating on writing good code, developers end up counting spaces. When it comes to enforcing neatness, just make sure that the code looks neat and is indented without becoming neurotic about it. In summary, a good rule of thumb is to make the standards simple and easy to follow: the developer should be able to look up all the coding standards on one or two sheets of paper.

CHAPTER 7

User Interface Design

In a graphical environment like Windows, the user interface takes on a prominent role that it didn't have in old command-line environments like DOS. While the functionality behind a piece of software is still what counts the most, the fact is that the user interface can make or break an application. If the user feels frustrated and confused by what he sees on the screen, he won't get very far with the software and probably won't ever discover the powerful features that you spent hours developing. If the design of the interface follows industry standards and is intuitive to the average user, they'll feel right at home and will sing the praises of your great application. Don't forget, if you're programming in Windows with Visual Basic, the only way the end user can interact with your software is through the graphical user interface, or GUI.

By sticking to a few simple design standards, it will be easy to build user-friendly applications without having to put too much thought into it. While the user interface is important, we don't want it to become so overwhelming that it consumes all of your energy—energy that you need to save for the meat of the application. In this chapter, we'll lay out some simple design protocols that can help you build applications that your users will feel comfortable with and hopefully cause them to send praises your way. The focus on this chapter is not the "how" of building a user interface; in other words, we won't be talking about how to add a form to a project or put controls on it. In this book, we are assuming that you have already learned these techniques elsewhere, so we will instead be focusing on the "what" of a good interface design.

The Elements of a Good User Interface

One of the fortunate facts of life when programming in Visual Basic is that Microsoft has made many of the tools that they use in building GUIs available in VB as controls. Another free benefit we get from programming in Windows is that Windows *defines* many of the user interface elements, such as forms, command buttons, and common dialogs. But this brings us to a mild conflict—within the constraints set by Windows, Visual Basic gives the developer complete freedom to design the user interface. This is both good and bad. It promotes creativity, which helps propel the art of designing user interfaces to new heights. On the other hand, too much freedom can lead to programmers developing UIs that are downright ugly. This might mean a screen that has bright colors or one that is cluttered with too many controls. The choices made may hinge on a variety of factors, including the preferences of the developer as well as constraints set by the data the program is working with. This means that it's important to add a user interface design protocol to your set of coding standards.

When thinking about the elements of a good user interface, we can start by considering what is already popular in the software world. Many large companies have spent a lot of money trying to figure out how to build a user-friendly interface, so it's a good idea to follow their lead. By sticking to a *general* method of user interface design, you can ensure that any computer user with a reasonable level of experience will be able to use your application without being confused by the layout of the forms. If we're talking about building a program for use in the business world, or by scientists and engineers, we also want to build a professional-looking application. Let's identify some of the elements of popular software products that we can incorporate into a Visual Basic application:

- *The splash screen*: Almost every off-the-shelf or professional application displays a "splash screen" when it launches. This practice came about as way to keep the user happy while the program went about its time-consuming initialization business. The splash screen displays the program name, the company that developed it, copyright and version information, as well as some type of graphics. Splash screens are so ubiquitous in Windows that a program is expected to have one. If a program doesn't have one it seems unprofessional. You don't want your users to think that you're some backyard hacker, so it is a good idea to include a splash screen even it your program doesn't need it.

- *A main window*: If your program has more than one form, it should have a centralized main screen where the user can access just about every function the program has. There are a few options available for the main window, but they will all have several elements in common. We can have an *MDI* or multiple document interface, where the main window functions as a container for document forms that contain the actual data the user interacts with. We can have an *SDI* or single document interface. This is similar to the MDI in that the main form is a container for a document window. However, in this case there can only be one document open at a time.

- *A pull-down menu system*: Even though Windows has been moving to a more and more graphical approach with push buttons and icons, you should include a pull-down menu system that at least duplicates some of the functions available on toolbars or with buttons. A user of a Windows application expects it.

- *A toolbar*: Toolbars have become a popular user interface element, particularly since the release of Windows 95. A toolbar provides a user-friendly, one-step way to access frequently used functions. These days just about every Windows application has a toolbar on the main window. You shouldn't build a form that has a menu system without a toolbar to accompany it.

- *ToolTips*: A ToolTip is a text string that will display on screen when the user rests the mouse pointer over a control. The ToolTip provides a description of what the control does, for example, *Save* if the user clicks the button with the image of a floppy disk on it.

- *A status bar*: A status bar gives a main window a complete feel and can be used to display helpful or important information to the user. For example, if you're using a word processor to type a document the status bar might tell you what page you are on or what line of the page you're currently typing.

- *Good tab order*: Users expect to be able to move around the controls of a form by using the tab key. Make sure that you keep the tab order moving in a logical fashion, especially if you go back later and add new controls in the middle of the screen.

- *Form position*: When designing your forms, think about the position in which they will appear on the screen. If startup position is set to Windows default, each time the form is loaded it will appear wherever on the screen the operating system decides to place it. It's a good idea to set startup position to either center screen or center owner.

- *A control box and Min and Max buttons*: It's a good idea to follow Windows convention and put these buttons on every form. They provide the user with the ability to minimize, maximize, and close the form. Since these buttons are standard in Windows, the user will know what to do with them if she has any computer experience, and placing them on your forms helps give your application a professional appearance.

- *Conventions used for command buttons*: Most Windows programs follow the same convention for the arrangement given to common command buttons. This includes *OK-Cancel*, *Yes-No-Cancel*, *Save-Cancel*, and *Abort-Retry-Ignore*. The buttons should be shown on the screen in the same left-to-right order in which they are listed here. Users get accustomed to using a specific order and might move around the screen clicking buttons quickly. For example, if the buttons are not in the expected order, the user may end up clicking the *No* button when he meant to click the *Yes* button. The way command buttons are arranged on your forms will give the user an impression of the application's level of professionalism. The arrangement of standard command buttons is no place to be creative, so follow the conventions that Microsoft uses.

- *Clear screen layout*: If a screen gets too crowded, that means it's a bad user interface design. This is a pressing problem that is seen in customized database applications for the business world. It's important to learn what a good data input screen should look like. You can find out by looking at the top sellers in areas such as personal finance or accounting software.

- *At most two tables on a single form*: It may be tempting to display a series of related data tables on the same screen. However, this can result in too much clutter. If you are working with two tables in a master-dependent relationship, this is acceptable. However, if there are more than two tables, use command buttons to allow the user to view the other tables either on a separate screen or on an area of the screen that is normally hidden. The goal is to keep forms as clutter-free as possible. This is because people digest information better when it is given to them in smaller bits rather than in large chunks.

A Main Window

To illustrate these principles, in this section we consider an application written to help run a carpet cleaning business. The application tracks customers, gives job estimates, and tracks equipment. The main window of the application is a form that provides a menu system and buttons that can be used to access the rest of the application (see Figure 7-1). There are a few things to notice about the layout of the screen:

- *The menu system*: This window has the standard Windows pull-down menu system found in almost any application.

- *A toolbar*: A toolbar with user-friendly buttons is found just *below* the menu system. The buttons on the toolbar are large so they are easy to spot. (Obviously, the size that can be given to each button will depend

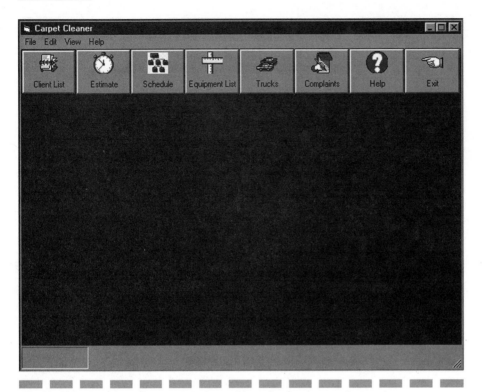

Figure 7-1 Example of a main window with toolbar, menu, and status bar.

on how much functionality you need to put on the toolbar. Try to keep it at a minimum so the program is clear and straightforward. My experience has been that users prefer the larger buttons by a wide margin.) The function of each button is made clear by a one-word description of what part of the program the button will open. The buttons are given a pleasant appearance with colorful, but not overwhelming, icons.

- *The middle of the window is blank*: For a database application like this one, the middle of the main window will function as a work area of sorts where the other forms that contain the data will be displayed.

- *A status bar*: A status bar is found at the bottom of the screen. We can use the status bar to display a message to the user.

- *Help is easily accessed*: The user can clearly spot a help button on the main toolbar, as well as the help pull-down menu.

Figure 7-2 A splash screen created in VB.

The Splash Screen

At the beginning of this chapter we mentioned that every program should start with a splash screen. Our hypothetical carpet cleaning software is no exception. To add a splash screen, we open the Add Form dialog box from the Project pull-down menu in Visual Basic. Next, we select *Splash Screen*. Visual Basic will then add a ready-made splash screen to our project, which we can customize (see Fig. 7-2). Customizing the splash screen is easy; all you have to do is set the captions of the label controls that Visual Basic has put on the form. Visual Basic will set the values of the captions to the settings you specify in the Project Properties dialog, so you really don't have to do anything for the splash screen to work. To do this, open the Make tab of the Project Properties dialog. You can set the following information, which will appear on the splash screen:

■ *Application title* appears in the `lblProductname` caption.

■ *Version number* appears in the `lblVersion` caption.

If you want to customize it further, you can do so by working with the splash screen in the same way you would any other form. The splash screen is set to unload if the user clicks on it. If desired, you can change this behavior by editing the form `KeyPress` event and the frame `Click` event. I also add a timer to the splash screen and set the interval to 3,000 so the screen will unload in three seconds if the user doesn't take any action.

When the splash screen unloads, we want the user to see the main window. One way to do this is to set the startup object of the program to `Sub Main`. We then use the following steps:

■ Use the `Sub Main` procedure to show the splash screen.

■ Add a procedure called `UnloadSplash` to a standard code module in the project. Inside this routine, we show the main window and unload the splash screen.

■ In the `Timer` event of the timer control, we call the `UnloadSplash` procedure.

■ We replace the unload methods in the `KeyPress` and `Click` events of the splash form with a call to the `UnloadSplash` procedure.

For example, the code would look like the following:

```
'standard code module
Option Explicit

Public Sub Main()

 frmSplash.Show  'start the program by displaying a splash screen

End Sub

Public Sub UnloadSplash()
 'show the main form and unload the splash screen
 frmMain.Show
 Unload frmSplash
End Sub
```

The code in the splash screen form will look like this:

```
Option Explicit

Private Sub Form_KeyPress(KeyAscii As Integer)
 UnloadSplash
End Sub

Private Sub Form_Load()
 lblVersion.Caption = "Version " & App.Major & "." & App.Minor
  & "." & App.Revision
```

```
        lblProductName.Caption = App.Title
End Sub

Private Sub Frame1_Click()
  UnloadSplash
End Sub

Private Sub Timer1_Timer()

  UnloadSplash

End Sub
```

Displaying Data in Grid Format

When we are talking about database applications, the way in which the data is displayed is of central concern. There are many ways to do it, and I will suggest just one way here. It is a good, user-friendly method. The goal of our user interface design is to keep the user from being overwhelmed by the data while at the same time trying to show him as much data as possible. One way you meet these goals is to break the data into two forms. The first form, which is accessible directly from a button on the main window, displays the data in a grid format. The grid will display either the results of a query or the contents of an entire table; this choice will depend on the particular program at hand. In Fig. 7-3, we show an example of what a well-designed grid form should look like. This form has several key elements:

- The form caption displays either the name of the table that is open or a descriptive name reflecting the results of a query.

- A grid displaying the data is centered in the middle of the form. The grid is for viewing purposes only, and the user can select a row or record by clicking on the grid with the mouse.

- A series of command buttons is placed in the lower portion of the form that provide the user with a series of commands she can execute to manipulate the data. For our example, we have a New button, which the user can click to add a new record. The Edit button lets the user edit the currently selected record. Other buttons that may be included are Delete, Query, and Print. The specific nature of most of the buttons will be determined by each specific application. The form should have a Close button that the user can click to return to the main screen.

- The New and Edit buttons will open another window, which displays a single record. This secondary form can be used to add new records or edit the contents of an existing record.

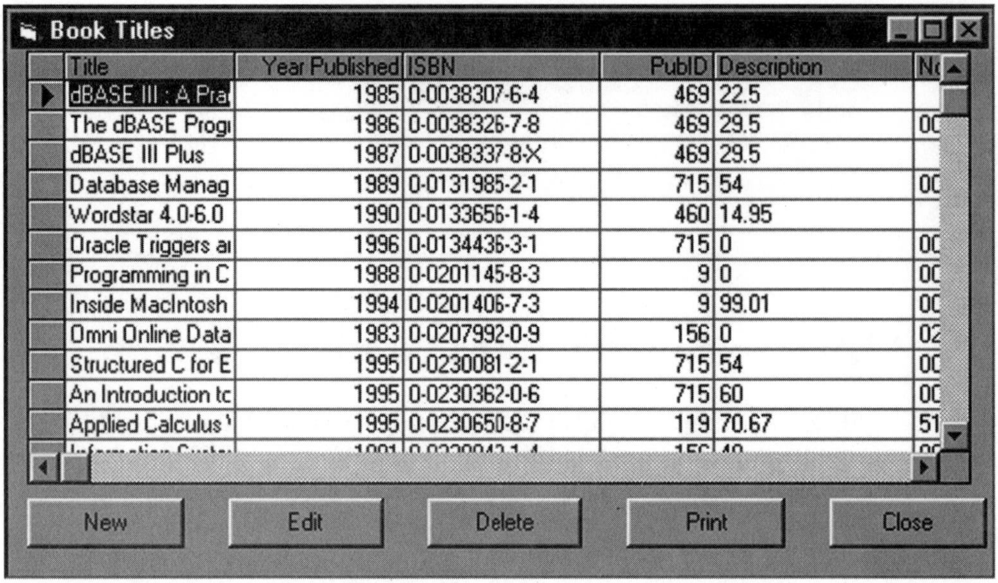

Figure 7-3 Displaying data in a grid format.

A grid form should also have a means for allowing the user to search the database. There are many extended data controls available on the market that have built-in searching capabilities. It is a good idea to use these on your forms. Otherwise, you should add your own Find or Search button that will let the user search the data grid based on the values of one or more fields. The Find button can be implemented by using the Find methods of a recordset object.

Displaying Individual Records

The grid form is a "gateway" form. It lets the user browse through the data and perform actions on that data as required. One of those actions is to add new records to the table or to edit an existing record. An example of a form to display a single record is shown in Fig. 7-4. A form of this type has the following elements or characteristics:

■ The form caption contains the table name. You can also include an identifying characteristic of the record here, such as ID or name.

■ The fields of the record are displayed neatly in text boxes, which the user can edit.

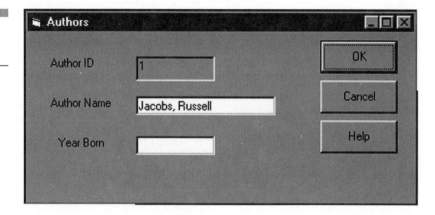

Figure 7-4
Displaying a single record.

- Each text box is clearly labeled.
- An OK button lets the user save any changes.
- A Cancel button lets the user back out or abandon the changes.
- A Help button lets the user access help from this dialog.
- The form uses good tab order (see Fig. 7-5). When the form loads, the cursor is present in the Author ID text box. When the user presses Tab, the cursor will move in this order: Author Name, Year Born, OK, Cancel, and Help.

Notice what the form does not show or allow:

- The data control, which acts as the data source of the form, is not visible to the user.
- This form can only be used to display one record. The grid form that we discussed in the previous chapter is used to navigate through the records of the database. The user selects the record that he is interested in viewing on the grid form, clicks the edit form, and then this form opens, displaying that particular record. If the user clicks *New* from the grid form, the data control on this form will add a new

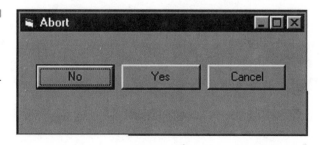

Figure 7-5
Placing command buttons in the wrong order.

record, which will blank out all of the data bound controls so the user can enter new data.

We will delay the specifics and our discussion of how to program database elements until Chapter 10. However, we can provide the following suggestions for building an application this way:

- You can use public variables to communicate between the forms. For example, we can use a variable to let the single record form know if the operation selected was *New record* or *Edit an existing record*. If the user is editing an existing record, we can also pass the value of the primary key to the single record form so it can display the appropriate record.

- The grid form can use the `Refresh` method of the data control to update the data displayed in the grid. This should be done whenever the user brings the grid form into view. We can do this by placing the call to refresh in the form's `Activate` event. That way, the grid form will reflect any changes made to the data in the single record form.

There are other ways to build a user interface and other ways to display and manipulate data. We are simply suggesting a protocol that can be adopted to provide the user with a standardized, friendly interface.

Judging User Expertise

The end user must be kept in mind during all phases of the design process. When thinking of the end user, always think of the worst possible case. The user interface should be such that users from the novice to expert levels can use the program without any problems. For more expert or so-called power users, you can provide added features such as customizable toolbars.

Prototyping

In the era of rapid application development, prototyping is taking on an ever larger role in interactions with the customer. Since it's easy to patch together a user interface, it makes sense to prototype an application. In this section, we explore the importance of prototyping.

Why Prototype an Application?   The main function of a prototype is to define system requirements. Prototyping helps build communication with the customer. When an application is prototyped, it will go through several successive iterations of increasing complexity. By providing the customer with a mock-up of the application early on, we can gauge and react to the customer's desires before the software is too developed. This process is continued throughout the development of the application, so the customer stays involved in the design process. This is better than surprising them with a piece of fully developed software after six months of programming. If they aren't happy, that's six months wasted. Prototyping helps maintain communication with the customer and helps ensure that progress is being made in a timely fashion—keeping the customer happy.

What to Include in a Prototype The idea of prototyping is to show the customer what appears to be a complete version of the software. Behind the scenes, all we have is a shell, in other words, a mock-up or model. This is easy to accomplish with Visual Basic. We can design several forms and load them with bogus data. The forms can be compiled into a "program" that we can show to the user, giving the customer a chance to see how the application would work before any real effort has been applied to the project.

It's important to approach prototyping as you would any aspect of software development. That means one thing: don't rush. RAD environments tempt a developer to rush out a real program as is. If we are talking about throwing together a few screens, the temptation to rush is even larger. The downside is that a poor design choice may be included in the prototype that ends up being part of the final product. The key to avoiding these problems is to approach prototyping with a requirements-gathering approach. Meet with the customer and have the customer define what they want. They can lay out what data will be tracked, how they expect to access them, and how they want the screens to look. The format of printed reports may be discussed. This information is then used by the developer to patch together a hollow shell of a VB program that will display the forms and some artificial (or maybe even real) data. A sample report can be included. When this is completed, you meet with the customer again and determine if the requirements have been met. If not, more work is put into the prototype. Once the customer is satisfied, work on the real project can begin. The prototyping process may involve several hit-and-miss attempts. How well things go will depend on the level of communication with the customer. In many cases, the prototype will evolve into the real application. This is especially the case when using a RAD development environment like Visual Basic.

Setting Expectations for Prototyping   Good communication is key when prototyping. The customer might want to work with the prototype on their own. It's important that they understand that the prototype is not a real program. To them, the forms on the screen and the colorful buttons convince them it's a real program. The customer needs to know that the prototyping process is simply an aid in defining the requirements of the project in the same way that a flow chart does. This is an important point. If the customer views the prototype as a real piece of software, they may end up pushing the development team into rushing the prototype into a production piece of software. Customers become impatient during software development. Remember that unless the customer has some history of software development behind them, the process of building a program will be a complete mystery. As far as they're concerned, if you have a form that shows up with some data, it's a working program. They may not fully appreciate that you need to spend the next two months putting code behind all of those buttons and grids. In the end, keeping the expectations of the customer realistic during the prototyping process requires good communication.

CHAPTER 8

Object-Oriented Design in Visual Basic

Introduction to Object-Oriented Programming

In recent years the traditional method of software development has been supplanted by *object-oriented* programming. In the context of software development, an object is a software component that combines data and the procedures that act on that data into a single entity. Objects provide a ready means to model the real world in software; after all, the real world is made up of a series of objects. With each object we can think of its *characteristics* or *attributes*, which will make up the data of the object. We can also consider what happens to the object or what kind of actions the object can initiate. These will be the *procedures* for the object.

Let's consider a specific example and think about the data and procedures that can be used to define the object. A familiar object from everyday life is the family automobile. We can start thinking about modeling a car in software by breaking it down into data and procedures. First, we consider the data of the car object, which are the characteristics or *properties* of the car. Here is a list of some of the properties the average car might have:

- Make
- Model
- Year
- Fuel capacity, in gallons
- Miles per gallon, city
- Miles per gallon, highway
- Current fuel, in gallons
- Oil type required
- Number of cylinders
- Money spent on fuel

Each of these data elements or properties of the car can be modeled by a simple data type. For example, we can define the model and fuel capacity in the following way:

```
Dim Model As String
Dim FuelCapacity As Byte
```

For the procedures that the car object will have, we can think about what happens to the car during its existence. Some of the things that happen to a car might include:

- Driving
- Going in for repairs
- Refueling
- Getting in an accident

Each of the items we've identified here can be modeled as software procedures. For example, we could develop a function that modeled driving. If we were interested in fuel consumption, we might track how many miles of city travel or highway travel the car accumulated and have the driving function return the number of gallons used. Our function definition might look something like this:

```
Function Drive(HighwayMiles As Integer, CityMiles As Integer)
   Return GallonsUsed
```

By analyzing each of the data elements and procedures in this way, we can build up a car object to model the behavior of a car under different driving conditions or to study its fuel use. While this is a good start, you might notice that many properties of the car object will have to be set over and over again in code. For example, if we were continually modeling Ford trucks, all of these trucks would have similar values for several of their properties or similar behavior for many of the procedures. It might therefore make sense to have an object named "Truck." You might also notice that a truck has characteristics that a car does not. Rather than having to redefine a new object that used all of the characteristics of a car with a few additions, it would be nice if we could use the car object as the basis for the truck object and *extend* it.

This brings us to the idea of *inheritance*. With inheritance, we can define a generic car object with the properties and procedures that we just defined. We can then define new types that inherit the car object but add their own additional data and procedures. Let's call the original object the *base* object. When the new object type inherits from the *base* object, it will have all of the base object's data and procedures as part of its characteristics. In other words, the truck object will already have `Model` and `FuelCapacity` without having to redefine them. However, the truck object might extend the car object with, say, the following properties and methods:

- ■ `Diesel`: A Boolean variable that can be set to True if the truck uses diesel fuel.

- ■ `TowCapacity`: An integer that tells us how many pounds the variable can tow.

- ■ `LoadCapacity`: An integer tells us how many tons the truck can hold.

I'm sure that you can think of some more. In the same way that we can use the car object as the base object for developing a truck object, we can use it to define several other objects as well, such as a sedan, mini-van, or any other type of automobile.

From the preceding discussion, you are probably beginning to see some of the power that an object-oriented approach to programming provides. By putting software code in objects we have a reusable component. By reusing components, we can build software in much shorter time periods, with less cost, and with more reliability.

Software Reuse Speeds Product Development

Once a piece of software is packaged in a reusable object it can be plugged into a new program without having to reinvent the wheel. This will save you an enormous amount of time when developing new software. An object-oriented approach can also provide a standardized way for interoperability, which means that components can be simply dropped into a program and used immediately without having to deal with the nuances of using code libraries. When you use objects, for example, a calendar object, you save a great deal of time by being able to simply drop the calendar into your project without having to code up a calendar yourself. Being able to choose from a wide collection of objects makes possible the speedy development of software at a lower cost.

Software Reuse Promotes Reliability

Once an object is designed, debugged, and thoroughly tested, it can be used over and over again without having to worry about the code that represents the object causing problems. Entire software projects can be built entirely from objects that are already known to be reliable. This means that the reliability of the project as a whole is increased. The time spent debugging and testing can also be reduced because they have already been done for each object in the program.

Structuring Your Data with Classes

When we thought about the car object, we noticed that we *classified* the objects, such as car and truck. This is the origin of the term *classes*. By using a class to define an object in software, we can classify objects by behavior (procedures or methods) and data (properties). We can also think about what might happen to an object: we can call this an *event*. An object is an *instance* of the class.

In the C++ language, a class is modeled on a type declaration. Without getting into how a class is used in C++, let's think about how we can represent a class in an abstract fashion. Let's return to the car example. Using the properties and methods that we defined in the introduction, we could build the class like this:

```
Class Car
 Properties
   Make As String
   Model As String
   Year As String
   FuelCapacity As Integer
   CityMPG As Integer
   HwyMPG As Integer
   Fuel As Integer
   FuelCost As Currency
   MoneySpentOnRepairs As Currency

 Methods
   Function Drive(HighwayMiles As Integer, CityMiles As Integer) Return
GallonsUsed
   Function GetRepairs(RepairType As Integer) Return Cost
   Function Refuel(Gallons As Integer) Return Cost

 Events
   Crash()
   End Class
```

We can then declare variables of type `Car`, as defined by the `Car` class above. Each of these variables will be an object, and we say that each object is an instance of the `Car` class. For example:

```
Dim Van As Car, Sedan As Car
```

The function of the class is to *define* the object. Once the object is defined, we can declare the individual instances of the object in our program. Because all of the objects of a particular class share the same properties, methods, and events, they will behave in the same way.

We can also use a class that functions only as a template. In this case, the class is known as an *abstract* class. Objects of the abstract class are never declared; the class is only used to define other classes, through inheritance. The methods and events of the abstract class may not even do anything: we can insert blank function definitions and only add the code to the inherited classes.

The Aspects of Object-Oriented Programming

The world of object-oriented programming is filled with terminology. This terminology can make object-oriented programming seem a lot more complicated than it really is. Some of the most important terms are described in this section.

Abstraction

By viewing a problem in a black box or hierarchical fashion, we can simplify software development by concentrating only on certain details of a problem. We can build an object as a series of black boxes without worrying about what's happening inside each box. This process is known as *abstraction*. Abstraction involves temporarily ignoring the details of how the black boxes work while we concentrate on structuring the object. Once the object is built at a higher level, we can fill in the details of each black box. The roots of abstraction go back to the idea of building modular software. In that case, we could define a software program as a series of steps represented only by function headers. Once the overall flow of the program was developed, then we could move on to filling in the details—that is, writing the code behind each of the functions.

Client and Server

Client and *server* are not really a part of the object-oriented language, but I've put them here because it's important that you know what we mean by the terms *client* and *server* in the context of objects. In the Windows environment, an application will make its objects available to other applications—this is called *exposing* the objects. The application that exposes its objects is known as the *server*. The applications that use these objects are known as *client* applications. When you develop a

Visual Basic application that uses the Word Basic object library, Microsoft Word functions as the server, while your application is the client. In Chapter 12 we'll see that Visual Basic allows you to develop server applications by building your own objects and making them available to other applications.

Encapsulation

Encapsulation means that the user of an object does not worry about how that object goes about performing its functions. Encapsulated data is not accessible outside of the object. The data in the object can only be manipulated by the methods of that object. The methods of the object can either be invoked by a message from another object or by another method that is part of the object itself. The goal of encapsulation is to hide the details of how the object works.

Information Hiding

In object-oriented software development, the user interacts with an object by performing certain operations on that object. The user cannot see the data or the implementation behind that object. The goal of information hiding is to promote software reuse. By hiding the details, we can modify the object without having any impact on any applications that use the object. The goal of object orientation is to reduce the interaction between the object and the user to an interface. The details of the object may change, but the interface stays the same. If the object is updated or changed, the user application does not care; to the user, the object seems the same. This saves time and money and keeps software headaches to a minimum.

Inheritance

In our introduction to this chapter we showed how we could use the car object to define other objects that were similar but had their own characteristics, such as a truck. The central characteristic of inheritance is the ability to use a set of characteristics and behaviors that are common to a wide variety of objects. We call a class that inherits the characteristics of the base class a *subclass*. The subclass is defined in terms of the base class that already exists. The subclass inherits all of the characteristics and behaviors of the base class as its own and can extend the functionality of the class by adding new characteristics and behaviors. Inheritance is a characteristic of object-oriented programming that contributes to faster and cheaper software development.

Polymorphism

Polymorphism means that a software operation can be applied to many different situations. For example, we might have a class called *shape* that represents three-dimensional objects. A useful method for 3-D shapes would be Volume, which returns the volume of the object. Different classes of shape objects, such as cubes and spheres, will use different methods for calculating volume. As another example, think about using the plus (+) symbol to concatenate strings or to add two numbers together. We can think of this as using the same object to perform two very different operations. When an operation can be used in several different ways, we call this *overloading*. Polymorphism allows a subclass to *override* a method of the base class to suit its own purposes. For example, we can have a base class called *Circle*. The Area method for the Circle class will return *Pi*(Radius squared)* for the area. We can develop a *Sphere* class and override the Area method to return the area of a sphere, *4*Pi*(Radius squared)*.

The idea of polymorphism contributes to the abstract approach of object-oriented development by letting the developer focus on using the method without worrying about how the method is implemented. Once the programmer figures out how the method will be used, the details inside can be built.

Is Visual Basic Object Oriented?

The question of whether or not Visual Basic is an object-oriented language is complicated. For the purist, the answer would probably be "not quite." One problem is that Visual Basic does not really support inheritance, although it provides a means for using polymorphism through interfaces. Another problem is that Visual Basic makes it to easy to *expose* data rather than hide it, an important characteristic of object orientation. You can develop a VB app and fill it with global variables that have free access to data throughout the program. The language also has a loose structure. For example, recall that in Chapter 5 we considered the ability to use variables without declaring them. As each new version of the language is released, many of these problems have been addressed. However, to maintain backward compatibility old practices are still allowed. Despite these weaknesses, when you consider the language in total, especially the more recent versions, we can say that Visual Basic is evolving into an object-oriented language.

More recent versions of Visual Basic have imposed a more rigorous structure on the language. For example, we can use `Option Explicit` to force variable declaration. In recent versions, we have also seen an explosion in VB's capacity to build and use objects. Classes have been greatly expanded, including the ability to implement subclassing through interfaces. While a programmer can still define a property as a public variable, the option of using property procedures instead promotes the concept of data hiding. Objects built with classes can be used as abstract objects by other applications without regard to the internal workings of the class. We can use Visual Basic to build ActiveX controls, which are objects that use encapsulation and data abstraction to the fullest. For example, a developer isn't concerned with the code or data implementation that lies behind a calendar control.

COM

If you've been anywhere around the software development world in the past couple of years, no doubt you've heard about *COM* and *DCOM*. If you've been programming in Windows, you're already somewhat familiar with COM through OLE and ActiveX. COM stands for *component object model*, and it represents a standardized method of communication between objects. Under COM, objects can only communicate by means of an interface that they provide. The internal workings of the object are invisible to clients—they can only see and manipulate the interface. COM provides this standard through a set of base classes upon which all objects are built. Developers use a set of abstract classes that define the component interface. Recalling the definition of abstraction in an object-oriented environment, this means that COM builds these classes as if they were a set of black boxes—or function headers. COM specifies how information gets in and out of the box, but the internal workings of the box are defined by the developer. Since the implementation details are hidden from the client and the client knows the interface of the object through COM, the client can communicate with the object through the use of the COM standard.

One of the benefits of COM is that it allows objects to evolve while maintaining the same interface for backward compatibility. Client applications can continue to use new versions of an object without worrying about how the internal implementation has changed. This permits developers of objects to increase the functionality of the object while at the same time promoting software reuse.

Another term floating around software circles these days is DCOM, or the *distributed* component object model. This is an extension of COM that allows objects to work across a network. This is done by using what is known as a remote procedures call, or *RPC*. RPC allows a client application to access objects that are on a remote machine without having to worry about the fact that it is on a network.

COM and the Registry

In Windows, each COM object uses a unique 128-bit number that is known as the *ClassID*. This value is stored in the registry, where it can be used by client applications to look up the component. As long as the component maintains the same ClassID and interface the client application can continue to use newer versions of the component. This is an important means by which COM promotes software reuse.

Code Reuse versus Component Reuse

Throughout this discussion of objects, you may be thinking back to the concept of a code library. A code library is a set of related software functions that other programmers can use in their software development work. A code library provides some of the benefits of object-oriented programming, especially by providing reusable code. However, the concept of code reuse does not provide the standardized means of communication that is imposed by component reuse. A standard like COM imposes an interface that is used by all objects. This means that any object in Windows automatically knows how to communicate with any other object. Another problem with code reuse is that it does not provide true abstraction and encapsulation. In many cases, you might even have the source code of the library available for modification. This prevents the library from keeping its internal implementation hidden from the user. Code reuse also does not depend on the notion of classes, which means that the code cannot be extended through the use of inheritance and polymorphism. Component reuse, on the other hand, depends on these concepts in a fundamental way. This makes software reuse easier and less costly.

Existing Methodologies

There are several object-oriented design methods known throughout the industry, and here we will give a brief overview of some of the well-known techniques. One of the most famous of these is the *Grady Booch* object-oriented design method. This method uses Booch diagrams that show the interactions between different objects. Object-oriented design allows the developer to show how objects are derived from base classes and how these objects interact. The Booch method provides object diagrams and object partitioning along with the relationships of the behavior of each object. This method is the most mature method of object-oriented design.

The *Coad/Yourdon* method illustrates the behavior of objects by naming methods on classes. These methods are defined by what is known as a service chart. A service chart has flowcharts and state transition charts. Interactions among objects are tracked by message connections. This method allows the entire system to be described in a single diagram, with a system of built-in layers.

The *Object Modeling Technique* or Rumbaugh method, consists of three models. These are the object model, the dynamic model, and the functional model. The object model displays classes and their properties, which include operations and relationships between classes, such as inheritance and association. The dynamic model provides state transition diagrams for each class. The functional model is a data flow diagram. This method is considered easy to follow, but it is a relatively new model that is still in development.

The *unified modeling language* is a methodology that combines Booch, Rumbaugh, and the Jacobsen use-case driven object-oriented model. Use-case diagrams are used to show the software as seen by the end user. Class diagrams show the structure of the classes within the system, while object diagrams are used to show the objects in the system (remember, an object is a specific *instance* of a class). This model also includes state diagrams to show the states an object can have, along with any state transitions.

Practical Object Modeling in Visual Basic

In Visual Basic, a class is implemented by using a class module. A class module can be added to any VB project by selecting *Add Class Module* from the Project pull-down menu. A class module looks very similar to a standard code module, and in many ways it is. The class will be represented by a code window in the design environment with a general declarations section. You build your class by defining the properties, methods, and events for the class. The properties and methods of the class will be implemented by `Sub` and `Function` procedures. It is here that the similarity with a standard code module ends.

When you write code in a standard code module, the rest of the program uses that code by calling the `Subroutine` and `Function` procedures in that module. With a class, however, the code cannot be used in this manner. The function of the class is to define new objects that can be declared in a Visual Basic program. You declare an object variable that is a specific instance of the class. You can then program with that object, using the properties, methods, and events that were defined in the class module. When you add a class module to your project, the first thing you should do is open the properties window for that class and set the Name property. The value of the Name property will be used to declare objects of the class, so it's important to give the class a meaningful name. If you wish to use Hungarian notation begin the name of each class with the lowercase prefix *cls*.

Properties and Methods

The simplest way to implement a property in a class module is to declare a public variable in the general declarations section. This does not provide true encapsulation, however, so we will not use this method. Instead, we will define our properties by using *property procedures*. A property procedure is a special kind of procedure that provides access to a private variable that will store the property. Property procedures come in pairs. These are as follows:

- `PropertyGet`: A `PropertyGet` procedure returns the value of the property. `PropertyGet` is a function, so you return the value of the property by assigning it to the procedure name.

■ `PropertyLet`/`PropertySet`: A `PropertyLet` or `PropertySet` procedure assigns a new value to the property. In this book, we will use `PropertyLet` procedures.

The property value is stored in a private variable declared in the general declarations section of the class. For example, suppose we had a class called `clsCircle`. One property a circle can have is its radius. To implement the property, we use the following code:

```
Option Explicit

Private mRadius As Double
Public PropertyGet Radius() As Double
 Radius = mRadius
End Property

Public PropertyLet Radius(ByVal dblNewValue As Double)
 mRadius = dblNewValue
End Property
```

The private variable, `mRadius`, is used to hold the property value. Since the variable is private, it is hidden from the user, providing encapsulation. Private variables that store property values are often prefixed with an *m*. This is used to tell us that it is a member variable of the class. The `PropertyGet` function returns the value of `mRadius` to the user. `PropertyLet` assigns the property a new value. Note that property procedures can be used for data validation or to ensure that business rules are being followed. For example, we can check to make sure that the user has entered a valid value for the `Radius`:

```
Public PropertyLet Radius(ByVal dblNewValue As Double)

 If dblNewValue > 0 Then
    mRadius = dblNewValue
 Else
   MsgBox "Error : Must Enter a Positive Radius."
   End If

End Property
```

Declaring and Instantiating an Object

To use a class in Visual Basic, we must declare an object variable. This can be done using a `Dim`, `Static`, `Private`, or `Public` declaration. However, object variables must be declared using `As New`. For example, to declare a `clsCircle` object, we would use this code:

```
Dim objCircle As New clsCircle
```

Using `As New` is called instantiating the object. In this case, we declared and instantiated the object in a single step. This can also be done in two separate steps, which adds a little clarity. In that case, you first declare the object in the same way that you declare any variable in Visual Basic. You will then need to use a `Set...New` statement to instantiate the object before it can be used. For example:

```
Dim objCircle As clsCircle

Set objCircle = New clsCircle
```

Once the object has been declared, we can begin to use its properties. The properties of the `clsCircle` object can be referenced by using the same "dot" syntax that is used to reference the properties of a Visual Basic object. To set the radius we write:

```
objCircle.Radius = 12.5
```

Methods A class wouldn't have much functionality if it just had properties, so we will probably want to add some methods as well. Adding a method to a class module is simple. All you need to do is add a public `Sub` or `Function` procedure. Returning to the `clsCircle` object, recall that we can figure out the area and circumference for a circle. To implement these operations, we add two `Function` procedures. The code in the class module now looks like the following:

```
Option Explicit

Private mRadius As Double
Private Const PI = 3.141593

Public PropertyGet Radius() As Double
 Radius = mRadius
End Property
Public PropertyLet Radius(ByVal dblNewValue As Double)
 mRadius = dblNewValue
End Property

Public Function Area()
 Area = PI * (mRadius) ^ 2
End Function

Public Function Circumference()
 Circumference = 2 * PI * mRadius
End Function
```

The `Sub` and `Function` procedures in a class module can do just about anything and be just about any length. It's just a coincidence that they are one-line procedures like the properties in this case. However, if you take a look at the class module, you see that this class implements a complete circle object. Despite the fact that this is a very simple example, we've illustrated all of the elements that you need to know about to start building classes in Visual Basic. Here is some code that uses the clsCircle object:

```
Dim objCircle As clsCircle
Dim dblArea As Double, dblCircumference As Double

Set objCircle = New ACircle

objCircle.Radius = 6.25
dblArea = objCircle.Area
dblCircumference = objCircle.Circumference
```

Events

No object in Visual Basic would be complete if it did not have the ability to raise events. Since this is the case, Visual Basic allows you to add events to your class modules. When designing the class, all you need to do is declare the event and then cause the event to occur at the appropriate time. This is called *raising* the event, and Visual Basic provides the RaiseEvent keyword for this purpose. It is up to the object variable to respond to the event. First, let's see how to add an event to a class module. Adding an event to a class module requires two steps:

■ Declare a public event in the general declarations section of the class.

■ At the appropriate point in code in the class module, raise the event.

Let's return to the example at the beginning of the chapter. We will write a simple class in Visual Basic to represent a car. The code looks like this:

```
Option Explicit

'private variables to hold property values
Private mMake As String
Private mModel As String
Private mYear As String
Private mFuel As Double
Private mFuelConsumption As Double

Public Event OutofGas()

Public Property Get Make() As String
  Make = mMake
```

```
End Property

Public Property Let Make(ByVal strNewValue As String)
  mMake = strNewValue
End Property

Public Property Get Model() As String
  Model = mModel
End Property

Public Property Let Model(ByVal vNewValue As String)
  mModel = vNewValue
End Property

Public Property Get Year() As String
  Year = mYear
End Property

Public Property Let Year(ByVal strNewValue As String)
  mYear = strNewValue
End Property

Public Property Get Fuel() As Double
  Fuel = mFuel
End Property

Public Property Let Fuel(ByVal dblNewValue As Double)
  mFuel = dblNewValue
End Property

Public Property Get FuelConsumption() As Double
  FuelConsumption = mFuelConsumption
End Property

Public Property Let FuelConsumption(ByVal dblNewValue As Double)
  mFuelConsumption = dblNewValue
End Property

Public Sub Drive(dblMiles As Double)

  Dim dblGallons As Double

  dblGallons = dblMiles / mFuelConsumption

  If dblGallons > mFuel Then
     mFuel = 0
     RaiseEvent OutofGas
  Else
     mFuel = mFuel - dblGallons
  End If

End Sub
```

In this class, we have an event we have named OutofGas, which we will raise when the car runs out of gas. The event is declared in the general declarations section of the class:

```
Public Event OutofGas()
```

The event is raised in the `Drive` method. If the gallons consumed on this drive exceed the number of gallons in the car, which we represent by the `Fuel` property, we use the `RaiseEvent` to let the user of the class object know that the car is out of gas.

To use the event, we must declare the object using the `WithEvents` keyword. We do this in the general declarations section of a form:

```
Option Explicit
Private WithEvents objFord As clsAuto
```

The event will now be available in the code window of the form. If we click open the object drop-down list of the code window, we'll see a listing for `objFord` just like we would for a command button or a text box. If we select it, we'll see the `OutofGas` event in the events drop-down list, which is on the right side of a code window. We can respond to the event by placing code in the procedure:

```
Private Sub objFord_OutofGas()
  MsgBox "You Ran Out of Gas!"
End Sub
```

We can then program the object. In a command button, we make the car run out of gas:

```
Private Sub cmdDrive_Click()
Dim dblMilesTraveled As Double

Set objFord = New clsAuto

objFord.Make = "Ford"
objFord.Model = "Truck"
objFord.FuelConsumption = 15
objFord.Fuel = 10
dblMilesTraveled = 160
objFord.Drive (dblMilesTraveled)

End Sub
```

Events can also be used when validating data in property procedures. Returning to the circle example, we can raise an error event if the user doesn't enter a positive value for the radius:

```
Public Event DataError(intErrorFlag As Integer)

Public Property Let Radius(ByVal dblNewValue As Double)
```

```
If dblNewValue > 0 Then
    mRadius = dblNewValue
Else
    RaiseEvent DataError(BADRADIUS)
End If

End Property
```

Interfaces and Implements

In Visual Basic, when we are talking about class modules the term *interface* refers to the properties and methods of that class. You may recall that an object-oriented language provides a means for building a new object that *inherits* the properties and methods of another object. While Visual Basic does not directly provide a means of inheritance in the way that the C++ language does, we can use the `Implements` keyword to build a class and specify additional interfaces that the class will use. For all practical purposes, this allows us to use inheritance.

To see how the concept of inheritance might be used, consider the following example. Suppose that we wanted to model simple three-dimensional solids in a software program. There are several shapes we can think of. We have a cube, a ball, a cylinder, and a cone, for example. Despite the differences between each of these shapes, they have many characteristics and operations in common. For example, we might want to know the volume or surface area of the object. In code, we could declare the objects in the following way:

```
Dim objCube As Cube
Dim objBall As Ball
Dim dblLength As Double, dblRadius As Double

Set objCube = New Cube
Set objBall = New Ball

dblLength = 6.5
dblRadius = 4.25

MsgBox "Volume of Cube is " & CStr(objCube.Volume(dblLength))
MsgBox "Volume of Ball is " & CStr(objBall.Volume(dblRadius))
```

This type of design is wasteful because we have defined two different classes, `Cube` and `Ball`, that implement the same method, `Volume`. There are probably many functions that the two objects have in common. It makes more sense to take a different design approach, one that will allow us to define the functions and properties that are common to all three-dimensional solids. (Notice that each type of solid uses and responds to the same method, Volume, but the algorithms that implement this method are different for each object. This is an example of a function that is *overloaded*.) We can place the common properties and methods, or interface elements, in a base class. We will call the base class ISolid. The ISolid class will define the common properties and methods for the interface but will not contain any code. The interface class acts as the definition of a solid object. We can then build other classes, such as Cube, that will *implement* the solid object. The interface class is known as an abstract class because it has no code behind the definitions. The convention is to use a capital *I* as the first letter of the name of an interface class.

The interface class for our 3-D object might look something like this:

```
Option Explicit

Public Function Volume() As Double

End Function

Public Function SurfaceArea()

End Sub

Public Sub Draw()

End Sub
```

Notice that while we have defined some methods of the solid object, there is no code in any of the procedures. This is consistent with the idea of building an abstract class. To use the abstract class, we will build classes to represent several shapes: a cube, a ball, a cylinder, and a cone. To implement the ISolid class, each of these classes will use the following line of code in the general declarations section of the class:

```
Implements ISolid
```

The volume and surface area of each type of solid will be calculated differently. To specify that a class is implementing a method or property of an interface class, we tell Visual Basic the interface class name as well as the procedure name. For example, the Volume function header for the ball class would look like the following:

```
Public Function ISolid_Volume() As Double
```

We can then put the code specific to finding the volume of a ball in this function. Each shape can also extend the ISolid class by adding its own properties, methods, and events. The ball, cylinder, and cone classes look like this:

```
'Ball class, implements the abstract class ISolid.

Option Explicit

Implements ISolid

Private mRadius As Double
Private Const PI As Double   = 3.14593

'Implement the volume function
Public Function ISolid_Volume() As Double
 ISolid_Volume = (4 / 3) * PI * (mRadius) ^ 3
End Function

'Implement the ISolid SurfaceArea function
Public Function ISolid_SurfaceArea() As Double

   ISolid_SurfaceArea = 4 * PI * (mRadius) ^ 2

End Function

'Implement ISolid Draw method
Private Sub ISolid_Draw()
 'Code here to draw the ball
 'in a picture box
End Sub

'Radius-a property of a ball object
Public Property Get Radius() As Double
 Radius = mRadius
End Property

Public Property Let Radius(ByVal dblNewValue As Double)
 mRadius = dblNewValue
End Property
```

The cylinder class will look like this:

```
Option Explicit

Implements ISolid

Private Const PI As Double = 3.141593

'properties of cylinder
Private mRadius As Double
Private mHeight As Double

'procedures to implement ISolid class
Public Function ISolid_Volume() As Double
   ISolid_Volume = PI * (mRadius) ^ 2 * mHeight
End Function
```

```
Public Function ISolid_SurfaceArea() As Double
  'return lateral surface area
  ISolid_SurfaceArea = 2 * PI * mRadius * mHeight
End Function

Public Sub ISolid_Draw()
 'code to draw cylinder
End Sub

Public Property Get Height() As Double
 Height = mHeight
End Property

Public Property Let Height(ByVal dblNewValue As Double)
 mHeight = dlbNewValue
End Property
```

And the code for the cone object is as follows:

```
Option Explicit

Implements ISolid

Private Const PI As Double = 3.141593

'member variables of cone class
Private mRadius As Double
Private mHeight As Double
Private mSLength As Double

'procedures to implement ISolid class
Public Function ISolid_Volume()  As Double
 ISolid_Volume = (PI / 3) * (mRadius) ^ 2 * mHeight
End Function

Public Function ISolid_SurfaceArea() As Double
 ISolid_SurfaceArea = PI * Radius * mSLength
End Function

Public Sub ISolid_Draw()
 'code to draw cone goes here
End Sub

Public Property Get Radius() As Double
 Radius = mRadius
End Property

Public Property Let Radius(ByVal dblNewValue As Double)
 mRadius = dblNewValue
End Property

Public Property Get Height() As Double
 Height = mHeight
End Property

Public Property Let Height(ByVal dblNewValue As Double)
```

```
   mHeight = dblNewValue
End Property

Public Property Get SLength() As Double
 SLength = mSLength
End Property

Public Property Let SLength(ByVal dblNewValue As Double)
 mSLength = dblNewValue
End Property
```

There are three things to notice about the ball, cylinder, and cone classes:

- Each class implements the ISolid object. This means that each class will inherit the properties and methods of the ISolid class. In this case, this includes the Volume, SurfaceArea, and Draw procedures.

- Each class that implements the ISolid class does so in its own unique way. This provides us with a means for overloading the Volume and SurfaceArea procedures.

- Each class extends the ISolid object by providing its own unique members. For example, the cylinder object has height and radius properties that are not part of the ISolid class.

We can now write code to program objects of all three types:

```
Private Sub cmdSolids_Click()

 Dim myball As Ball
 Dim ColaCan As Cylinder
 Dim IceCreamCone As Cone

 Set myball = New Ball
 Set ColaCan = New Cylinder
 Set IceCreamCone = New Cone

 myball.Radius = 4.25
 MsgBox "Surface Area of Ball is " & myball.ISolid_SurfaceArea
 MsgBox "Volume of Ball is " & myball.ISolid_Volume

 ColaCan.Radius = 3
 ColaCan.Height = 6
 MsgBox "Volume of Can is " & ColaCan.ISolid_Volume
 MsgBox "Surface Area of Can is " & ColaCan.ISolid_SurfaceArea

 IceCreamCone.Height = 5
 IceCreamCone.Radius = 3
 IceCreamCone.SLength = 5.83
 MsgBox "Volume of Cone is " & IceCreamCone.ISolid_Volume
 MsgBox "Surface Area of Cone is " & IceCreamCone.ISolid_SurfaceArea

End Sub
```

Using Callbacks

In Visual Basic, a *callback* can be used to support *asynchronous* processing. Asynchronous processing allows code to be processed while the user moves on to other tasks instead of waiting for the code to finish executing. A callback works by having Windows call a function periodically. For example, the API has a function called `EnumWindows`. To work with this function, you must provide your own function, which will serve as the callback function. By passing the handle of a parent window, you can use the `EnumWindows` function to locate all of the child windows. Each time it locates a child window, it will call your callback function. The Visual Basic declaration of `EnumWindows` looks like this:

```
Public Declare Function EnumWindows Lib "user32" (ByVal lpEnumFunc As
    Long, ByVal lParam As Long) As Long
```

The first parameter, `lpEnumFunc`, is a pointer to your callback function. `lParam` is a user-defined parameter. Each time `EnumWindows` locates an open window in your system it will make a call to the callback function you have defined. The parameters passed to your callback function are defined by the API function. In the case of `EnumWindows`, the callback function must take three parameters. We could define the function header like this:

```
Public Function GetWindowHandles(lngHandle As Long, lngData As Long,
    lngReturn As Long)
```

We can place code inside this function to respond to the `EnumWindows` function. You could use it to count the number of open windows, for example. When we call the `EnumWindows` function, we must provide the address of the callback function that we will use. This is done with the `AddressOf` operator:

```
lResult = EnumWindows(AddressOf GetWindowHandles, lValue)
```

The `EnumWindows` function now has the address of the callback function that you wrote. This will provide it with the means to call your function every time it encounters a window.

Collections of Objects

Visual Basic permits you to work with collections of objects. You may already be familiar with some of the Visual Basic collections like forms and controls. This idea can be extended to the objects you create as well, providing you with another powerful programming tool. Let's say that we had a class called Student that represents a student for a local high school database. We can define a collection class to hold a list of students:

```
Private Students As New Collection
```

We can use the members of a standard VB collection to manipulate the students. We declare individual students as objects of the Student class type. For example, we can use the Add method of a collection to add a new student to the list:

```
Dim MyStudent As Student
Set MyStudent = New Student
Students.Add MyStudent

Students.Item(Students.Count).Name = "Sandra Smith"
Students.Item(Students.Count).SSN = "999-99-9999"
Students.Item(Students.Count).Class = "Junior"
```

We can display the student collection in a list box by looping through the collection:

```
Dim Person As Student

Set Person = New Student

For Each Person In Students

  lstStudentList.AddItem Person.Name

Next Person
```

The Dependent Class and Dependent Collection Class

We can take this idea a bit further by introducing what is known as a *dependent class* and a *dependent collection class*. The dependent class will function just like every class we've developed so far. The dependent collection class will provide wrapper functions for the normal collection methods, such as Add. In our example, we can declare a local variable to hold the collection:

```
Private mColStudents As Collection
```

In the student class, we can then provide the wrapper functions. For example, we build a wrapper function called `AddStudent`:

```
Public Function AddStudent(Key As String, Name As String, Class As
String) As Student

    Dim objNewStudent As Student
    Set objNewStudent = New Student

    objNewStudent.Key = Key
    objNewStudent.Name = Name
    objNewStudent.Class = Class

    'add the student to the collection
    mColStudents.Add objNewStudent

    'release this object
    Set AddStudent = objNewStudent
    objNewStudent  = Nothing

End Function
```

We can also build wrapper functions for the collection Item, Count, and Remove methods.

Ownership and Lifetime As They Relate to Collections of Objects

Lifetime and scope affect object variables in the same way they affect variables. Public object variables are available to the entire project. Private object variables are only available in the module in which they are declared. You can also declare local objects, which are known only to the procedure in which they have been declared.

Collections of objects present a special case. The collection may have wider scope and lifetime than individual objects that we use to access the members of the collection. In the previous example, we declared a collection variable that had module-wide scope. In the `AddStudent` function we declared a local object variable called `objNewStudent`. This local variable has local scope, and as such it goes out of existence when the function ends. However, the collection lives on, and the student that the `objNewStudent` variable represented *temporarily*, continues to exist as part of the collection. To access it, we would have to declare a new object variable and set a reference to it, by using its key, for example.

EXAMPLE: A BANK SIMULATION PROGRAM

Now let's illustrate how to build an application that uses class modules to build objects. We'll create a simple bank simulation program that will simulate a day at the bank. Customers will come into the bank and make deposits or withdraw cash from their accounts. Our bank is small; it only has one teller.

To run the simulation, we will need to track the following items:

- A list of customers

- A list of bank accounts

- A list of customers who are waiting in line at the bank

- The total cash on hand at the bank

- The time of day

When the simulation starts, the time of day will be set to 9:00 a.m. It will run until 3:00 p.m., at which point the bank will close. Let's think about how we would do this. We can use a Do While loop, which might go something like this:

```
Set Time to 9:00 a.m.
Do While Time < 3:00 p.m.
  Check the customer line
  If there is a customer in line then
    Process that customer
  End if
  Increment the time
Loop
```

This simple loop is pretty much all there is to it. To build the program, we will have to figure out the following items:

- How to represent a customer and account

- How to pass time

- How to decide when a customer comes in or leaves the bank

- How to process a deposit or withdrawal

- How to represent the customer line

Once the program is complete, we could build on it to create a more complicated simulation. For example, we could add more tellers, allow new customers to come in and open accounts, and more.

The user interface for the simulator will be simple. It will display a list of customers in line and a list of accounts and balances at the bank (see Fig. 8-1). The user starts the simulation by clicking the Run button.

Figure 8-1
The Bank Simulator screen.

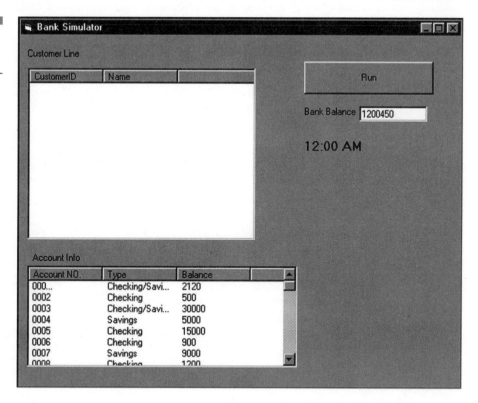

The classes in the simulation program will be pretty simple. The customer class will track the bank account number, customer name, and address of each customer. The code is as follows:

```
Option Explicit
Private mName As String
Private mCustomerID As String * 12
Private mAddress As String
Private mInBank As Boolean

Public Property Get Name() As String
 Name = mName
End Property

Public Property Let Name(ByVal strNewValue As String)
 mName = strNewValue
End Property

Public Property Get InBank() As Boolean
 InBank = mInBank
End Property

Public Property Let InBank(ByVal blnNewValue As Boolean)
```

```
  mInBank = blnNewValue
End Property

Public Property Get Address() As String
  Address = mAddress
End Property

Public Property Let Address(ByVal strNewValue As String)
  mAddress = strNewValue
End Property

Public Property Get CustomerID() As String
  CustomerID = mCustomerID
End Property

Public Property Let CustomerID(ByVal strNewValue As String)

  If Len(strNewValue) <= 12 Then
    mCustomerID = strNewValue
  Else
    MsgBox "Cannot Set Customer ID"
  End If

End Property
```

We will also define an `Account` class to track the setup of the account at the bank:

```
Option Explicit

Private mCustomerID As String * 12
Private mType As String
Private mBalance As Currency

Public Property Get CustomerID() As String
  CustomerID = mCustomerID
End Property

Public Property Let CustomerID(ByVal strNewValue As String)
  mCustomerID = strNewValue
End Property

Public Property Get AccountType() As String
  AccountType = mType
End Property

Public Property Let AccountType(ByVal strNewValue As String)
  mType = strNewValue
End Property

Public Property Get Balance() As Currency
  Balance = mBalance
End Property

Public Property Let Balance(ByVal curNewValue As Currency)
  mBalance = curNewValue
End Property
```

```
Public Function WITHDRAWAL(Amount As Currency) As Boolean

 If Amount < mBalance Then
    mBalance = mBalance - Amount
    WITHDRAWAL = True
 Else
    WITHDRAWAL = False
 End If

End Function
Public Sub Deposit(Amount As Currency)
 mBalance = mBalance + Amount
End Sub
```

The customers and accounts will be maintained in two collections. We will load the collections from a database (see Chapter 11, "Making Databases and Objects Work Together"). For now, we will simply assume that the collections have been loaded with the data. The collection variables are declared in a standard code module:

```
Public colAccounts As New Collection
Public colCustomers As New Collection
```

Each collection can be used to loop through accounts or customers, respectively.

To run the simulation, we have created a Sub procedure called RunSimulation. The routine sets the start time to 9:00 a.m. and uses a Do While loop to run through the day. The loop continues until the time is 3:00 p.m. The code is as follows:

```
Public Sub RunSimulation3()

 frmBank.tmrAddCustomer.Enabled = True

 'set time to 9:00 a.m.
 datTime = TimeSerial(9, 0, 0)

 'update time display for user
 frmBank.lblTime = CStr(datTime)

 'get the current hour
 intHour = Hour(datTime)

 'run the simulation until 3:00 p.m.
 Do While intHour < 15

  'Process the customer line
  Call ProcessCustomer
  'increment the clock and update user display
  datTime = DateAdd("n", 1, datTime)
  intHour = Hour(datTime)
  frmBank.lblTime = CStr(datTime)
  'process events so timer event can fire
  DoEvents
```

```
Loop

    frmBank.tmrAddCustomer.Enabled = False

End Sub
```

Each time through the loop, the Sub procedure ProcessCustomer is called. ProcessCustomer will check to see if a customer is waiting in line and if so will retrieve that customer and take care of his or her transaction. Once the customer is processed, the time is incremented by one minute by calling the DateAdd function. We then update the time displayed to the user in the lblTime label of the program's main form. The last line of the loop calls the Windows function DoEvents so events waiting on the event queue are processed.

We call DoEvents because we are using a Timer control to add customers to the line. The Timer control fires once per second. The code in the tmrAddCustomer Timer event is listed here:

```
Dim dblRandom As Double
 Dim intHour As Integer
 Dim objPerson As New clsCustomer
 Dim blnAddCustomer As Boolean
 Dim temp

 Static MaxCustomers As Integer
 intHour = Hour(datTime)
 dblRandom = Rnd * 100

 blnAddCustomer = False

 If (intHour > 11) And (intHour < 13) Then

    If dblRandom > 50 Then

     blnAddCustomer = True

    End If

 ElseIf dblRandom > 75 Then

   blnAddCustomer = True

 End If

 If blnAddCustomer Then

    Set objPerson = ReturnCustomer
    lstCustomerLine.ListItems.Add
    temp = lstCustomerLine.ListItems.Count
    lstCustomerLine.ListItems.Item(temp).Text = objPerson.CustomerID
    lstCustomerLine.ListItems.Item(temp).SubItems(1) = objPerson.Name
 End If
```

First, we retrieve the current hour. This is because the bank will be busier between the hours of 11:00 a.m. and 1:00 p.m. Next, we obtain a random number. Depending on the value of the random number and the time of day, we will allow a new customer to enter the bank. The first `If` statement tests the time of day to see if we are operating during the peak hours. If so, we check the value of the random number; if it is greater than 50 we will add a customer to the line. We set the Boolean variable `blnAddCustomer` to True if this is the case. The `Else` part of the `If` statement handles nonpeak bank hours. During these hours, the chance of a customer coming in is reduced, so we use a restricted range of the random number to set `blnAddCustomer` to True.

At the bottom of the procedure, if `blnAddCustomer` is True, we call the `ReturnCustomer` function to add a customer to the line. `ReturnCustomer` is a function that has a return type of one of the class modules we created, `clsCustomer`. To set an object variable equal to the return value of a function that has an object data type, we use the `Set` statement:

```
Set objPerson = ReturnCustomer
```

We will maintain the customer line in a List View control. The next line of code adds a new item to the `lstCustomerLine` List View control. A List View control has a `ListItems` collection, which represents the items in the list. Next, we use the Count property of the `ListItems` collection of the List View to obtain the position of the new customer in the line:

```
lstCustomerLine.ListItems.Add
temp = lstCustomerLine.ListItems.Count
```

The next line of code adds the customer ID (the bank account number) and the customer name to the List View control:

```
lstCustomerLine.ListItems.Item(temp).Text = objPerson.CustomerID
lstCustomerLine.ListItems.Item(temp).SubItems(1) = objPerson.Name
```

Let's go back to the `ReturnCustomer` function, which was used to retrieve a customer and add it to the list. The code for this function is as follows:

```
Public Function ReturnCustomer() As clsCustomer

 Dim objPerson As New clsCustomer
 Dim intKey As Integer
```

```
Do
intKey = Int(MAX) * Rnd + 1
Set objPerson = colCustomers.Item(CStr(intKey))
If objPerson.InBank = False Then
  objPerson.InBank = True
  Set ReturnCustomer = objPerson
  Set objPerson = Nothing
  Exit Function
End If

Loop

End Function
```

The function uses a Do loop to find a customer at random. The customers are stored in a collection called colCustomers. All customers have a Boolean property, InBank, that we can test to see if they are already in the bank. The first line uses the random number function to obtain a random number between 1 and *MAX*, where *MAX* is the total number of customers:

```
intKey = Int(MAX) * Rnd + 1
```

Next, we set the objPerson object variable equal to the randomly selected customer:

```
Set objPerson = colCustomers.Item(CStr(intKey))
```

If this customer isn't in the bank, then we put him in the bank and return the customer to the tmrAddCustomer function. Notice that we release the memory allocated for the objPerson object variable by setting it equal to Nothing:

```
If objPerson.InBank = False Then
    objPerson.InBank = True
    Set ReturnCustomer = objPerson
    Set objPerson = Nothing
    Exit Function
    End If
```

If the current customer was already in the bank, we go back to the top of the loop and try again until we find a customer who hasn't been in.

The next routine to look at is ProcessCustomer. This routine is called in the Do loop of the RunSimulation procedure. The code looks like this:

```
Public Sub ProcessCustomer()

 Dim waittime As Single
```

```
Dim settime As Single
Dim strAccountNum As String * 12
Dim intTransactionType As Integer
Dim curAmount As Currency
Dim objAccount As New clsAccount

'get first customer in line
If frmBank.lstCustomerLine.ListItems.Count > 0 Then

    strAccountNum = frmBank.lstCustomerLine.ListItems.Item(1).Text
    frmBank.lstCustomerLine.ListItems.Remove (1)

    'process the transaction
    intTransactionType = 2 * Rnd + 1
    curAmount = Rnd * 100

    If intTransactionType = WITHDRAWAL Then
        curAmount = -1 * curAmount
    End If

    Set objAccount = colAccounts.Item(strAccountNum)
    objAccount.Balance = objAccount.Balance + curAmount
frmBank.lstAccounts.ListItems.Item(CInt(strAccountNum)).SubItems(2)
  = CStr(objAccount.Balance)
  End If

  'insert delay
  waittime = Timer
  settime = waittime + INTERVAL
  Do While waittime < settime
    waittime = Timer
  Loop

End Sub
```

The first line of the procedure is an `If` statement, which checks to see if anyone is in line. You will recall that when a customer gets in line, we place her in the `lstCustomerLine` List View control. We can check to see if anyone is in line by testing the Count property of the `ListItems` collection of the control. If there is a customer in line, we obtain the customer's account number and then remove the first customer from the line:

```
strAccountNum = frmBank.lstCustomerLine.ListItems.Item(1).Text
frmBank.lstCustomerLine.ListItems.Remove (1)
```

Next, we have to pick a transaction and dollar amount. We will only allow two types of transactions, a deposit or a withdrawal. We will again use the random number generator to determine which type of transaction this is and how much cash to use:

```
'process the transaction
intTransactionType = 2 * Rnd + 1
```

```
'get a random currency amount
curAmount = Rnd * 100

'if this is a withdrawal, set cash amount to negative value
If intTransactionType = WITHDRAWAL Then
        curAmount = -1 * curAmount
End If
```

We set the cash amount to a negative value for withdrawals so they can be deducted from the customer's account balance. This is done in the next two lines:

```
Set objAccount = colAccounts.Item(strAccountNum)
objAccount.Balance = objAccount.Balance + curAmount
```

The `colAccounts` variable is a collection. The collection contains the customer accounts, which are represented by the `clsAccounts` class. The `objAccounts` variable is an object variable of type `clsAccount`. We use the Item method of the `colAccounts` collection to get the desired account. This is done by specifying the account number. In the next line, we update the display for the user. The customer accounts are stored in another List View control, which we have named `lstAccounts`:

```
frmBank.lstAccounts.ListItems.Item(CInt(strAccountNum)).SubItems(2)
   = CStr(objAccount.Balance)
```

To mimic a real bank transaction, we will need to pass some time before returning to the `RunSimulation` procedure. The last piece of code inserts a time delay:

```
'insert delay
 waittime = Timer
settime = waittime + INTERVAL

Do While waittime < settime
  waittime = Timer
Loop
```

The `Timer` function returns the number of seconds since midnight. We use the `settime` variable to set the length of the delay. `INTERVAL` is a constant that can be modified to make the simulation run at different speeds.

This simulation illustrates how we can break the application up into three tiers. The data for the program will be loaded from a database. After we cover database processing in Chapter 10, we will return to this program in Chapter 11 to see how we can put the objects defined here together with our classes through a database. The user interface represents one tier, while the database represents the tier on the database server. We can place the class definitions and any interaction with the database in the middle tier. In Chapter 12, we will learn how to create an in-process ActiveX control, or DLL. What we would do is place the class definitions in the DLL along with the routines needed to interact with the database. The DLL could then be placed on an intermediate server. The program we have here really wouldn't change much, except that we would have to set a reference to the DLL before declaring the class variables. We can use this type of structure to hide the data processing from the user interface tier of the code.

Implementation

CHAPTER 9

Database
Design for
Visual Basic

Visual Basic is well suited for building database front ends and, in particular, front ends for Microsoft Access databases. As a result, a large percentage of Visual Basic development in the real world is geared toward developing database applications. When building a database application, you should put as much care into designing the database as you would in designing the software itself. When designing your tables, records, and queries, you are still working with objects, and the way these objects are designed will have as great an impact on your application as would any class or control.

Great care needs to be used when building the database to ensure that it has a solid structure and good relationships between the tables. Designing a database in this way will involve the process of *normalization*, which will help keep the data organized in an efficient manner. It will also involve the construction of indexes and queries, which will aid users when they sort and retrieve data or work with subsets of the data. Once the database design is completed, you can start thinking about the software, that is, using Visual Basic to build the front end. The front end will be the forms and code that will be used to manipulate the database.

In this chapter, we'll focus on what elements a Microsoft Access database will have, and investigate some good design principles that should be followed when structuring the data. This is by no means a complete examination of Microsoft Access; we will be focusing on the elements that will be used in Visual Basic coding. As such, we will not cover Access forms, reports, and modules. We'll conclude the chapter by seeing how the Visual Data Manager can be used to build a database. In the next chapter, we'll discuss how to write Visual Basic code to manipulate the database.

Overview of Database Design

A database is a place to store data. When working with Microsoft Access, a database is just a single file with an .mdb extension. Inside that file you'll find all the objects needed to store and manipulate information. This will include tables, queries, forms, and reports. If the user has Microsoft Access or a run-time version of Access installed, the database can include everything the user needs, including forms and the code behind them.

At this point, you might be asking yourself, "If an Access database has everything in it, why do I need to use Visual Basic?" The answer depends on the situation, and as a developer you'll have to use your judgment in deciding which tool to use. Typically, Visual Basic is good to use if you want to have a self-contained application, where the user is not required to have any preexisting tools like Access. In this case, as far as the user is concerned the Access database is just a file that comes with your app. Another consideration is performance. Since Visual Basic can be native code compiled, a Visual Basic program will typically perform very well, usually better than an Access application. In the end, the choice may simply come down to preference; many programmers would rather write VB apps than use Access. No matter what language you choose to develop in, the first step is to determine what data needs to be stored and how to organize it.

Determining the End User's Needs

The first step in designing a database is to meet with the customer and discuss what his needs are. Some items to keep in mind during the initial planning stage are as follows:

- What specific data elements need to be stored? This will include items such as name, address, or monthly salary.

- What possible ranges will the data elements take? As you should do when declaring variables in code, when designing the database you'll need to make sure that it can hold the largest possible value (which is still valid) that the user might enter. You'll also need to keep efficiency in mind; variables with larger ranges take more storage space.

- How can each data element in the database be uniquely identified?

- How can the data be organized so as to break it down into different tables?

- How will the different categories of data interact? In other words, how do the individual tables relate to one another?

- In what ways will the user want to sort the data?

- What types of queries will the user want to "ask" the database?

- What types of reports will need to be generated?

- Does the user have MS Access or some other database on her system?

- Will the user need to transfer data between different storage formats, that is, between different types of databases?

- Will the application be a local app or client/server?

The design of the database needs to be taken just as seriously as any step in the software development cycle. Also, you should have the design of the database completed before you move on to building the application in Visual Basic. This will help ensure that the software development cycle moves as smoothly as possible. If there are problems in the database, redesigning the data means redesigning your software as well, which can turn into a real headache.

Organizing the Data

Once you've determined what data needs to be stored, the next step is to organize that data into distinct but related categories that can be turned into tables (see the next section). The user might already have some idea of how he wants this done, but chances are you will have to make sure the data is arranged in such a way as to maintain efficiency and develop good relationships between each category. Consider a database for a local high school that will track students, the classes offered, and the classes each student is taking. Let's say the school administrator wanted to track the following information:

- Social security number
- Name, address, home phone, and the parents' work phone for each student
- The grade level, date of enrollment, and expected date of graduation for each student
- A list of classes offered by the school, with class name and scheduled time
- The classes each student is taking

  Looking at this data, we can divide it into three distinct categories:

- *Students*: This table will maintain the list of students and store the social security number, name, address, phone number, grade level, date of enrollment, and expected date of graduation for each student.
- *Classes*: This table will maintain the list of classes offered by the school.
- *Schedules*: This table will track which classes each student is enrolled in.

When we actually build the database, each of these categories would become a table in the database. The tables will be related through indexing.

The Elements of a Database

As I said earlier, an Access database file can contain just about everything the user needs to store, view, and manipulate data. If you open an MDB file with Access, you'll find that it contains the following elements:

- *Tables*: This is where the data is actually stored. A table is a collection of information relating to a specific category. Tables are arranged in a row-column format, with each row representing a *record* and each column representing a *field*. A record is a single entity of related data. For example, in a list of students a particular student record will contain all of the information for one particular student. Each piece of information is a field, such as *Name*, *Address*, or *Phone Number*. Typically, a table will be indexed, which will allow the database to uniquely identify each record and sort the data.

- *Queries*: A query is basically a question you can ask about a database. For example, you might ask, "How many students are in the sophomore class?" Queries usually return a subset of the data in a table, or they can combine the data from several different tables. Queries can be built in Microsoft Access or in code using a special language called structured query language (SQL). We'll be discussing SQL in the next chapter.

- *Forms*: Access allows you to build forms to provide a user interface as part of the database. Since we'll be building our forms with Visual Basic, we will ignore forms in Access.

- *Reports*: Access reports provide a format for viewing and printing data. You can use the Data Report object in VB to build reports, so we won't be talking about Access reports.

- *Macros*: A macro is a single command that allows you to perform several tasks in Access at once.

- *Modules*: An Access module is a code module, just like in Visual Basic.

Let's start by looking at tables.

Organizing Data into Tables

An Access database is a single-disk file, and the database file contains data stored in one or more tables. Each table represents a collection of related data, such as an employee list, a list of office locations, or a list of job positions. Data in tables is organized in a row and column format, much like an Excel spreadsheet. As mentioned, each row in the table is called a record. A record is a collection of data that belongs to a single object in the table. Each column in the table represents a field, which is an individual piece of data, such as somebody's phone number. A record could represent an employee, a customer order, an item in inventory, or any other object. The individual characteristics of the object are the fields. Let's consider a simple example. A table that tracked product inventory for an office supply store might contain the following fields:

- Product ID
- Product name
- Description
- Quantity

The table will then contain one column for each of these fields. The products that the user enters into the database will be the rows or records in the table, and each record will have a value specified for each of these fields. When data has been entered in the table, it might look something like this:

Product ID	Product Name	Description	Quantity
1001	Computer disks	3.5-inch "floppy" diskettes, IBM formatted	2,000
1002	Pencils	No. 2 pencils	300
1003	College-ruled notebook	100-page college-ruled notebook	50
1004	Office desk	ABC company office desk	5

The row identified by *ProductID 1002* represents an individual record in this table, while each column, for example, *Product Name*, is a field in the table.

In summary, there are two things to remember about tables:

- Each row or record is an individual object stored in the table, such as an employee.

- Each column or field represents one aspect of a record, such as name or phone number.

Data Types in an Access Database

Each field in a table will have a data type, just like a variable in Visual Basic. In fact, generally, the data types used in Access correspond pretty well to the data types used in Visual Basic. This means that you will think about the same kinds of issues that you would when choosing Visual Basic variables. That means giving a field a meaningful name and weighing efficiency issues. Some good ideas to keep in mind:

- *Use good judgment when selecting a field size.* There are two considerations here, and you've faced this before when choosing data types for a VB program. First, you want to make sure that you allocate enough space for the range of values the data might take. For example, when storing the population of a city, an integer will not be large enough, so a long integer would be a better choice. Another consideration, however, is that we don't want to waste disk space when we can avoid it. When saving test scores with a range of 0 to 100, it is more efficient to store this as type `Byte` rather than using an integer, which takes two bytes of storage. On today's computers, where hard disk space is cheap, this isn't as much of a concern as it was in the past.

- *For numbers that don't require calculations, use text fields.* Examples of when using text fields is a good idea include social security numbers, part serial numbers, and phone numbers.

- *Think about sort order.* If this is a field that will be used in an index, think about how a particular data type will sort. For example, a text string will sort differently than a number.

- *Give meaningful, descriptive names to each field.* An Access field name can be up to 64 characters in length. You should give field names a reasonably sized but descriptive name. Don't use Hungarian notation when naming fields; just give a straightforward name that you would use in everyday language. Don't forget, the user will see the field names when working with the database. This means you should avoid using cryptic field names.

There are ten types of fields that you can use in Access:

- *Text*: Use for strings or numbers that don't require calculations. A Text field can be up to 255 characters in size. The default size is 50 characters.

- *Memo*: A Memo field is used to hold large chunks of text data when you think the field will require more than 255 characters. A Memo field can hold up to 64,000 characters.

- *Number*: Number fields hold numeric data. The field size for a Number field corresponds to the Visual Basic data types. In other words, you can have an Integer, Long Integer, Byte, Single, or Double. See Chapter 5 for a summary on the range of the VB numeric data types.

- *Date / Time*: A Date/Time field can store dates in the range of January 1,100, to December 31, 9999.

- *Currency*: The Currency field is the same as the Visual Basic currency type. It stores numeric data with four decimal places.

- *AutoNumber*: An AutoNumber field is used by Access to automatically provide a number to identify each record. Each time you add a record to the database, Access increments the value it will place in the AutoNumber field.

- *Yes / No*: The Yes/No field corresponds to the VB Boolean data type. Yes/No fields display in Access with a check box, with checked meaning *Yes* and unchecked meaning *No*.

- *OLE Object*: An OLE Object field is a large binary field that can store data such as pictures or sound files.

- *Hyperlink*: This type of field can store a web link.

- *Lookup wizard*: This lets you create a field that can be used to select a value from a list of choices in another table. For example, you could have a table that stored the state abbreviations for the 50 U.S. states. In another table, say a list of customers, when entering the address of each customer the State field could be a lookup field that retrieves the values from the *U.S. States* table.

Fields

Each field in the table will have the following properties:

- Name
- Type
- Size

- Ordinal position
- Validation text
- Validation rule
- Default value

We discussed the name, type, and size properties of a field in the section "Organizing Data into Tables" earlier in this chapter. Let's explore some of the other attributes that a field can have, focusing on items that will concern you in Visual Basic.

OrdinalPosition   The ordinal position property will determine where a field will appear when you load the table in a data grid. This is done in a left-to-right order. While you can arrange the order of fields in your grid during design or run time, things will be easier if you think about the order that you want the data to appear on screen when you are designing the table.

Validation Rule   The validation rule determines what type of data will be accepted in the database. For example, if we had a field to track the hourly wage of an employee, we could define a validation rule that made sure that the pay rate was at least the minimum wage. We could use the following validation rule:

```
>= 5.25
```

This would ensure that the wage had to be at least $5.25 per hour. When tracking a Text field, we can provide a list of valid choices. For example, if we were maintaining a list of college students we could use the following validation rule for `Class`:

```
IN(FR,SO,JR,SR)
```

This way, the user will only be able to enter one of the choices from this list. You can also use the `Like` keyword to test for similar text strings or to validate date ranges.

ValidationText   If the validation rule is violated, we can specify a message to display to the user by setting the ValidationText property. If the user did not enter one of the class abbreviations that we specified in our list, we could display the error message:

```
Class Must Be One of FR,SO,JR, or SR.
```

AllowZeroLength　If you want to allow the user to enter a null value for a field, select the *AllowZeroLength* check box.

Indexes

A table will have one or more indexes. The primary key is used to determine the default sorting order of the table and to uniquely identify each record. Indexes can also be used for speedier access to a record. This is just like using a Rolodex to store your phone numbers or, you guessed it, looking up a subject in the index of a book. By categorizing and ordering the names in your phone number list, you can locate them much more quickly and easily. An index in the table works much the same way.

Each index is made up of one or more fields in a table. For example, if we had a list of students we could use the social security number of each student as the primary key. This is because each student has a unique social security number. Indexes can also consist of more than one field. Indexes can also be used to relate two different tables, to achieve a different sorting order, or to speed searching on frequently used fields. Keep in mind that a large number of indexes can add a lot of overhead to a database, so they should be used judiciously.

The Primary Key　Each table must have a way to uniquely identify the data it contains. This is done by specifying a primary key. Just like any other index, a primary key can be made up of just a single field or it can contain multiple fields. Use a single field if a table contains one field that can uniquely identify each record.

Sometimes more than one field will be required to uniquely identify a record. Earlier, we considered a class schedule at a local high school. A table that tracked the classes each student was taking might contain the following fields:

- Social security number
- Class ID
- Class name
- Homework grade
- Test grade

Obviously, the social security number field cannot be used because a student will likely enroll for more than one class. Class ID can't be used because several students will sign up for the same class, say, "History." In this case, to uniquely identify a record we need to consider two fields, social security number and class ID. This will ensure that every record in the table is unique, that each student only signs up for a class once, and that every student can sign up for multiple classes.

In summary, each record in the table will have its own unique value for the primary key. If possible, use a single field to define the primary key. If a record can't be uniquely identified with a single field, however, multiple-field primary keys can be used.

Foreign Keys and Relating Tables   If a field is used as the primary key of one table and it is included as a field in a second table, that field is known *in the second table* as a *foreign key*. The power of a database is the ability to relate the data in one or more tables, and it is the foreign key that helps us do this. For example, consider a vendors table and a related table of products that the vendors supply. Let's say the vendors table had the following fields:

Vendors

Vendor ID

Name

Address

Phone number

Contact person

Terms

Now let's consider the products table. The products table has its own primary key, Product ID, but is related to the vendors table by the Vendor ID field. Vendor ID is the primary key of the vendors table, so it is a foreign key in the products table. The products table might look like the following:

Products

Product ID

Description

Vendor ID

Quantity

Storage location

In summary, foreign keys are used to define relationships between common fields of data in two or more different tables.

One-to-Many Relationships   The type of arrangement we described in the previous section is known as a *one-to-many* relationship. One record in the vendors table, which can be thought of as the master table, relates to multiple records in the products table, which can be thought of as a lookup table.

Queries

A query is a question that the user can ask about the data. A query can be used to sort the data in a particular way or to retrieve a subset of the data. Queries are where the power of a relational database really becomes apparent. The most common query is called a Select query. A Select query can be used to retrieve a subset of the data in a table and to join data from multiple tables together. Some sample queries could include the following: How many customers are from California? How many cars in the inventory are blue? Who are the students in the junior class?

Queries can be built in Access with the query wizard, manually, or through code. We will be concerned with building queries in Visual Basic code. This is done by using a special language called structured query language, or SQL. In the next chapter we'll see how to use SQL in a VB program.

Views

When working inside Access, there are different ways to look at the structure of the database, that is, there are different views. This includes design view, which enables you to build the structure of a table or query. Datasheet view displays the data in a table or query in a spreadsheet, that is, in row-column format.

Stored Procedures

Stored procedures provide you with a way to perform various functions on a database. Basically, a stored procedure is an SQL query that is stored as a part of the database rather than including it in code. A stored procedure fits in with the idea of object-oriented design and encapsulation by hiding what's going on in the database from the rest of the application. This provides a data layer that is separate from the Visual Basic code. This means that we can change the implementation of the data processing without having to change the VB code. This compliments nicely the idea of object-oriented design. Remember that we want to relate between objects only though an interface while not worrying about how each object is actually implemented. The specifics of stored procedures will depend on the database management system (DBMS) that you are using.

Normalization

In the previous sections we saw how to organize data into tables and how those tables are related through indexing. This type of arrangement is what makes relational databases so powerful, and understanding how to organize your data in this way is central to maintaining the integrity of your database. Splitting your data into different tables is known as normalization.

The central goal in normalization is to avoid placing data in a table that should be placed in a table of its own or that should be calculated at run time or when generating reports. For example, in a database that tracked customer orders, it would not be advisable to place the products ordered by the customer in the same table that maintains the list of customers. Every time a customer placed a new order the customer's phone number and address would be added again for each product, making the database bloated and inefficient. It would make more sense to place this data in its own table, say, OrderDetails, and relate the two tables through indexing.

There are three types of normalization used by most programmers. We'll explore each of these by considering the following simple example. Let's say that we needed to design a database to track the club membership of the students at a local high school. We might track the following information:

- Student ID number
- Last name
- First name
- Phone number
- The clubs each student belongs to
- Membership dues, monthly and annually

First Normal Form

The most fundamental type of normalization is known as *first normal form*. The central idea behind first normal form is making the fields in a table *atomic*. Generally, for a field to be atomic it must meet two conditions. First, it cannot store a listing of values in a single column or field. Second, the table must not have repeating fields of data, such as Order1, Order2, and Order3.

In our example, let's say we started our design by building a students table that looked like this:

Student ID	Last Name	First Name	Phone	Clubs	Monthly Dues	Dues/ YR
0001	Jones	Sandra	555-5555	Chess, Drama, Debate	$25	$300
0002	Smith	Frank	555-9010	Tennis, Chess	$15	$180
0003	Garcia	Stephanie	555-7363	Tennis, Ski Club	$10	$120
0004	Newman	Chris	555-4990	Debate	$5	$60

The data in the Clubs field violates first normal form because we have a list of values for almost every student. This is not desirable because it places limits on what we can do with the data. For example, we might want to view students who belong only to the chess club and to do so would require parsing the Clubs field for each student.

We could organize the data by placing, say, three Club fields in the table:

Student ID	Last Name	First Name	Phone	Club1	Club2	Club3	Monthly Dues	Annual Dues
0001	Jones	Sandra	555-5555	Chess	Drama	Debate	$25	$300
0002	Smith	Frank	555-9010	Tennis	Chess		$15	$180
0003	Garcia	Stephanie	555-7363	Tennis	Ski Club		$10	$120
0004	Newman	Chris	555-4990	Debate			$5	$60

However, as you can see, this arrangement could cause lots of problems. Many students might belong to more than three clubs, and this database can't handle that situation without the programmer going in and adding a new field. Also notice that many students don't belong to the maximum number of clubs so the database is wasting a great deal of space. This really wouldn't help our searching criteria either; we would have to check all three club fields to extract the members of the chess club. By using only one Club's field with a single value for each record, we can place the database in first normal form:

Student ID	Last Name	First Name	Phone	Club	Monthly Dues	Annual Dues
0001	Jones	Sandra	555-5555	Chess	$10	$120
0001	Jones	Sandra	555-5555	Drama	$10	$120
0001	Jones	Sandra	555-5555	Debate	$5	$60
0002	Smith	Frank	555-9010	Tennis	$5	$60
0002	Smith	Frank	555-9010	Chess	$10	$120
0003	Garcia	Stephanie	555-7363	Tennis	$5	$60
0003	Garcia	Stephanie	555-7363	Ski Club	$5	$60
0004	Newman	Chris	555-4990	Debate	$5	$60

In summary then, for a database to be in first normal form it must meet these conditions:

- All fields must be atomic.
- Columns should not be repeated in a table.

Second Normal Form

While we have improved the situation, our sample table design is far from optimal. You might notice, for example, that we are wasting a lot of space with repeated data. The last name, first name, and phone number fields are entered for every record, which is not necessary or efficient. It would make more sense to split the database into two tables, one that contained student information and another that contained the clubs each student belonged to. The two tables could then be related by the student ID field.

This brings us to the concept of *second normal form*. In second normal form, all nonprimary key fields in each table are directly dependent on the primary key. Data that is not directly dependent on the primary key should be moved to a separate table.

In our example, the most sensible arrangement would be to first create a students table that tracked student ID, last and first name, and phone number. The table would look like this:

StudentID	Last Name	First Name	Phone
0001	Jones	Sandra	555-5555
0002	Smith	Frank	555-9010
0003	Garcia	Stephanie	555-7363
0004	Newman	Chris	555-4990

The primary key in this table is *StudentID*. Each field that we have put in the table, Last Name, First Name, and Phone number, is completely dependent on the primary key—which specifies who the student is. Another way to look at this is that for each student ID there is one and only one last name, first name, and phone number.

The clubs table will contain all the clubs each student belongs to. To relate the two tables, we'll use the primary key from the students table, StudentID, which will be the foreign key for the clubs table. The primary key for this table would be the StudentID + Club fields. The clubs table would look like this:

StudentID	Club	Monthly Dues	Annual Dues
0001	Chess	$10	$120
0001	Debate	$10	$120
0001	Drama	$5	$60
0002	Chess	$5	$60
0002	Tennis	$10	$120
0003	Ski Club	$5	$60
0003	Tennis	$5	$60
0004	Debate	$5	$60

The database is now in second normal form. To summarize, for a database to be in Second Normal Form the following must be true:

■ Each table should only contain data that is directly related to the primary key. Fields that are only indirectly related should be placed in a separate table.

Third Normal Form

You'll notice that the clubs table contains the monthly and annual dues required for each club. Storing the data in this manner is a waste of space because we can derive the annual dues from the monthly dues with a simple calculation. Also, whenever the monthly dues change we would have to go into the annual dues field and update the value in the table.

This brings us to the concept of *third normal form*. In third normal form, all nonkey fields must be independent of one another. This means that a field that contains data derived or calculated from other nonkey fields in the table is kept out of the table. Instead, the calculation is done at run time. The calculated data can be displayed on forms or reports as necessary without wasting space in the table and having to go in and write to the database every time the calculation changes.

It makes more sense to calculate the annual dues at run time or when displaying a report. The annual dues field should be removed from the clubs table, so the clubs table would then look like this:

Student ID	Club	Monthly Dues
0001	Chess	$10
0001	Debate	$10
0001	Drama	$5
0002	Chess	$5
0002	Tennis	$10
0003	Ski Club	$5
0003	Tennis	$5
0004	Debate	$5

Third normal form is the easiest type of normalization to implement. Just remember one simple fact—if a field is derived from data in another field leave it out of the database. Calculate the value at run time for display on a form or generate the value in a report.

Here is a summary of normalization:

- *First normal form*: Never allow a single field to contain a listing of values, and never create repeating fields.
- *Second normal form*: Every nonkey field depends on the primary key, and the database is in first normal form.
- *Third normal form*: Third normal form requires that each nonkey field in the table be independent of the other nonkey fields. Never create a field whose value can be calculated from the values stored in the other fields. A table must be in second normal form before it can be in third normal form.

There are higher levels of normalization; however, third normal form is adequate for most database designs.

Denormalizing a Database

While you should use the first three forms of normalization when designing most databases, there are occasions when normalization is not the best design approach. Let's return to our example of the students and clubs table. To locate the clubs for a particular student, we have to look up the student record and then retrieve the clubs for that student from the clubs table. If our data set is particularly large, this may end up being a slow process. On an inadequate computer system the drag of such a search operation may outweigh the benefits achieved by normalization. In this case, it might be easier to simply use first normal form, where all the records are centrally located in one table.

Another situation where normalization may not be the best approach involves the use of calculated fields. There could be a situation where you will need to design a report that can't be built in such a way as to perform the calculations you need when the report is generated. In this case, it would be easier to store the calculations in a table and simply have the report read those values. There also could be a situation in which the calculations slow down the report so much that it's more user friendly to place the calculations in the database. Once this is done, the report will load much faster.

As a final example, consider the requirement of first normal form that we avoid repeating fields. If the number of repeating fields is always constant, it may make more sense to keep the repeating fields in the table rather than splitting them off to another table or creating multiple records. For example, if we tracked multiple phone numbers for a client it makes more sense to have three phone number fields, Phone1, Phone2, and Phone 3, rather than splitting the phone numbers off into a separate table.

In any case, the decision to denormalize a database should not be taken lightly. If you decide to denormalize a database, keep the following in mind:

■ You should have a strongly compelling reason to do so. Generally, normalization will increase the efficiency of a database.

■ The reason for denormalizing should be carefully documented. This will prevent a new programmer from coming along and normalizing the database, which will probably be his first impulse.

Using the Visual Data Manager

One way to create a database is to use the *Visual Data Manager*, which is available as an add-in from Visual Basic (see Fig. 9-1). The advantage

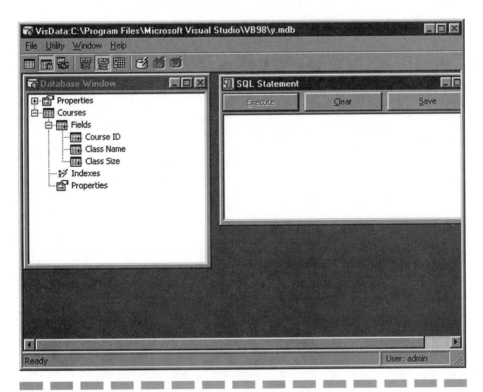

Figure 9-1 The Visual Data Manager.

of using the Visual Data Manager is that you don't need to have MS Access installed in order to create an Access database. The first step is to create the database file, which is done by executing the following steps:

- Select *New* from the File pull-down menu.
- Specify the type of database you want to create. We will select Microsoft Access Version 7.0 MDB.
- Type in the name you want to give the file, and click the *OK* button.

When the database is created, you'll see the database window open on the screen with one object, labeled *Properties*. You can click open the *Properties* icon to view and edit certain properties of the database.

Adding a Table

To add a new table to the database:

- Select the *Properties* icon in the database window.
- Right-click and select *New Table*.

The Table Structure window will then appear on your screen (see Fig. 9-2).

Adding Fields to the Table

Now we can add fields to the table. To add a field, follow these steps:

- Click the *Add Field* button. A new dialog will open (see Fig. 9-3).
- Specify the field name, which can be up to 64 characters in length.
- Specify the data type for the field. This will be one of the Access data types that we discussed in earlier.
- Specify field size, if appropriate.
- If you will allow zero length or null data for this field, click the *AllowZeroLength* box.
- If this field will be required, click the *Required* box.
- Specify the OrdinalPosition if desired. If you don't, Access will assign OrdinalPosition based on the order in which the fields are added to the database.
- Specify the ValidationRule and ValidationText for this field.
- Enter a default value (DefaultValue).
- Click the *OK* button.

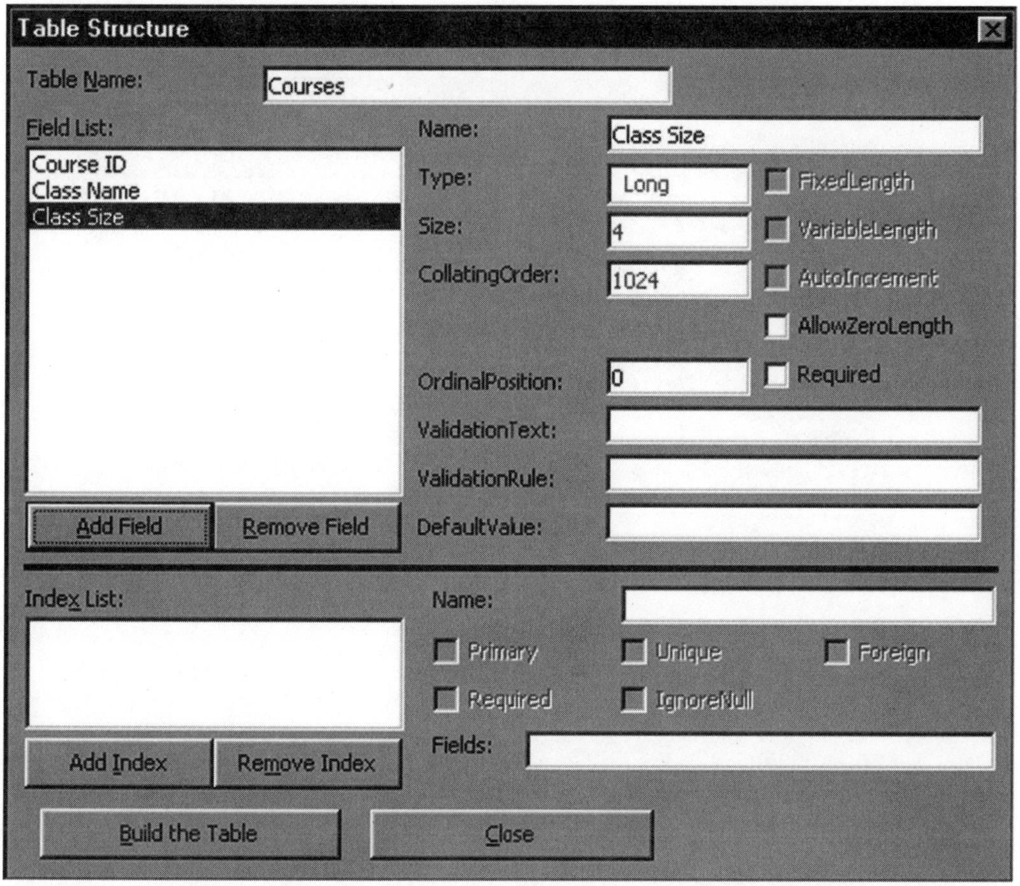

Figure 9-2 Building a table.

Once the fields have been added to the table, you can define one or more indexes for the table. This is done by clicking the *Add Index* button. The `Add Index to...` dialog will open, as shown in Fig. 9-4. You can specify if the index is a primary index, if the index will require unique values, or if it will allow null values. Select the fields you want to include in the index from the Available Fields list. You must also specify a name for the index.

Repeat each of these steps as necessary to create your tables and fields. The Visual Data Manager also provides facilities for building and saving SQL statements and viewing and editing the data in your tables. We will be doing these tasks with Visual Basic.

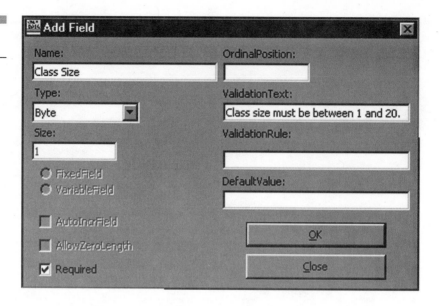

CHAPTER 10

Data Access

Most applications that are of any practical use must offer the ability to save and retrieve disk files. One reason for Visual Basic's popularity is the ease with which it handles files of all types, be they text files, binary files, or Access databases. With Visual Basic, there are two general categories of files that we will be working with. The first type we are concerned with are nondatabase or flat files. In this chapter we'll first tackle sequential files, which are just plain text files. We'll use Visual Basic's new file system objects to open, manipulate, and save these types of files. Next we take a look at random access files, which are files that contain records of data of identical length. Then we'll consider binary files, which are accessed byte by byte.

In the second part of this chapter we will take a look at using Visual Basic to manage relational databases. We'll start by using the data control to connect to and manipulate databases. Next, we'll investigate working with databases in code, including making comparisons of the different technologies, such as OLE DB and ADO, and then review SQL. Finally, we'll tackle some multiuser considerations.

Flat Files

Visual Basic allows the programmer to work with *flat files*, which are simply nondatabase-type files. A flat file is "flat" because it has no relationships within the file or with other files in the way that a relational database like Microsoft Access does. A flat file can be just about anything, from a simple text file to an image. Visual Basic allows you to work with three basic types of flat files:

- Sequential files
- Random access files
- Binary files

In the following sections we'll see how to open, manipulate, and save these types of files.

Sequential Files

A sequential file is a plain-text file. To work with sequential files, Visual Basic provides a set of objects known as *file system objects*. These objects will allow you to perform manipulations of text files, such as writing a line of text or making a copy of the file.

Setting a Reference to the File System Objects To use the file system objects in a project, you must first set a reference. Open the References dialog from the Project menu and select *Microsoft Scripting Runtime*. There are three file system objects we will use to work with sequential files:

- FileSystemObject
- File
- TextStream

The FileSystemObject The FileSystemObject can be used to perform what I would describe as bookkeeping operations on files. For example, a FileSystemObject can be used to create a file, delete a file, copy a file, or create a new folder. When working with sequential files, we'll typically use the FileSystemObject to create and open files. The following table describes some useful properties and methods of the FileSystemObject.

Property/Method	Description
CopyFile	Makes a copy of a file.
CopyFolder	Makes a copy of a folder.
CreateFolder	Creates a new folder.
CreateTextFile	Creates a new text file.
DeleteFile	Deletes a specified file.
DeleteFolder	Deletes a specified folder.
FileExists	Returns True if a specified file exists.
GetAbsoluteFileName	Returns the complete path, file name, and extension of a file.
GetBaseName	Returns file name without path and extension.
GetFile	Returns a pointer to a file.
GetFileName	Returns the file name and extension without path.
MoveFile	Moves a file to a new folder or drive.
OpenTextFile	Opens a file that can be used to read and write text strings.

The FileObject The next object we will use to work with sequential files is called the FileObject. A FileObject can be used to point to a particular file by calling the GetFile method of a FileSystemObject. Once this is done, the FileObject can be used to retrieve important information about a file, such as the file attributes or the date the file was created. When working with sequential files, a FileObject can be used to open the file as a TextStream, which is then used to read and write to the file. Some properties and methods of the FileObject are listed in the following table.

Property/Method	Description
Attributes	Returns the attributes of a specified file, as integer. Return values include Normal(0), ReadOnly(1), Hidden(2), System(4), Directory(16), or Archive(32).
Copy	Makes a copy of the file.
DateCreated	Returns the date the file was created.
Delete	Deletes the file that the File object currently points to.
Move	Moves the file to a new folder or drive.
OpenAsTextStream	Opens a file and returns as TextStream for reading and/or writing.
Path	Returns the complete directory path, file name, and file extension.
ShortName	Returns the file name and extension without the directory path.
Size	Returns the length in bytes of the file as type Long.
Type	Returns the file type as string, for example, "Text Document".

The TextStream Object The TextStream object can be used to read and write character strings to a text file. Some useful properties and methods of the TextStream object are listed in the following table:

Property/Method	Description
AtEndOfLine	Flags True if the end of line is reached.
AtEndOfStream	Flags True if the end of TextStream has been reached (i.e., end of file).
Close	Method that closes the file.
Column	Returns the current position of the TextStream cursor as the column number of the current line.

Property	Description
Line	Returns the current line number of the TextStream, as type `Long`.
Read	Reads characters from a TextStream. Specify the number of characters to read as a `Long`.
ReadAll	Reads the complete file into a string.
ReadLine	Reads a single line of text.
Skip	Skips a number of characters, pass as type `Long`.
SkipLine	Skips over a single line of text in the file.
Write	Writes a text string to the file.
WriteBlankLines	Writes a number of blank lines into a file.
WriteLine	Writes a line of text into the file. Differs from Write because it will write an end-of-line character after the end of the string.

Creating a Simple Form to Manipulate Sequential Files Let's see how to put these file system objects together into a functional application that can read and write sequential files. This is a bare-bones application, but by examining the code here you'll know just about all you need to use Visual Basic to work with sequential files. The code is placed in a single form.

The declarations section of the form has the variables that we will need to open and manipulate the sequential file. Recall that we need three objects to work with sequential files: a FileSystemObject, a FileObject, and a TextStream Object. The following code shows the declarations of these variables:

```
Option Explicit

Private strFileName As String
Private fsoFile As New FileSystemObject
Private MyFile As File
Private MyTextStream As TextStream
```

Since a FileSystemObject is a Visual Basic object, we must use the New keyword when declaring a variable of this type. This will dynamically allocate the memory for this object.

Opening a Sequential File To open a sequential file using the file system objects, we need to go through the following steps:

■ If this is a new file, we need to create it with the FileSystemObject.

- Next, we need to return a reference to the file with the GetFile method of the FileSystemObject.
- Finally, we can open the file as a TextStream.

We will use the Open File command button to open the file, and we'll give the user the opportunity to create new files by typing in a nonexistent file name. The code behind the Open File command button looks like this:

```
Private Sub cmdOpenFile_Click()
On Error Resume Next
 CommonDialog1.ShowOpen
 strFileName = CommonDialog1.FileName
 If (Trim(strFileName) = "") Then Exit Sub      'if user clicks cancel,
    file name is blank string
 If (fsoFile.FileExists(strFileName) = False) Then
     'file not there, ask the user if he wants to create it
     Dim resp As Integer
     resp = MsgBox("File Does Not Exist. Create?", vbYesNo)
     If resp = vbYes Then
        'create the file
        Call fsoFile.CreateTextFile(strFileName)
     Else
        Exit Sub
     End If
 End If

 'get a reference to the file
 Set MyFile = fsoFile.GetFile(strFileName)

 'test to make sure file is not too big
 If MyFile.Size > 32768 Then
  MsgBox "Error : File is too large to open. Max file size is 64k."
  Exit Sub
 End If

 Set MyTextStream = MyFile.OpenAsTextStream(ForReading)
 'read it in
 Text1.Text = MyTextStream.ReadAll
 MyTextStream.Close

 txtFileName.Text = strFileName
 txtLastModified = MyFile.DateLastModified
 txtSize = MyFile.Size
 txtFileType = MyFile.Type

End Sub
```

I've used a common dialog control to provide the user with standard Windows file open/save dialogs. In the first two lines of this procedure, I use the common dialog to allow the user to specify which file she wants to open. Then I check to see if the value returned by the FileName property of the common dialog is a blank string. If it is, that means the user selected the *Cancel* button, so I exit the routine without doing anything.

If the user has specified a file name, we then use the FileExists method of the FileSystemObject to test if the file is one that already exists or if the user typed in the name of a nonexistent file:

```
If (fsoFile.FileExists(strFileName) = False) Then
    'file not there, ask the user if she wants to create it
```

If the file does not exist, and the user has indicated that she wants to create a new file, we can use the CreateTextFile method of the FileSystemObject to create the file. The code looks like this:

```
Call fsoFile.CreateTextFile(strFileName)
```

CreateTextFile takes three parameters:

- `FileName As String`
- `Overwrite As Boolean`. This is an optional parameter. If you leave this parameter blank, it takes the default value of True.
- `Unicode As Boolean`. This is also an optional parameter, with a default value of False. Accepting the default value of False will create a file using the ANSI standard character set that uses one byte per character file. Setting this value to True creates a two-byte-per-character Unicode file.

Once we've either established that the file exists or created a new file, the next step is to get a reference to the file. This is done by using the GetFile method of the FileSystemObject to return a file:

```
Set MyFile = fsoFile.GetFile(strFileName)
```

GetFile takes a single parameter, `FilePath As string`, and returns a file.

Before opening the file, recall that a multiline text box can only hold 32 KB worth of text. We can use the Size property of the file object to check the size of the file and restrict ourselves to opening files of the correct size:

```
'test to make sure file is not too big
 If MyFile.Size > 65536 Then
  MsgBox "Error : File is too large to open. Max file size is 64k."
  Exit Sub
End If
```

Now we're ready to open the file. This is done by using the OpenAsTextStream method of the `File` variable.

```
Set MyTextStream = MyFile.OpenAsTextStream(ForReading)
```

OpenAsTextStream has the return type of TextStream and takes the following parameters:

- IOMode As IOMode. **Default value is** ForReading. **Other possible values include** ForAppending **and** ForWriting.
- Format As TriState. **An optional parameter.**

The next piece of code in the procedure using the ReadAll method of the TextStream object to fill the text box with the contents of the file. ReadAll returns a string, which we can use to set the Text property of the text box. Then we close the TextStream.

```
'read it in
Text1.Text = MyTextStream.ReadAll
MyTextStream.Close
```

In the last part of the procedure, we show how the file object can be used to obtain information about a file. For this program, we simply display the date the file was last modified, the size of the file in bytes, and the type of file:

```
txtFileName.Text = strFileName
txtLastModified = MyFile.DateLastModified
txtSize = MyFile.Size
txtFileType = MyFile.Type
```

Saving a Sequential File   Now we need a way to let the user save the text file. This is done with the code in the Save File command button. First, we reopen the TextStream, this time to write to the file. Then we use the Write method of the TextStream object to write the contents of the text box to the file. The code looks like this:

```
Private Sub cmdWriteFile_Click()
On Error Resume Next

 Set MyTextStream = MyFile.OpenAsTextStream(ForWriting)
 MyTextStream.Write (Text1.Text)
 MyTextStream.Close
 MsgBox "File " & strFileName & "has been saved."

End Sub
```

Random Access Files

Visual Basic also allows you to handle files built on records, which are user-defined types that contain one or more fields. Before getting into the details of using random access files, we must understand user-defined types.

A user-defined type can be described as a data structure that contains several fields. Each field can be a standard Visual Basic type, or you can have a field based on another user-defined type. For example, suppose we were tracking a list of employees. We could define the following type to hold each employee:

```
Type  Employee
   ID As Integer
   FirstName As String * 20
   LastName As String * 40
   PhoneNumber As String * 13
   Position As String * 20
End Type
```

We could extend the `Employee` type by defining a `Job` type as follows:

```
Type Job
 WorkType As Integer
 Title As String * 10
End Type
```

By changing the `Position` field in our original definition of `Employee`, we can access the new `Position` type:

```
Type Employee

   ID As Integer
   FirstName As String * 20
   LastName As String * 40
   PhoneNumber As String * 13
   Job_Title As Job

End Type
```

Notice that we have defined our string fields as fixed-length strings. For example, `FirstName` is defined as a string of 20 characters. This is because each record in a random access file must have the same length in bytes. The behavior of the strings will follow that described for fixed-length strings in Chapter 5. While the program is running, if the string assigned to this field is not actually 20 characters, it will be padded with blanks. If we had a variable-length string, the extra blanks would not be added and we would end up with a record of a different size. When we read the file, Visual Basic would not be able to determine this information and would read the data incorrectly. In general, user-defined types can have variable-length strings or arrays, but, remember, if you are going to use the type with a random access file, use fixed-length strings and arrays.

Declaring Variables and Accessing the Fields of a User-defined Type Once you've defined your types, declaring variables is done just as it is with any of the Visual Basic standard types. For example, we could define a variable of type Job and one of type Employee:

```
Public MyJob As Job
Public Worker As Employee
```

You can also have arrays of user-defined types. In that case, our variable declarations would look like this:

```
Public Positions(10) as Job
Public Workers(20) As Employee
```

To access the fields of a user-defined type, you use the "dot" syntax. The name of the variable is followed by a period and then by the name of the field you want to access. Let's say we wanted to create a new variable of type Position and initialize the fields. We could use the following code:

```
Dim MyJob As Job

MyJob.WorkID = 12
MyJob.Title = "Accountant"
```

To access the elements of an array of user-defined types, we use the following syntax:

```
Dim Workers(10) As Employee

Workers(1).FirstName = "Susan"
Workers(1).Job_Title.Title = "Electrical Engineer"
```

Opening a Random Access File Random access files are opened by using the Open statement. The syntax of the Open statement for use with a random access file is as follows:

```
Open filename For Random [Accessaccess] [locktype] As [#]FileNumber
  Len = RecordLength
```

The Access parameter is optional. It can be used to specify the operations that can be performed on the file. It can be one of *Read*, *Write*, or *Read Write*. Locktype, which is also an optional parameter, can be *Shared*, *Lock Read*, *Lock Write*, and *Lock Read Write*.

FileNumber is an integer. A file number cannot be one that is already in use elsewhere in the program. You can manually specify the value used here, but you should use the `FreeFile` function to allow the system to obtain the next available file number. The following code can be used to obtain a file number:

```
Dim intFileNum As Integer

intFileNum = FreeFile

File numbers can be in the range of 1 to 511.
```

The final parameter, `Len`, is the length of each record read from or written to the file. To obtain the length of a record, we use the `LenB` function, which returns the length of the variable in bytes as a long. For example, to obtain the length of the `Employee` type we defined earlier, we could use the following code:

```
Dim lngFieldLength As Long
Dim Worker As Employee
lngFieldLength = LenB(Worker)
```

Now we have everything we need to open a file. Let's say that we wanted to open a file called *Employees.dat* that contained a set of employee records. The code would look like this:

```
Dim intFileNum As Integer
Dim Worker As Employee
Dim lngFieldLength As Long

lngFieldLength = LenB(Worker)

intFileNum = FreeFile

Open "Employees.dat" For Random As intFileNum Len = lngFieldLength
```

Reading and Writing Records   When reading from or writing to random access files, you do so a record at a time. To read from a file, you use the `Get` statement. The `Get` statement has the following syntax:

```
Get [#]filenumber,[position], recordbuffer
```

If you call `Get` without passing the `Position` parameter, the next record following the last `Get` or `Put` statement will be read. The first record in the file is at position 1. In the following code, the code opens a random access file and reads the data into an array of user-defined types, while displaying the fields Last, First, and Title in a List View control.

```
Option Explicit

Type Employee
 Last As String * 20
 First As String * 10
 Phone As String * 13
 Title As String * 20
 Date_Hired As Date
End Type

Private Sub cmdRead_Click()

 Dim intFileNum As Integer
 Dim lngRecLength As Long
 Dim i As Integer
 Dim MyEmployees(1 To 100) As Employee
 Dim NumRecs As Integer
 Dim itmEmployee As ListItem

 intFileNum = FreeFile
 lngRecLength = LenB(MyEmployees(1))

 Open "C:\Employees.dat" For Random Access Read As #intFileNum Len =
   lngRecLength
 For i = 1 To 100
  Get #intFileNum, , MyEmployees(i)
  Set itmEmployee = lstEmployees.ListItems.Add(, , MyEmployees
    (i).Last)
  itmEmployee.SubItems(1) = MyEmployees(i).First
  itmEmployee.SubItems(2) = MyEmployees(i).Title

Next i

Close #intFileNum

End Sub
```

When the user clicks the *cmdRead* command button, an available file number is obtained by using the `FreeFile` function and the length of a record is determined:

```
intFileNum = FreeFile
lngRecLength = LenB(MyEmployees(1))
```

Next, we open the file for reading:

```
Open "C:\Employees.dat" For Random Access Read As #intFileNum Len
  = lngRecLength
```

Next, a `For` loop is used to read the data into the array `MyEmployees` with the `Get` statement, and then the Last, First, and Title fields are displayed in a List View control. Note that we read an entire record at a time rather than the individual fields:

```
For i = 1 To 100

  Get #intFileNum , , MyEmployees(i)
  Set itmEmployee = lstEmployees.ListItems.Add(, , MyEmployees
    (i).Last)
  itmEmployee.SubItems(1) = MyEmployees(i).First
  itmEmployee.SubItems(2) = MyEmployees(i).Title

Next i
```

Notice that when using the Get statement, we have omitted the Position parameter. This causes the next record to be read in sequence, in the order that the records were written to the file. Note that omitting the commas in a Get statement will cause a syntax error. To write to a random access file, use the Put statement. The syntax for the Put statement is as follows:

Put [#] filenumber, position, variablename

You can write to files using the Put statement in the same way that we used Get to read from the file.

Binary Files

The final type of flat file we will look at is the *binary* file. A binary file is simply a stream of bytes. Binary files can represent images, text, numbers, or just about any type of data defined by the programmer. When using binary files, it is up to the programmer to keep the information straight since there is no specification of record length as in a random access file. There are at least four situations when you should consider using binary files:

- *For writing variable-length records.* Recall that in the last section we built our data types with fixed-length strings. If you will be using variable-length strings, then use a binary file.

- *For storing numerical data.* It is more efficient to store numbers in a binary file than to use text files that will use a byte for each digit. For example, the integer 20,000 will require two bytes of storage in a binary file, but if we stored it as a text string it would require five bytes.

- *For storing large chunks of binary data, like an image.*

- *When small file size is important.*

Creating and Opening a Binary File   A binary file can be opened by using the `Open` statement with the following syntax:

```
Open filename For Binary As [#] filenumber
```

Writing to a Binary File   To write to a binary file, use the `Put` statement. We defined the `Put` statement in the section on random access files earlier in this chapter. Recall that the function takes three parameters:

- `Filenumber`—required; a valid file number.
- `Position`—optional; for binary files, specify the byte number at which writing is to begin.
- `variablename`—required; the name of the variable containing the data to be written to disk.

Reading from a Binary File   To read from a binary file, we use the `Get` statement. Recall that the `Get` statement takes the same three parameters as `Put`:

- `Filenumber`—required; a valid file number.
- `Position`—optional; in the case of binary files, this is the byte number at which reading begins.
- `variablename`—required; the name of the variable to read the data into.

EXAMPLE: A SIMPLE PROGRAM TO READ AND WRITE NUMERICAL DATA

We will now consider a simple program that can read and write integers to a binary disk file. Using a binary file will save disk space because each value will only require two bytes of storage. If we used a sequential file, the numbers would be stored as text strings and would require more disk space.

The form will create a grid of integer values and allow the user to save these values to a file. By clicking a *Read File* button, the user can read the values from a file and load them into the grid. The code is as follows:

```
Option Explicit
Dim NumRows As Integer
Dim NumCols As Integer
```

```vb
Private Sub cmdWriteFile_Click()

Dim strFileName As String
Dim intFileNum As Integer
Dim i As Integer, j As Integer
Dim intVal As Integer

strFileName = InputBox("Enter File Name", "Binary Files")
If Trim(strFileName) = "" Then
  MsgBox "No File Name Entered"
  Exit Sub
End If

intFileNum = FreeFile

Open strFileName For Binary As intFileNum

For i = 1 To NumRows - 1
 flxData.Row = i
 For j = 1 To NumCols - 1
  flxData.Col = j
  intVal = CInt(flxData.Text)
  Put intFileNum, , intVal
 Next j
Next i

Close intFileNum
MsgBox "File Written"
End Sub
Private Sub cmdReadFile_Click()

Dim strFileName As String
Dim intFileNum As Integer
Dim i As Integer, j As Integer
Dim intVal As Integer

strFileName = InputBox("Enter File Name", "Binary Files")

If Trim(strFileName) = "" Then
  MsgBox "No File Name Entered"
  Exit Sub
End If

intFileNum = FreeFile

Open strFileName For Binary As intFileNum

 For i = 1 To NumRows - 1
  flxData.Row = i
 For j = 1 To NumCols - 1
  flxData.Col = j
  Get intFileNum, , intVal
  flxData.Text = CStr(intVal)
 Next j
Next i
Close intFileNum

MsgBox "File Read."
End Sub
```

The form used in this project has three command buttons. By clicking the Load Data button, the user can fill the grid with numerical values. If the user clicks on *Write File*, he will be prompted to enter a file name where he wants to save the data. If he entered a file name, the FreeFile function is used to obtain a valid file number, and the file is opened for binary access:

```
intFileNum = FreeFile
Open strFileName For Binary As intFileNum
```

Next, we use two nested For loops to step through the grid. Data is accessed from a FlexGrid control in text format, so we use the Cint function to convert the data into an integer. Next we use the Put statement to write the value to the file:

```
For i = 1 To NumRows - 1
  flxData.Row = i
  For j = 1 To NumCols - 1
   flxData.Col = j
   intVal = CInt(flxData.Text)
   Put intFileNum, , intVal
  Next j
Next I
```

Finally, we close the file:

```
Close intFileNum
```

Reading the data from a file into the grid is accomplished in much the same way, this time using the Get statement to read the value into an integer variable:

```
For i = 1 To NumRows - 1
  flxData.Row = i
  For j = 1 To NumCols - 1
  flxData.Col = j
  Get intFileNum, , intVal
  flxData.Text = CStr(intVal)
 Next j
Next I
```

Using INI Files in a VB Application

Many programs use an initialization file to set program parameters or initialize variables at startup. An INI (extension *.ini*) file can be stored as a sequential access or text file, and the data can be read in the Sub Main procedure or form load event. Typically, an INI file is broken into different sections, which are delimited by brackets. You can create and work with INI files by using the file system objects described at the beginning of the chapter. A typical INI file looks like this:

```
[Visual Basic]
vbpath=D:\VB
CBTPath=D:\VB
ReportDesign=1
BooksExePath=D:\VB\VBOnline
MainWindow=0 0 800 74 1
PropertiesWindow=606 218 194 350 9
ToolBar=0
ColorPalette=72 505 0 0 0
CustomColors=16777215 16777215 16777215
ProjectWindow=399 70 348 452 9
ToolBox=4 78 0 0 1
RecentFile1=F:\Program Files\Microsoft Visual Basic\QuickBid for
Windows 95\CleanWorks
RecentFile2=D:\VB\samples\picclip\Redtop.vbp
RecentFile3=D:\VB\samples\graphics\Blanker.vbp
RecentFile4=C:\Crescent\QuickPak\Input\CALDLG.VBP
DebugWindow=118 124 454 423 0

[ToolboxBitmaps32]
Excel.Sheet.5=D:\VB\vb32.exe,100
Excel.Chart.5=D:\VB\vb32.exe,101
Word.Document.6=D:\VB\vb32.exe,102
Word.Picture.6=D:\VB\vb32.exe,103

[Add-Ins32]
DataFormDesigner.DFDClass=0
```

The file can be read line by line with a TextStream object. Each string will then need to be parsed and the settings read. When placing an entry into an INI file, you search the file for the appropriate section and use the TextStream object to write to the file.

Working with Databases

One of the most popular uses of Visual Basic is building database front ends. This will continue to be the case with version 6.0, which has added enhanced capabilities with OLE DB technologies and new features like the Data Environment. This includes an extended data control, new and improved data-aware controls such as grids and list boxes, as well as the capability to build an Access-like report right in VB. I think most developers will greet the reporting capabilities with a sigh of relief because they provide an alternative to difficult-to-use third-party reporting tools. Let's start by taking a look at the data control.

Using the Data Control

Most VB programmers are familiar with the data control. Version 6.0 of Visual Basic comes with two data controls: the old reliable data control that you may already be familiar with, and a new control known as the ADO data control (ADO stands for *ActiveX Data Objects*). ADO is the latest in database technologies from Microsoft, the earlier versions being RDO and DAO. In this section, we will focus on using the ADO control. If you learn how to use the ADO data control, you'll be able to use the older "plain" data control because it's a simpler tool. We'll be getting into the specifics of ADO technology later in this chapter; right now we just want to understand the steps required to use the ADO control in a program.

Setting a Reference to the ADO Data Control   The regular data control is one of the VB standard controls that loads with every standard VB project. The ADO data control, however, must be added to your project. This can be done by following these steps:

- Open the Components dialog from the Project pull-down menu.
- Select *Microsoft ADO Data Control 6.0 (OLE DB)*.
- Click the OK button to accept the changes.

When the Components dialog closes, the ADO data control will be added to your toolbox. The ToolTip text for the ADO data control is *Adodc*.

The Properties of the ADO Data Control   At first glance, the ADO data control (abbreviated ADodc) looks just like the old standard data control. It has four buttons that can be used to navigate the data set. A brief glance at the properties (see Fig. 10-1), however, reveals that the ADO data control departs somewhat from the data control of the past. If you compare the properties of the two controls, you will notice that the ADO control has the following new properties:

- *Cache size*: Cache size allows you to specify the number of records to cache when navigating through the `recordset`. Default setting is 50.
- *Command time out*: Command time out lets you specify the time in seconds that ADO will wait for a command to be returned before aborting.
- *Command type*: This is used as information for setting the RecordSource. It can be text, a table, or a stored procedure. Select

Figure 10-1
The Property Pages
dialog for the ADO
data control.

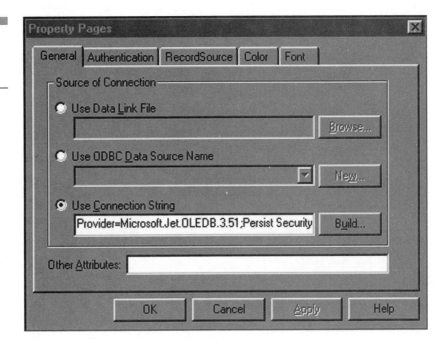

Text to use an SQL statement as the RecordSource for this control. If you select *table* or *stored procedure*, the name is specified in the RecordSource property.

■ *Connection string*: The connection string designates the data source name and tells which provider is being used, such as ODBC or Microsoft Jet 3.51. Other information specified in the connection string will include user name and password.

■ *Connection time out*: This is the amount of time to wait for the connection before aborting.

■ *Cursor location*: Cursor location lets you specify whether to use client-side or server-side cursors.

■ *Cursor type*: Cursor type sets the cursor type for the `recordset`. It can be *Open Keyset*, *Open Dynamic*, or *Open Static*.

■ *Lock type*: Lock type can set or return the type of locking used, that is, pessimistic versus optimistic. We will discuss locking in the section on multiuser applications near the end of this chapter.

■ *Max records*: This sets the maximum number of records to return with the `recordset`. If set to 0, there is no limit.

- *Mode*: Returns the mode of the current connection. It can be *Unknown, Read, Write, Read Write, Share Deny Read, Share Deny Write, Share Exclusive*, or *Share Deny None*.

- *Password*: A valid user password. It can be used to get authentication information for a password-protected database.

- *User name*: User name is a valid user name for the database. It can be used to get authentication information for a password-protected database.

The strength of the data control has always been that it gives the programmer the ability to build a database application with little or no coding. The amount of power we can build into our programs this way is taken to new heights with the extended capabilities of the ADO data control.

Setting the Connect Properties of the ADO Data Control   When programming a data control, the first item of business is to connect to the database. With the ADO control, the first step is to specify the connection source. When you open the Property Pages dialog for the ADO control, you'll see three options for connection source on the General tab (see Fig. 10-1):

- *Use Data Link File*

- *Use ODBC Data Source Name*: If you are using ODBC, click open the drop-down list and select the ODBC source. The choices include *MS Access 97 Database, dBase Files, Excel Files, FoxPro Files*, and *Text Files*.

- *Use Connection String*: The connection string includes information like the data source name, user name, password, default database, and cursor location. Click the *Build* button to open the Data Link Properties dialog (see Fig. 10-2). If you will be using Jet, click on the *Provider* tab and select *Microsoft Jet 3.51 OLE DB Provider*. On the Connection tab, you can specify the database file to use, such as *Biblio.mdb*. The user name and password required to log onto the database is specified here as well. The Advanced tab can be used to specify network settings and access permissions for the database.

Setting the RecordSource   You can set the RecordSource for your data control by clicking on the *RecordSource* tab. This is done after specifying the connection string. First, click open the *Command Type* drop-down list. Selections available include text, table, and stored procedure.

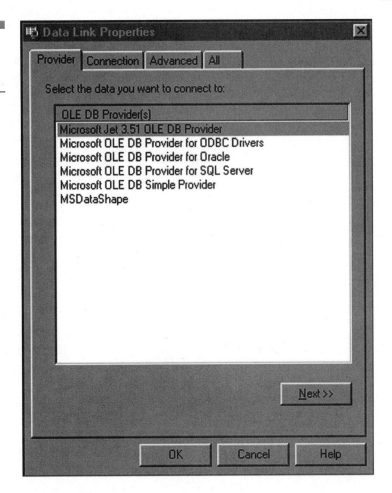

Figure 10-2
Setting the data link for an ADO Data Control.

Select *text* if you want to enter an SQL statement. If you select *table* or *stored procedure*, click open the *Table* or *Stored Procedure* drop-down list and select the appropriate object from the database.

Important Methods and Events of the ADO Data Control

While you can create a database app by simply dropping the ADOdc on a form and setting a few properties, it makes more sense to program the control to build a more robust application. To do this we need to be familiar with the methods and events of the control. Some useful methods and events are listed in the following sections along with some code samples.

EndOfRecordset   The EndOfRecordset event fires when the pointer is moved to BOF (beginning of file) or EOF (end of file). The adStatus parameter can be tested to detect error conditions. This event is also passed a recordset variable, which you can use to handle the BOF/EOF condition. For example, you could move the pointer to the first record.

```
Private Sub adoBookTitles_EndOfRecordset(fMoreData As Boolean,
  adStatus As ADODB.EventStatusEnum, ByVal pRecordset As
ADODB.Recordset)
  If adStatus = adStatusOK Then
    'Code to handle OK
    pRecordset.MoveFirst
  ElseIf adStatus = adStatusErrorsOccurred Then
    'code to handle error condition
  ElseIf adStatus = adStatusCantDeny Then
    'code for cant deny
  Else
    'code for other conditions
  End If
End Sub
```

Error   The Error event fires when a data access error occurs but no code is executing. In other words, the error arises from the actions of the data control. The Error event works much like the Err object (see Chapter 13). The error number, description, and source are passed.

FieldChangeComplete   This event fires after the data in a field has been changed.

MoveComplete   The MoveComplete event fires when the recordset has moved to a new row. You can test the adReason parameter to determine the cause of the move, such as add new record, delete, or move previous. The pError parameter can be tested for error conditions. The adStatus parameter can be tested to see if status is OK or if an error has occurred.

Refresh   Use the Refresh method to reopen or reconnect to the database. For example, if another user has added a new record to the database you can issue a call to the Refresh method to show the most recent version of the recordset. In the following code, we use the Refresh method in the form activate event:

```
Private Sub Form_Activate()

  adoBookTitles.Refresh

End Sub
```

WillChangeField The WillChangeField event occurs before the value of a field is changed. You can use this event for data validation and to abort if necessary.

WillChangeRecord This event is fired before the record is changed. The adReason parameter can be used to test why the event was fired. The adStatus parameter can be set to allow or cancel the change. For example, we can prompt the user and ask him if he wants to save the changes:

```
Private Sub adoBookTitles_WillChangeRecord(ByVal adReason As
ADODB.EventReasonEnum, ByVal cRecords As Long, adStatus As
ADODB.EventStatusEnum, ByVal pRecordset As ADODB.Recordset)

  Dim intResponse As Integer

  intResponse = MsgBox("Record Changed, Save Changes?", vbYesNo)

  If intResponse = vbNo Then
      adStatus = adStatusCancel      'user wants to abandon changes
  End If

End Sub
```

If we set adStatus to adStatusCancel, any changes the user entered will be abandoned.

WillMove WillMove is fired before the data control moves to a new record. This can happen when the user clicks *data control* or another record in a data grid or when you use one of the move methods of the recordset. The adReason parameter can be used to check the reason that the cursor is being moved. In the following example, we use a Select Case statement to initiate different actions based on the reason the user is moving the record pointer:

```
Private Sub adoBookTitles_WillMove(ByVal adReason As
ADODB.EventReasonEnum, adStatus As ADODB.EventStatusEnum, ByVal
  pRecordset As ADODB.Recordset)

Select Case adReason

  Case adRsnClose:
     'code here is for when the user is closing the connection

  Case adRsnMove:
     'code here for when the user moves to another record

  Case adRsnMoveFirst:
     'code here for when the user moves to the first record
```

```
'either by clicking the movefirst button of the ado control
'or from a call to the movefirst method of the ado control's
  recordset

Case adRsnMovePrevious:
  'code here for when the user clicks the move previous button
  'or a call to the MovePrevious method of the recordset has been
    invoked
  End Select

End Sub
```

RDO and DAO

As Visual Basic has grown and developed, Microsoft has introduced different objects that could be used to program databases. In this section, we will briefly review the older technologies. The first of these was DAO, or *data access objects*. DAO allows you to use the Jet engine to work with Access databases or ODBC drivers. You can also support so-called ISAM databases such as Paradox or work with files like Excel. DAO can also be used with ODBC, which can bypass the Jet engine to execute queries in a server, such as Oracle. You can use DAO with the standard data control or by declaring and programming data access objects in code. These include the `Workspace` object, the `database` object, and the `recordset` object. In order to use DAO in code, we must set a reference. Set a reference to the Microsoft DAO 3.51 Object Library from the References dialog of the Project menu.

In the following example, we open the *Biblio.mdb* database with data access objects so we can add the data from the titles table to a list box. First, we declare a database object and use the OpenDatabase method of the `Workspace` object to point it to the *Biblio.mdb* file. Next, we use the OpenRecordset method to open the "Titles" `recordset`. We can then loop through the `rs` `recordset` and add each title to the list box, testing for end-of-file at each iteration of the loop.

```
Private Sub cmdLoadTitles_Click()

Dim db As Database
Dim rs As Recordset

Set db = opendatabase("C:\Program Files\Microsoft Visual
  Studio\Vb98\Biblio.mdb")
Set rs = db.OpenRecordset("Titles")

Do While rs.EOF = False

  lstTitles.AddItem rs("Title")
```

```
        rs.MoveNext

    Loop

    rs.Close
    db.Close

End Sub
```

RDO stands for *remote data objects*. RDO permits the access of remote data sources through the use of ODBC. Through RDO, you can use objects that can connect to a remote database and execute queries and stored procedures. RDO is more heavily weighted toward working with stored procedures and as such fits in with Microsoft's three-tiered development strategy.

While DAO and RDO are still supported, the fact is that ADO is the future of database technologies. As a result, we will focus on ADO and OLE DB.

OLE DB and ADO

OLE DB uses COM as a means of providing the interfaces necessary for database programming. ADO, which, as noted, stands for "ActiveX data objects," is the object interface to OLE DB. Since OLE DB is based on COM it provides a language-independent set of database objects.

OLE DB can be used with a wide variety of data sources. This includes data sources that are not relational databases, such as Microsoft Excel. The interfaces that OLE DB provides adapt to the data source. So, regardless of whether you use an Access database, SQL Server, or an Excel spreadsheet, OLE DB will adjust its functionality to the appropriate level. This flexibility means that OLE DB is not restricted to use with the Jet engine. While you can still use Jet if desired, you can also use OLE DB for ODBC connections.

ADO is what programmers will use when developing their software. We have already seen how to use the ADO data control. ADO can also be used to program objects in code. Since ADO combines the functionality of DAO and RDO, if you have only worked with one of these models in the past using ADO may take some adjustment. ADO offers support for remote data services. RDS is a client-side component that can be used to provide support for cursors, middle-tier caching of `recordsets`, and remote `recordset` functionality.

Seven objects comprise ADO:

- *Connect*: This object is used to maintain an active connection to a data source. A connection object can be used to return `recordsets`, process database transactions, or execute other commands. If you are used to DAO, note that you will use the Connect object to open a database rather than the database object.

- *Recordset*: This is the familiar `recordset` of the past, with some slight modifications. A `recordset` is used to return the results of a query. The `recordset` object contains all of the functionality necessary to manage a data set. `Recordsets` can be opened without opening a connection, but it's good programming practice to use a connection to open the data source.

- *Field*: This is the fields collection of the `recordset`.

- *Command*: A Command object is used to maintain information about a command. Some properties of the Command object are Active Connection, Command Text, Parameters, and Properties collections.

- *Parameter*: ADO maintains a Parameters collection that specifies the input and output parameters for parameterized commands.

- *Error*: ADO maintains an Errors collection. This collection contains the error information from the provider. The Errors collection can contain multiple errors at one time.

- *Property*: The property object is an object that has the provider-defined attributes of the ADO object. This can include a `recordset` or connection.

Managing Cursors   Something new that you may have noticed with the ADO data control is the ability to manage cursors. The cursor type can be set with the CursorType property of the `recordset` object. The CursorType property must be set before opening the `recordset` or you can pass the cursor type with the open method of the `recordset`. The default cursor type is forward only. Other cursor values are OpenDynamic, OpenKeyset, and OpenStatic. A forward-only cursor provides a single pass through the data. To enable forward and backward movement as well as the ability to add, edit, and delete records, use an OpenDynamic cursor. A dynamic cursor allows you to see manipulations of the data by other users. The OpenKeyset cursor works like a dynamic cursor, except that you will not be able to see changes made by other users. A static cursor returns a copy of the data.

Another important property is the CursorLocation property. CursorLocation can be `adUseServer` or `adUseClient`. Using a client-side cursor can cause a burden on the network; however, it may improve performance as seen by the client. A client-side cursor will return entire rows of data, while a server-side cursor will only return the requested data. Note that not all data providers will support all cursor types. If a data provider does not support the selected cursor type, another type may be returned.

Creating an OLE DB Provider   You can use the OLE DB technology to create and expose OLE DB objects. This is done by first setting a reference to the Microsoft OLE DB Simple Provider 1.5 Library. You will then add two classes to your project. The first class has its DataSourceBehavior property set to None. A second class needs to be added to the project, and you set its DataSourceBehavior property to OLEDBProvider. This class will function as an interface or abstract class, as we described in Chapter 8. Put the following `Implements` line in the general declarations section of the class:

```
Implements OLEDBSimpleProvider
```

The methods of the `OLEDBSimpleProvider` class have now been added to your project.

Creating a VB 6 Data Source   You can also create a vbDataSource-type class with Visual Basic. This will allow you to expose ADO `recordsets` to client applications. To do this, create a new class module and set the DataSourceBehavior property to vbDataSource. You will need to set a reference to the ActiveX Data Objects library to use ADO. Visual Basic will create a method of the class called `GetDataMember`. This function is used to return an ADO data object to the client. For example, you can declare private `recordset` variables in the class module. You can then return references to those objects in the `GetDataMember` function. `GetDataMember` takes two parameters, `DataMember As String` and `Data As Object`. You can use the `DataMember` string to decide which object to return, and you return the object by pointing the `Data` object variable to it. The following code illustrates how this might be done:

```
Private mStudents As ADODB.Recordset
Private mTeachers As ADODB.Recordset

Private Sub Class_GetDataMember(DataMember As String, Data As Object)

    Select Case DataMember
```

```
   Case "Students"
      Set Data = mStudents
   Case "Teachers"
      Set Data = mTeachers
   Case Else
      Set Data = Nothing
 End If

End Sub
```

When you add a class module to your project, you can select *Data Source* from the Add Class Module dialog box.

Using ActiveX Data Objects in Code   To use ActiveX data objects in code you must set a reference. This is done by opening the References dialog box from the Projects pull-down menu. Select *Microsoft ActiveX Data Objects 2.0 Library*. ActiveX Data Objects can now be declared in your code. To manipulate the data, you will use a connection object and a recordset object. These are declared using the ADODB class. For example, we could declare a Connection object and an associated recordset with the following code:

```
Dim myrecordset As ADODB.Recordset
Dim myconn As ADODB.Connection
```

Just like any other object in VB, we must use the SET... New keywords to instantiate the objects. The following code continues our example:

```
Set myconn = New ADODB.Connection
Set myrecordset = New ADODB.Recordset
```

Opening a Database   You open a database by using the Open method of the Connection object. Connection objects can be used to open a DSN-based connection or a non-Data Source Name-based connection. The specifics will depend on your database management system. For example, if we are using the Microsoft Jet engine, we can specify this by setting the Provider property of the Connection object:

```
myconn.Provider = "Microsoft.Jet.OLEDB.3.51"
```

The database can then be opened with a call to the Open method:

```
myconn.Open "Data Source=C:\Employees.mdb"
```

The provider can be specified with the data source in the Open method. This lets us specify both pieces of information in one go:

```
strDataBase = App.Path & "\Biblio.mdb"

myconn.Open "Provider=Microsoft.Jet.OLEDB.3.51;" _
      & "Data Source=" & strDataBase
```

In this case, the data source was located in the same directory as the application. We built a string representing the path and file name of the database before using the Open method.

Opening the `recordset`   Now we have an open data source. To work with the records, we will use the `recordset` variable. A `recordset` also has an Open method. To use it, we specify the table or an SQL statement, along with the Connection object we want to use. To open the authors table of the *Biblio.mdb* database, we could use the following statement:

```
myrecordset.Open "Select * from Authors", myconn
```

In the next section, "Embedded and Dynamic SQL," we'll discuss SQL statements. SQL statements can be used in the `recordset` Open method to retrieve a subset of the data. At this point, we are ready to work with the data. The fields in a `recordset` can be accessed by placing the field name in parentheses:

```
txtName.text = myrecordset("Author")
```

An alternative method is to use the `!` character followed by the field name:

```
txtName.text = myrecordset!Author
```

You'll see later that when we write SQL statements fields with spaces are placed in between brackets. The same is done here:

```
txtYear.text = myrecordset![Year Born]
```

Navigating the `recordset`

We can use the Move methods of the `recordset` to move from row to row. There are five Move methods:

- *Move*: Moves a specified number of records. Pass the number of records as a Long.

- *MoveFirst*: Moves the pointer to the first record in the recordset.

- *MoveLast*: Moves the pointer to the last record in the recordset.

- *MoveNext*: Moves to the next record.

- *MovePrevious*: Moves to the previous record.

You can test for the end-of-file or beginning-of-file conditions by using the EOF and BOF properties of the recordset. In the following example, we loop through the recordset until end-of-file is reached:

```
Do While Not myrecordset.EOF
 lstAuthors.AddItem myrecordset!Author
 lstYears.AddItem myrecordset![Year Born]
 myrecordset.MoveNext
Loop
```

The MoveNext method is used at the bottom of the loop to move to the next row.

Closing the Connection and Recordset   Once you are done with a connection, you should close the Connection object and any associated recordsets. This is done by using the Close method. We should then release the object variables by setting them to Nothing. This is illustrated with the following code:

```
myrecordset.Close
myconn.Close

Set myrecordset = Nothing
Set myconn = Nothing
```

Searching a Recordset   To search a recordset, we use the Find method. The Find method takes the following parameters:

- Criteria: This is a string representing the search criteria. For example, to find the Author record with the Author field for James Dean, we would use a statement like "Author = 'James Dean'"

- SkipRecords: SkipRecords is a long that can be used to specify how many records to skip, if any.

- SearchDirection: The default is adSearchForward. It can be set to adSearchBackward.

- Start: This is the start position for the search. If left blank, it starts at the current record.

Updating Data Obviously the `recordset` would not be of much use if we could not add new records or edit the records already there. To edit the `recordset`, we must set the LockType (see the section "Multiuser Considerations" later in this chapter for a comparison of locking methods). The default is read-only. You specify the LockType in the `Open` statement for the `recordset`. For example:

```
myrecordset.Open "Select * from Authors", myconn, , adLockOptimistic
```

We can add a new record by issuing a call to the AddNew method:

```
myrecordset.AddNew
```

The fields of the `recordset` can then be filled in:

```
myrecordset("Name") = txtName.Text
myrecordset("Address") = txtAddress.Text
myrecordset("Phone") = txtPhone.Text
```

To save the data, we use the Update method:

```
myrecordset.Update
```

To edit a record, simply set the new field values and then save the changes with a call to the Update method:

```
Myrecordset("Author")  =  "J.Edgar Hoover"
myrecordset.Update
```

Deleting Records Records can be deleted by using the Delete method. For example, suppose we have a contacts database, and we wanted to delete all contacts from the state of Washington. We could use a Do loop:

```
Do While rs.EOF = False
  rs.Delete
  rs.MoveNext
Loop
```

Stored Procedures A stored procedure is a procedure that is built into the database. A stored procedure can be used for a complex query. As an example, consider the following stored procedure in an SQL Server database:

```
CREATE PROCEDURE spUserCount AS
 declare @usrcount as int
 select @usrcount = count(*) from LoginData
 return @usrcount
GO
```

We can execute this procedure in Visual Basic by using an ADODB recordset. The code will look like the following:

```
Dim conn As ADODB.Connection
Dim RS As ADODB.Recordset

Set conn = New ADODB.Connection
Set RS = New ADODB.Recordset

conn.Open "UserData", "User", "PassMe"
RS = conn.execute "Call spUserCount", numRecs, adCmdStoredProc
```

Here we used the Execute method of the Connection object to run the stored procedure. The result set is passed to the RS `recordset` variable.

Embedded and Dynamic SQL

A query can be used to retrieve a subset of the information stored in a database. Users can retrieve the data in a different sort order, retrieve only a subset of the fields in a table, or retrieve a set of records that only meet a specified criterion. Data from different tables can even be combined and displayed to the user. It is the query that helps bring out the power of storing information in a database.

One way to work with queries is to use a special language, known as structured query language or SQL. SQL is an especially powerful tool to use when writing VB apps. It allows you to build the queries at run time in response to user requests. This is called *dynamic* SQL. We can also create and use queries that are part of the database itself. These are called *embedded queries*.

We will investigate both types of queries in this section. First, we'll learn about SQL and see what the rules are for building SQL statements. Then, we'll see how SQL is used in a simple VB program to run queries against an Access database. Finally, we'll take a brief look at embedded SQL.

Building Select Queries

There are several types of queries that you can use when working with Access databases. The most common type of query is known as a Select query. A Select query allows us to specify which rows and columns to return from a table or tables and in what order to sort the records. We can also construct queries to update records, add new records to the database, or delete a set of records. For many of our examples, we'll consider a phone number database that stores the names, addresses, and phone numbers of clients in a table called *contacts*.

We can start by imagining a simple query that only specifies which fields to return from the table. This is the minimal Select statement that can be used. At this point, we won't be worried about filtering the records returned. This type of query will have two elements, a Select clause and a From clause. The Select clause specifies which fields to return from the table, while the From clause specifies the name of the table where the data can be found. An SQL statement of this type has the form:

```
Select Field From Table
```

We can build a query like this to retrieve the names in our contact database:

```
Select Name From Contacts
```

When specifying more than one field in a query, place commas between each field name. The syntax of the SQL statement then becomes:

```
Select Field1, [Field2], ...[FieldN]  FROM Table
```

For example, to return names and phone numbers from the contacts table of the phone database, we would write a query like this one:

```
Select Name, Phone from Contacts
```

To return every field in a table, you use an asterisk in place of the field list. To return all fields from the contacts table we write:

```
Select * from Contacts
```

If there are one or more blank spaces in the name of a field, enclose it in square brackets. Suppose that the contacts table has a field named *zip code*. We can retrieve this field in a query with the following statement:

```
Select Name, Phone, [Zip Code] from Contacts
```

We can also specify the table name for each field, though this is optional. You will do this when building queries from multiple tables. The table name for each field is specified using the "dot" syntax, `table-name.fieldname`. For example, we could rewrite the preceding query like this:

```
Select Contacts.Name, Contacts.Phone, Contacts.[Zip Code] from
  Contacts
```

Again, you won't do this unless you are building a query that retrieves fields from more than one table. To specify a query that returns every field from the table, we again use an asterisk:

```
Select Contacts.*
```

Aliasing

You can rename or *alias* field names that are returned by a query. This is done with the `As` keyword. For example, consider the *Biblio.mdb* database that ships with Visual Basic. The publishers table has a Name field and a Company Name field. Suppose that we wish to display the Name field as `Division`. We could write the query like this:

```
Select Name As Division, [Company Name] from Publishers
```

Aliasing is helpful when you are building a query with fields from multiple tables. Different tables may have fields with the same name. By using an alias, you can provide meaningful and unique names for each field.

Restricting the Records Returned with a Where Clause

Usually, when building a query, you will only want to return a subset of the records that are in the table. This will be based on the values contained in certain fields. For example, in a table of students you may only want to look at the students who are in the junior class. With this type of query, the records returned will be chosen based on a criterion that you supply with a `Where` clause. The form of the SQL statement then becomes:

```
SELECT Field1, [Field2], . . . ,[FieldN] FROM Table WHERE Expression
```

The expression used in a `Where` clause will be a conditional expression similar to that used in an `If` statement in Visual Basic. Like an `If` statement, the `Where` clause will use comparison operators as a filter. These are *greater than* (>), *less than* (<), *equal to* (=), *greater than or equal* (>=), and *less than or equal* (<=). We can also use an inequality operator, <> or not equal, !=. The expression will compare a field to some value we are using as a filter. Comparison values must follow these rules, based on the data type:

- Strings must be delimited by single quotation marks.
- Dates must be delimited by the # character.
- Numeric values are not delimited.

The field name supplied does not need to be returned with the query. We consider each type of data with the two following examples.

EXAMPLE: SEARCHING TEXT OR STRING FIELDS

Returning to the example in the previous section, say we wanted to return records from the contacts table only if the client was living in California. We could use this SQL statement:

```
Select * from Contacts where State = 'CA'
```

Note that single quotation marks are used to delimit the comparison value, which is a string.

Now suppose that we were building the SQL statement in a Visual Basic program. We could have the user select which state she wants to retrieve from a combo box. The SQL statement can be built up as a string variable, which we can use as the data source for a data control or `recordset` variable. We still need to enclose the string representing the state in quotation marks. We can do this with the following code:

```
Dim strState As String, strQuery As String
Dim strQuote As String
```

```
strQuote = "'"

strState  = cboStateList.Text

strQuery =  "Select * from Contacts where State =  " & strQuote &
strState & strQuote
```

Fields That Contain Date/Time Data

Dates in an SQL statement are delimited with the # character. Consider an orders table for a small business. This table has a field named Date that records the date the order was placed. If we only want to return orders placed since March 1, 1998, we can use the following query:

```
Select * from Orders where Date > #3/1/98#
```

Recall that the * character specifies that this query will return every field in the table.

EXAMPLE: NUMERIC FIELDS

As another example, let's return to a table that maintains a list of students. This table has string fields for last name and first name and a numerical field that holds the students' grade point average (GPA). For our query, say we only wanted to return students with GPAs greater than 3.5. This can be done with this SQL statement:

```
Select Last, First from Students where GPA > 3.5
```

Remember, numerical values do not need to be delimited by quotation marks.

Using the `Like` Operator

Partial string searches can be done using the `Like` operator. You can use the `Like` operator in SQL statements to compare text strings with wildcards or a character list. To return all students whose last name starts with *J*, we can write:

```
Select * from Students where Last_Name  Like 'J%'
```

The wildcard character % tells the query engine to return any string that begins with *J*. Single-digit wildcards can be built with the underscore character. For example,

```
Select Name From Contacts Where State Like 'C_'
```

will return contacts from any state beginning with the letter *C*.

You can also use `Like` to compare text fields to a list of characters. A character list is delimited in brackets. For example, suppose we wanted to return all records from the contacts table where the name of the person was Tim or Tom. The SQL statement would look like this:

```
Select * from Contacts where Name Like 'T[io]m'
```

Like can also be used to leave out records that have characters found in a character list. This is done by including the ! character at the beginning of your list. The following statement returns all names that start with *S* but only those that do not have *a* or *u* as the second letter:

```
Select * from Contacts where Name Like 'S[!au]*'
```

So names like Susan or Sam would not be returned by the query.

Returning Records That Fall Only within a Certain Range

When working with numerical values or dates, you can define an inclusive range of values by using the `Between` operator. This is used in conjunction with the `And` keyword. To return the records for all cub scouts between the ages 7 and 10, we write:

```
Select Name, Age from Scouts where Age Between 7 And 10
```

where `Scouts` is the name of the table and `Name, Age` are fields within the scouts table. The `Between` operator also works with date fields:

```
Select * from Orders where Date Between #1/1/98# And #12/31/98#
```

This query would return all orders placed in the year 1998.

Using the IN Operator

You can use the `IN` operator in your SQL statement to select among a group of values. This is basically a shorthand for using the `OR` operator several times. The list of choices is placed in between parentheses. As an example, let's write an SQL statement that selects contacts from California or Texas. Using the IN operator, it would look like the following:

```
Select Name, Phone from Contacts Where State IN ('CA','TX')
```

You can include as many values in the IN clause as there are test cases. This will save you a lot of typing and make your SQL statements easier to read if there are several OR choices.

Sorting the Records Returned by a Query

You can add an ORDER BY clause to an SQL query to tell the query engine how to sort the records. This can be based on whatever field you choose and is not necessarily determined by indexing. You do this by specifying which field or fields to sort on. Returning to the previous example of a scouts table, suppose we want to sort the scouts by age. We can do this by rewriting the query as follows:

```
Select Name, Age from Scouts where Age Between 7 And 10 ORDER BY Age
```

If we wanted to sort by name, the query would read as:

```
Select Name, Age from Scouts where Age Between 7 And 10 ORDER BY Name
```

ORDER BY sorts records in ascending order by default. To sort the same query in reverse order, you can add the DESC keyword:

```
Select Name, Age from Scouts where Age Between 7 And 10 ORDER BY Name
  DESC
```

Note that the field that you sort on with the ORDER BY clause does not need to be returned with the query. For example, we can still sort the scouts by age but only return their names and phone numbers:

```
Select Name, [Phone Number] From Scouts ORDER BY Age
```

Building More Complicated Queries with Logical Operators

We can extend the Where clause by using the AND, OR keywords to combine one or more expressions. Suppose we wanted to return records from the contacts table if the person lived in California, and she was entered in the database after November 1, 1998. The following statement would return the desired records:

```
Select Name, Phone from Contacts where State = 'CA' AND Date >
    #11/1/98#
```

If we want to return phone numbers for contacts in California and Texas, we can use the OR keyword:

```
Select Name, Phone from Contacts where State = 'CA' OR State = 'TX'
```

We can also use the NOT operator to keep certain records out of a query. To retrieve all clients except those from Texas, we could write:

```
Select Name, Phone from Contacts Where NOT State = 'TX'
```

We can build up more and more complicated queries by combining the logical operators. This is done in the same way as when constructing an If statement.

Grouping Records

Often it will be necessary to group records together. This can be done by using a Group By clause. This type of clause is used with an Aggregate function. Aggregate functions are functions that can be applied to a data set to perform some operation, such as counting the number of records. For example, if we wanted to count the number of students who had a GPA greater than 3.0, we could use the Count function:

```
Select Count(*) As "Honor Roll Students" From Students Where GPA > 3.0
```

We have used the As keyword to give a name to the field that will contain the result of the Count function. Other Aggregate functions include SUM, AVG, MIN, and MAX. The Group By clause can be used with an Aggregate function to group the records together. For example, we can group the students together by class (*Fresh, Soph, Junior, Senior*) and use the Count function to count the number of students in each class:

```
Select Name, Count(*) As "Number of Students" From Students GROUP BY
    Class
```

Editing, Adding, and Deleting Records

SQL can be used to update, add, or delete groups of records in a single statement. To update a group of records, we use an `Update` statement. The syntax is as follows:

```
UPDATE Table SET Field = Value [Where Condition]
```

A typical `Update` statement might look like the following:

```
UPDATE Contacts SET State = 'AZ' WHERE ContactID > 188
```

We use the `Update` keyword to tell the query engine that we will be updating the records. Next, we specify the table that we want to update. The `Set` clause specifies which field or fields to change, and the `Where` clause is used to define a criterion to select which records to update. In this example, we have specified that all contacts whose ID is greater than a certain value have the value in the state field set to *Arizona*. We can also update to a single record. For example, consider an inventory table named *Products*. We can change the price for a single item in the inventory with this statement:

```
UPDATE Products SET Price = 6.5 WHERE ProductID = 'A300L29'
```

To add records to a table with an SQL statement, you can use the `INSERT` keyword. You can specify the values that each field will take by using the `VALUES` keyword. The syntax is as follows:

```
INSERT INTO Table (Field List) VALUES (Value List)
```

For example, to add a record to the contacts table, we can use this statement:

```
INSERT INTO Contacts (ContactID, LastName, FirstName) VALUES
                (200,'Jones','Tim')
```

Deleting a record or group of records is done with a `Delete` statement. A `Delete` statement uses this syntax:

```
DELETE FROM Table WHERE Expression
```

To delete all contacts whose state of residence is California, we can use this statement:

```
DELETE FROM Contacts WHERE State = 'CA'
```

Each of these statements can be built up with more complexity in the same way that a `Select` statement is by following the same rules used in `Select` statements.

Joining Data from Different Tables

Up to this point we've been building simple queries that retrieve a subset of data from one table. However, the ability to relate data in two tables is at the core of database design, and the design of queries would not be complete without the ability to join the data from tables together. This is done with a `Join` statement. There are two types of joins. To distinguish between them, we will consider an example. Consider a database with a customers (see Fig. 10-3) table and an orders table. The orders table has the orders each customer has placed. However, not every customer has placed an order (some may have requested a catalog but not yet ordered).

- *Inner Join*: When an inner join is created, only records that have a match in both tables are included in the result of the query. If we

Figure 10-3 The Customers table.

build an inner join on the database in our example, the only records that will be included are those that match for both tables, which means that only the customers who have placed an order are listed.

- *Outer Join*: With an outer join, all records from a master table are included in the result, while only the matching records from a lookup table are included. In this case, all customer records are listed, regardless of whether or not they placed an order. The fields from the orders table will simply be blank for those customers.

To perform an inner join, you use a `Select` statement and specify the criteria you want to use to join the tables in the `Where` clause. As an example of an inner join, consider the *Biblio.mdb* database that ships with Visual Basic. The titles table and the publishers table can be linked on the pub_id field. An inner join would look like this:

```
Select Titles.*, Publishers.pub_id, Publishers.Name  From Titles,
   Publishers Where
                    Titles.pub_id = Publishers.pub_id
```

Notice that we used the familiar "dot" syntax to specify which table we are talking about. Using the asterisk tells the query engine to retrieve all fields from the titles table, while the query will only return the pub_id and Name fields from the publishers table.

When building an outer join, you can use a left join or a right join. This tells the query engine which table is the "master" table and which table is the "lookup" table. An outer join uses the `ON` keyword instead of a `Where` clause. For example, let's build a query with the titles table as the "master." This means that the query will return every title record, regardless of whether or not there is a matching publisher record. The query will look like this:

```
Select Titles.*, Publishers.* From Titles Left Join Publishers On
   Titless.pub_id = Publishers.pub_id
```

A right join works the same way, except the other table is considered the "master." To use the publishers table as the master and the titles table as the lookup, we can write the following SQL statement:

```
Select Titles.*, Publishers.* From Titles Right Join Publishers On
   Titles.pub_id = Publishers.pub_id
```

At this point, we're ready to illustrate how to use SQL in code with an example.

The Complaints Program

Overview

In this section, we examine a VB application created to track complaints made to a janitorial company. The program is shown in Fig. 10-4. The complaints program illustrates how you can use SQL in code to filter the records that the user sees. The complaints program uses *Complaints.mdb*, a database designed to track customer complaints for a janitorial company.

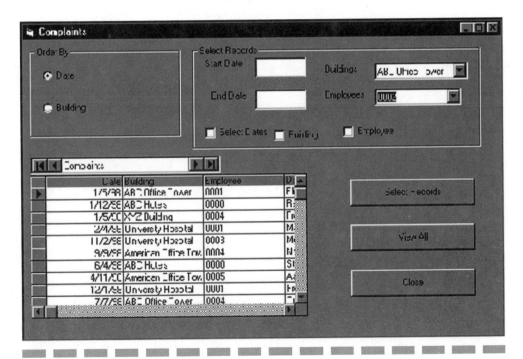

Figure 10-4 The Complaints program.

The Complaints Table

Inside *Complaints.mdb* you will find the tables *buildings*, *employees*, and *complaints*. The complaints table has the following fields:

Field	Type	Description
Date	Date/Time	Date the complaint was filed
Building	Text	Name of the customer who filed the complaint
Employee	Text	SSN of the employee assigned
Description	Memo	Description of the complaint

The buildings and employees tables will function only as lookup tables in this project.

What the Program Will Do

The complaints program will display the data from the database in a grid format on screen. It will allow the user to select sort order by building or date. The user will also be able to make the following choices:

- Show only those records for a specified date range
- Show only those records for a specified building
- Show only those records for a specified employee
- Use some combination of the above
- View all records in the default sort order that would be specified by the primary key

Entering Code for the Complaints Form

The first thing we will need is a variable to build the SQL statement. We add this code to the general declarations section of the form:

```
'string variable to hold SQL statement
Private strQuery as string
```

The All command button lets the user view all the records in the table. The code in the cmdAll command button Click event looks like this:

```
Private Sub cmdAll_Click()

On Error GoTo Err_cmdAll

 strQuery = "Select * from Complaints"
 datComplaints.RecordSource = strQuery
 datComplaints.Refresh
 optDate.Value = False
 optBuilding.Value = False
 Exit Sub

Err_cmdAll:
 MsgBox Err.Description & "  Occurred in cmdAll Click."
 Resume Next
End Sub
```

If the user clicks the *Date* option button, he can view only the records that fit within a specified date range. The Click event contains the following code:

```
Private Sub optDate_Click()
On Error GoTo Err_optDate

 strQuery = "Select * from Complaints Order By Date"
 datComplaints.RecordSource = strQuery
 datComplaints.Refresh
 Exit Sub

Err_optDate:
 MsgBox Err.Number & "Occurred in optDate Click"
 Resume Next
End Sub
```

By clicking on the *Building* option button, the user can view the complaints logged for a specific building. The following code is in the optBuilding Click event:

```
Private Sub optBuilding_Click()
On Error GoTo Err_optBuilding

 strQuery = "Select * from Complaints Order By Building"
 datComplaints.RecordSource = strQuery
 datComplaints.Refresh
 Exit Sub

Err_optBuilding:
 MsgBox Err.Number & "Occurred in optBuilding Click"
 Resume Next

End Sub
```

The Select Records button is used to execute the query. The following code is in the cmdRunQuery Click event:

```
Private Sub cmdRunQuery_Click()
On Error GoTo Err_cmdRunQuery

 strQuery = "Select * from Complaints "

 If chkDate.Value Then

     strQuery = strQuery & "where Date Between #" & txtStartDate.Text

         & "# And #" & txtEndDate.Text & "#"

 End If

 If chkBuilding.Value Then

 If chkDate.Value Then
   strQuery = strQuery & " AND "
 Else
   strQuery = strQuery & " WHERE "
 End If
 strQuery = strQuery & " Building = '" & dbBuildings.Text & "'"

 End If

 If chkEmployee.Value Then

 If chkDate.Value Or chkBuilding.Value Then
   strQuery = strQuery & " AND "
 Else
   strQuery = strQuery & "  WHERE "
 End If
 strQuery = strQuery & " Employee = '" & dbEmployees.Text & "'"

 End If

 strQuery = strQuery & " ORDER BY Date"
 datComplaints.RecordSource = strQuery
 datComplaints.Refresh

 Exit Sub

Err_cmdRunQuery:

 MsgBox Err.Description & " Occurred in cmdRunQuery Click"
 Resume Next
End Sub
```

Executing the Complaints Program

Let's say we wanted to run the complaints program. When the form first loads, you would see the complaints records listed in the grid in no particular order. Click on the *Date* option button in the *Order By* frame, and you'll see the records listed by date.

Now let's say that we wanted to view the complaints entered in the months of January and February. You can do that by using these steps:

- Click on the *Start Date* text box and enter 1/1/98.
- Click on the *End Date* text box and enter 2/28/98.
- Click the *Select Dates* check box.
- Click the *Select Records* command button.

The grid will then be updated to include only those records with a date in this range. The user could open the Buildings drop-down list and choose a building, say *University Hospital*. She then clicks the *Building* check box and then the *Select Records* command button. You would then see listed the complaints for University Hospital entered between the specified date range.

How the Complaints Program Works

The complaints program works by building up an SQL statement based on user choices. Let's examine the code in each Click event.

Code in the cmdAll Click Event

Let's start by taking a look at the code in the cmdAll command button. When the user clicks this button, the grid displays all of the records in the complaints table. To see how this works, let's take another look at the code:

```
Private Sub cmdAll_Click()

On Error GoTo Err_cmdAll

  strQuery = "Select * from Complaints"
  datComplaints.RecordSource = strQuery
  datComplaints.Refresh
  optDate.Value = False
  optBuilding.Value = False
  Exit Sub


Err_cmdAll:
MsgBox Err.Description & "  Occurred in cmdAll Click."
  Resume Next
End Sub
```

The first step is to build the SQL statement. To display all the records from the complaints table, we need to build an SQL statement with a Select clause that tells us which fields to include from the table and a From clause that tells us which table to get the records from. Recall that we can use the * character to tell the Jet engine to retrieve all fields. So we can use this SQL statement:

```
strQuery = "Select * from Complaints"
```

To use an SQL statement with a data control, you simply assign the SQL statement as the data control's record source. The RecordSource property is of type String, so this is why we use a string variable, strQuery, to hold the SQL statement. Next, you need to issue a call to the data control's Refresh method to requery the database. This is what we did with these two statements:

```
datComplaints.RecordSource = strQuery
datComplaints.Refresh
```

The final statements reset the option buttons and check boxes to reflect that all of the records are displayed.

Code in the Option Button Click Event

When the user clicks on the optDate option button, the following code is executed:

```
Private Sub optDate_Click()
On Error GoTo Err_optDate

  strQuery = "Select * from Complaints Order By Date"
  datComplaints.RecordSource = strQuery
  datComplaints.Refresh
  Exit Sub

Err_optDate:
  MsgBox Err.Number & "Occurred in optDate Click"
  Resume Next

End Sub
```

The first statement builds the SQL statement and assigns it to the string variable strQuery:

```
strQuery = "Select * from Complaints Order By Date"
```

In the `Select` clause, we specify that we want to return all fields from the table:

```
Select *
```

In the `From` clause, we specify that we want the records from the complaints table. The SQL statement now reads:

```
Select * from Complaints
```

Finally, we specify that we want to sort the records based on the values of the Date field. Recall that sort order is ascending by default:

```
Select * from Complaints Order By Date
```

The last two statements assign the SQL string to the `datComplaints` data control record source and then call the Refresh method to update the data structure of the data control:

```
datComplaints.RecordSource = strQuery
datComplaints.Refresh
```

The `optBuilding Click` event works in a similar manner.

Code in the `cmdRunQuery` Click Event

When the user clicks the `cmdRunQuery` command button, the following code is executed:

```
Private Sub cmdRunQuery_Click()
On Error GoTo Err_cmdRunQuery

 strQuery = "Select * from Complaints "

 If chkDate.Value Then

 strQuery = strQuery & "where Date Between #" & txtStartDate.Text _
        & "# And #" & txtEndDate.Text & "#"
 End If

 If chkBuilding.Value Then

  If chkDate.Value  Then
    strQuery = strQuery & " AND "
  Else
    strQuery = strQuery & " WHERE "
  End If
```

```
    strQuery = strQuery & " Building = '" & dbBuildings.Text & "'"

End If

If chkEmployee.Value Then

  If chkDate.Value Or chkBuilding.value Then
    strQuery = strQuery & " AND "
  Else
    strQuery = strQuery & "  WHERE "
  End If

  strQuery = strQuery & " Employee = '" & dbEmployees.Text & "'"

End If

strQuery = strQuery & " ORDER BY Date"
datComplaints.RecordSource = strQuery
datComplaints.Refresh

Exit Sub

Err_cmdRunQuery:
MsgBox Err.Description & " Occurred in cmdRunQuery Click"
Resume Next
```

End Sub This code builds an SQL statement with a Where clause to filter the records displayed in the grid. Since we are giving the user the ability to filter based on three fields, we need to use the AND keyword to add an expression to the SQL statement for each field the user has chosen to sort on.

In the first line of code, we initialize the SQL statement to include the Select clause and the From clause:

```
strQuery = "Select * from Complaints "
```

This tells the database engine that we want to include all fields from the complaints table.

Next, we test to see if the user clicked the chkDate check button:

```
If chkDate.Value Then
  strQuery = strQuery & "where Date Between #" & txtStartDate.Text _
       & "# And #" & txtEndDate.Text & "#"
End If
```

If the user clicked the chkDate check box, chkDate.Value will evaluate to True and the code will be executed. Inside the If statement a Where clause is added to the strQuery variable. Here we specify that the records returned have a value in the date field in the range the user specified in the txtStartDate and txtEndDate text boxes. We use the

BETWEEN . . . AND keywords to specify an inclusive range, and the date values are delimited by the # character.

The next If statement contains the following code, which is executed if the user clicked the chkBuilding check box:

```
If chkBuilding.Value Then

   If chkDate.Value  Then
     strQuery = strQuery & " AND "
   Else
     strQuery = strQuery & " WHERE "
   End If
   strQuery = strQuery & " Building = '" & dbBuildings.Text & "'"

End If
```

First we test to see whether or not the user has also clicked the chkDate check box. If so, the keyword Where has already been added to the SQL statement, so we don't want to add it again. Also, we need to use the AND keyword to build a compound Where clause. If the chkDate button was not clicked by the user, the Else statement will execute, and we add the Where clause to the strQuery variable.

In the next line of code we specify that we want to filter records based on the value of the Building field. The records are filtered to the value the user selected in the dbBuildings DBCombo box, which is returned in the dbBuildings.text property. Comparison strings in SQL statements need to be enclosed in single quotation marks, so we append a single quotation mark before and after the dbBuidlings.text value.

The next piece of code executed is the following:

```
If chkEmployee.Value Then

   If chkDate.Value Or chkBuilding.value Then
     strQuery = strQuery & " AND "
   Else
     strQuery = strQuery & "  WHERE "
   End If
     strQuery = strQuery & " Employee = '" & dbEmployees.Text & "'"
End If
```

This code works just like the code for the chkBuilding check box. First, we see if the user clicked the chkEmployee check box. Then we test whether the chkDate or chkBuilding check boxes were also selected. If so, we need to append the "AND" keyword. If they weren't checked, we need to append the "WHERE" keyword. Finally, we build the SQL statement so that it will filter the records returned based on the value that the user selected for the Employee field, which is enclosed in single quotation marks because it is a text field.

The final piece of code includes these lines:

```
strQuery = strQuery & " ORDER BY Date"
datComplaints.RecordSource = strQuery
datComplaints.Refresh
```

First, we add an `Order By` clause to the SQL statement so the returned records are sorted by date. Then we assign the `strQuery` variable to the `datComplaints` RecordSource property and refresh the `datComplaints` data control to display the filtered records in the grid.

Embedded SQL

You can embed or save queries as part of your database. If you are building a database with the Visual Data Manager, type your query in the SQL Statement window (see Fig. 10-5). When you click the *Save* button, you will be prompted to enter a `QueryDef` name. You can then specify whether or not this is an SQL pass-through query. An SQL pass-through query is a query that you executed on the database without returning the rows. For example, you may want to update a set of records.

The query will be saved as part of the database. You will see it displayed in the database window or be able to view it within Access. The query can then be used as a record source, either for a data control or in code. You can also use queries created in Access as data sources for your project. An embedded query may not provide as much flexibility as using dynamic SQL.

Figure 10-5
Building an embedded SQL Statement with VisData.

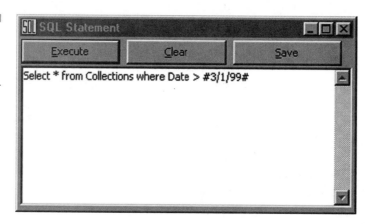

Multiuser Considerations

When developing multiuser applications, we need to concern ourselves with the problem of several users trying to access the same data at once. This is known as a *concurrency* problem. Concurrency problems are managed by using record locking. This prevents users from accessing a record for a certain period during which it is locked. While the record is locked, the user who locked the record can save his data. There are several types of locking that can be used with Visual Basic. Most of the time you will choose between "pessimistic" and "optimistic" locking.

Pessimistic Locking

The first type of locking strategy is known as *pessimistic locking*. This can be done by setting the LockType property of an ADO data control to `adLockPessimistic`. This locks the record immediately after a call to the Edit method has been issued. The record remains locked, and therefore inaccessible to other users, until the record is saved with an Update method.

Optimistic Locking

Another type of locking strategy we are concerned with is known as *optimistic locking*. This type will lock the record for a shorter time period. With optimistic locking, the record is only locked when a call to the Update method is issued. This type of locking may be less secure since other users can make changes to the record while the first user is editing it. You can use optimistic locking by setting the LockType property to `adLockOptimistic`.

Read-Only

The default LockType is `adLockReadOnly`. This makes the `recordset` read-only. This is useful in situations where data changes aren't necessary. For example, you can use read-only locking when generating a report.

Batch Optimistic

Batch optimistic locking is similar to optimistic locking. However, in this case, it requires the use of an `UpdateBatch` rather than the Update method. To use batch optimistic locking, set the LockType property to `adLockBatchOptimistic`.

Database Transactions

Database transactions enable the developer to make several changes with a single command. Transactions can be used to group together a set of program statements, which can then be canceled or "rolled back" if the transaction fails. This can help make your code more robust.

To use database transactions, there are three commands that can be used. These are `BeginTrans`, `CommitTrans`, and `RollbackTrans`. `BeginTrans` starts the transaction. `CommitTrans` is used in an attempt to commit the transaction, while `RollbackTrans` can be used to cancel it. Transaction methods are members of a connection object. A transaction should be used when a large number of commands or a large amount of data will be used. If the network goes down or the user's application crashes, the transactions are rolled back and data loss is avoided. The following example illustrates how to use the transaction methods.

```
Dim conMyConnection As ADODB.Connection
Dim rsDataSet As ADODB.Recordset

Set conMyConnection = CreateObject("ADODB.Connection")
Set rsDataSet = CreateObject("ADODB.Recordset")

myconn.Open "Provider=Microsoft.Jet.OLEDB.3.51;" _
    '   & "Data Source=" & strDataBase

myrecordset.Open "Select * from Authors", myconn, , adLockOptimistic

myconn.BeginTrans
myrecordset.AddNew
myrecordset("Author") = "Jimmy Carter"
myrecordset("Year Born") = myint

If myint < 1900 Then
    myconn.RollbackTrans
    MsgBox "TRANSACTION CANCELED"
    myconn.close
    myrecordset.close
    Set myconn = Nothing
    Set myrecordset = Nothing
    Exit Sub
End If
myrecordset.Update
myconn.CommitTrans
```

We have set dates of birth before 1900 as invalid. If the year set for this record is less than 1900, we issue a rollback for the myconn connection object.

EXAMPLE: PROGRAMMING THE ADO DATA CONTROL

To get a feel for how the ADO data control is used, let's build a simple application. The application we will build is a database app for a vending machine company (see Figure 10-6). Our hypothetical company maintains several soda and snack machines throughout town and needs to maintain an inventory of machines, food, and drinks as well as keep a record of the money collected from each machine. The database will include five tables, described in the following sections: customers, products, machines, suppliers, and collections.

Note: The code in this example will include error-handling routines. If you are not familiar with error handling in Visual Basic, you may wish to read Chapter 13 first. However, knowledge of error handling is not necessary to understand the operation of this program.

Figure 10-6
The Vending Machine Manager database app.

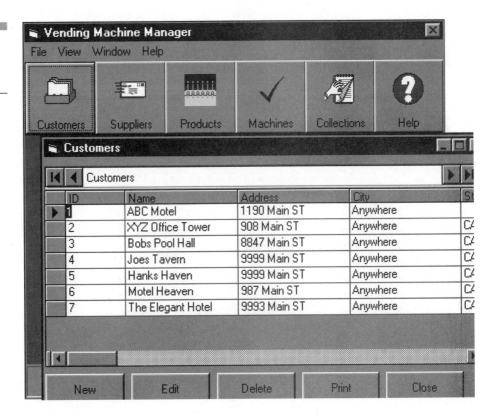

Customers

The customers table stores information about the clients, that is, the locations where vending machines are kept. This will include motels, office buildings, schools, and other assorted locations. The fields in the customers table are listed in the following table:

Field Name	Data Type	Size
ID	AutoNumber	Long
Name	Text	30
Address	Text	50
City	Text	50
State	Text	2
Zip Code	Text	10
Phone	Text	13
Fax	Text	13

Products

The products table will track the product inventory for the vending company. Here we will track each product and the quantity on hand. Each product will be tracked by a product number provided by the manufacturer. *Supplier* is a foreign key from a supplier's table; it's the AutoNumber field that uniquely identifies each supplier.

Field Name	Data Type	Size
ID	Text	10
Description	Text	50
Product Type	Text	20
Quantity	Numeric	Integer
Supplier	Numeric	Long

Machines

The vending company will have several machines on hand, including soda machines, gum machines, and snack machines. We need to track each machine along with its storage location. The storage location is a foreign key, provided by the ID field of the customers table.

Field Name	Data Type	Size
ID	Text	20
Description	Text	50
Type	Text	20
Storage Location	Numeric	Long

Suppliers

Here we will maintain a list of companies that supply the soda, candy, and chips for the vending company. This table looks just like the customers table. We could place both the customers and suppliers in the same table and add a type field to distinguish them, but I prefer to have the suppliers in a separate table.

Collections

The collections table will track the money collected from each machine on a weekly basis.

Field Name	Data Type	Size
Date	Date/Time	N/A
Customer	Numeric	Long
Customer Name	Text	50
Amount	Numeric	Currency

The Main Window

Now that we've defined the structure of the database, we are ready to start building the application. The first step is to create the main window, which we will use as a gateway to each table in the database, followed by other functions that the program will provide. These other functions will include printing reports, backing up the data, and other bookkeeping operations. We've built our main window with a pull-down menu system, command buttons for easy one-step access, and a status bar to display information to the user (see Fig. 10-7). For example, the user can open the customers table by clicking on the first command button. The main window doesn't do much; the code behind each button will typically be one or two lines, which calls another function or opens a form. For example, we are allowing the user to view the customers form

Figure 10-7
A main window.

by clicking the command button or by selecting *View Customers* from the pull-down menu. Each `Click` event looks like this:

```
Private Sub cmdOpenCustomers_Click()
 Call ShowCustomers
End Sub
```

The `ShowCustomers` function is a simple function placed in a standard code module to show the following form:

```
Public Sub ShowCustomers()
On Error GoTo errOpenCustomers:
 frmCustomers.Show
 Exit Sub
errOpenCustomers:
 MsgBox Err.Number & " " & Err.Description
 Resume Next
End Sub
```

The Customers Form

When the user clicks the *Customers* button, the application will display the data from the customers table in a grid format. The purpose of this form is to provide the user with a means to navigate the records in the table. We won't actually let the user manipulate the data, however. We will do that on a separate form. The customers form is displayed in Fig. 10-8.

The form has one ADO data control and one data grid. This is an OLE DB data grid, which is an OLE DB-aware version of the DB grid control. We can bind this type of grid to an ADO data control. This is done by setting the Data Source property of the grid. The ADO data control on this form is named `adoCustomers`, so we click open the data source property of the grid and set it to this value.

The customers grid has two command buttons, *New* and *Edit*, which can be used to add new records or edit records in the table. This is done by opening another form, called `frmEditCustomer`. If the *New* button is clicked, `frmEditCustomer` will add a new record to the database. If the *Edit* button was clicked, it will search for the record in question and display it for editing. We need a way to distinguish between these two situations, and we will do so by using a public variable of type Boolean.

Figure 10-8
The Customers form.

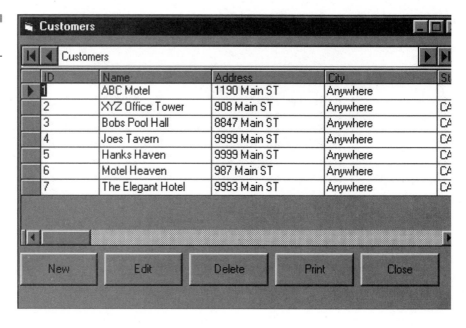

The variable will be set to True if we are going to edit a record that is already in the database. The code in the New Click event will look like this:

```
Private Sub cmdNew_Click()
On Error Resume Next
 'set the mode for new record
 blnEdit = False
 Call ShowCustomer
End Sub
```

If we are going to edit an existing record, we also need to pass the primary key to the frmEditCustomer form. This is also done with a public variable. The code in the Edit Click event looks like this:

```
Private Sub cmdEdit_Click()
On Error GoTo errEditClick
 'get the customer id
 lngCustomerId = adoCustomers.Recordset("ID")
 blnEdit = True
 Call ShowCustomer
 Exit Sub
errEditClick:
 MsgBox Err.Number & " " & Err.Description & " Occurred in Customer
   Edit Click Event."
 Resume Next
End Sub
```

The `ShowCustomer` procedure has one line, to show the `frmEditCustomer` form:

```
Private Sub ShowCustomer()
On Error Resume Next
 frmEditCustomer.Show
End Sub
```

The `frmEditCustomers` form is shown in Figure 10-9. This form lets the user enter data for a new record or edit the fields in an existing record. The form load event is used to determine whether or not we are going to add a new record. If this is an edit, it searches for the record specified by the primary key value stored in `lngCustomerID`:

```
Private Sub Form_Load()
On Error GoTo errFormLoad
 Dim intResponse As Integer
 'load state abbreviations into combo box
 Call LoadStates
 'check the mode
 'If the user wants to edit an existing record,
 'blnEdit will be set to TRUE
 If blnEdit = True Then
   'edit an existing customer
   'move to the first record
   adoCustomer.Recordset.MoveFirst
   'find the record in question
   adoCustomer.Recordset.Find "[ID] = " & frmCustomers.lngCustomerId,
     , adSearchForward
```

Figure 10-9
The `frmEdit`
`Customers` form.

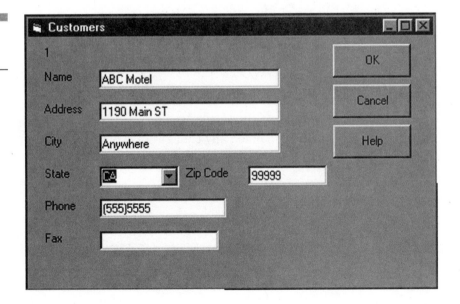

```
    If adoCustomer.Recordset.EOF Then
      intResponse = MsgBox("Error : Cannot Locate Record. Add New
        Customer?", vbYesNo)
      If intResponse = vbYes Then
        adoCustomer.Recordset.AddNew
      Else
       Unload Me
      End If 'response = yes
     End If  'end of file readed
    Else
      adoCustomer.Recordset.AddNew
    End If 'mode is edit
    Exit Sub
errFormLoad:
    MsgBox Err.Description & " " & "Occurred in frmEditCustomer
      FormLoad"
    Resume Next
End Sub
```

To search for the record, we use the Find method of the `recordset` object. If the end of the file is reached, this means that the record in question could not be located. We give the user the opportunity to add a new record if this is the case.

If the user clicks the *OK* button, we save the record by using the Update method of the `recordset` object. This is done with the following code:

```
Private Sub cmdOK_Click()
On Error GoTo errSvRecord
 'attempt to save the record
  adoCustomer.Recordset.Update
  Unload Me
  Exit Sub
errSvRecord:
  MsgBox Err.Number & Err.Description
  Resume Next
End Sub
```

If the user clicks *Cancel*, we use the Cancel method of the `recordset` object to abandon any changes that have been made:

```
Private Sub cmdCancel_Click()
On Error GoTo errCancel
  adoCustomer.Recordset.Cancel
  Unload Me
  Exit Sub
errCancel:
  MsgBox Err.Number & Err.Description
  Resume Next
End Sub
```

When the user clicks the `frmEditCustomers` form, control returns to the `frmCustomers` form, which displays the data in a grid format. We need to update the grid to reflect the most recent data when this happens. We can use the Refresh method of the ADO data control in the Form Activate method to make this happen:

```
Private Sub Form_Activate()
On Error Resume Next
  adoCustomers.Refresh
End Sub
```

CHAPTER 11

Putting It All Together

Making Databases and Objects Work Together

Now that we've had an introduction to database programming, we can turn to the problem of integrating objects and databases. The goal is to build a three-tiered program. The first tier of the application is the user interface or UI tier. The second tier of the application is the business or application logic tier. The second tier contains the classes and business rules or application logic that define how the classes behave. The third tier is the data processing tier.

Generally, we will build an ActiveX in-process component for the middle tier. This component will contain all of the classes that define the objects and logic of the program. The middle tier will also contain procedures for interacting with the database. This in effect hides the data processing from the UI portion of the application. The UI tier gets data for presentation to the user by declaring objects of the middle tier. In this brief chapter, we will consider how we will get the data from the database into the objects we have defined.

At the end of Chapter 8, we built a simple bank simulation program. When we presented the program we didn't say how we got the data, that is, the customers and all of the account information. We can do this in the middle tier by using ADODB connection and `recordset` objects. The object definitions that we built with our classes will correspond to the underlying structure of the database. By using a `recordset` object, we can loop through the `recordset` and load the data into a collection of objects. For the bank simulation, we do this for the customers and accounts collection with two procedures:

```
Public Sub LoadAccounts()

Dim conAccounts As New ADODB.Connection
Dim rsAccounts As New ADODB.Recordset
Dim objAccount As New clsAccount
Dim strKey As String

conAccounts.Provider = "Microsoft.Jet.OLEDB.3.51"
conAccounts.Open 'Data Source = D:\McGraw-Hill\Code Samples\Bank.mdb"

rsAccounts.Open "Accounts", conAccounts

Do While rsAccounts.EOF = False
  Set objAccount = New clsAccount
  objAccount.CustomerID = rsAccounts("CustomerID")
  objAccount.AccountType = rsAccounts("Type")
  objAccount.Balance = rsAccounts("Balance")
```

```
    strKey = objAccount.CustomerID
    colAccounts.Add objAccount, strKey
    rsAccounts.MoveNext
    Set objAccount = Nothing
Loop

rsAccounts.Close
conAccounts.Close

Set rsAccounts = Nothing
Set conAccounts = Nothing

End Sub

Public Sub LoadCustomers()

  Dim conCustomers As ADODB.Connection
  Dim rsCustomers As ADODB.Recordset
  Dim objCustomer As clsCustomer
  Dim intKey As Integer

  Set conCustomers = New ADODB.Connection
  Set rsCustomers = New ADODB.Recordset

  conCustomers.Provider = "Microsoft.Jet.OLEDB.3.51"
  conCustomers.Open "Data Source = D:\McGraw-Hill\Code Samples\
    Bank.mdb"

  rsCustomers.Open "Customers", conCustomers
  intKey = 1

Do While rsCustomers.EOF = False
  Set objCustomer = New clsCustomer
  objCustomer.CustomerID = rsCustomers("CustomerID")
  objCustomer.Name = rsCustomers("Name")
  objCustomer.InBank = False
  colCustomers.Add objCustomer, CStr(intKey)
  rsCustomers.MoveNext
  Set objCustomer = Nothing
  intKey = intKey + 1
Loop

rsCustomers.Close
conCustomers.Close

Set rsCustomers = Nothing
Set conCustomers = Nothing

End Sub
```

Each procedure works in the same way. For example, consider the LoadCustomers procedure. The first step is to open the database with the ADODB connection object. In this case, we are opening a local data source, but in practice you will probably open a data source that is on a remote server.

Once the recordset is connected, we can loop through it to read the data. Each time through the loop, we place the data in an object variable, objCustomers. This object variable is a clsCustomers variable. You will recall that we defined the clsCustomers class module in Chapter 8. Next, we add the customer to the colCustomers collection. We give each element of the collection a key value that can be used to retrieve a specific customer later on. In this case, we are simply keeping a running count of customers.

When the application is done presenting data to the user and going through any manipulation, we need to save the data back to the database. This is essentially done in the reverse order of what we did here.

Sharing Components

In the next chapter, we will see how to build ActiveX controls. The middle tier, which is represented by the classes and these routines to read and write data to the database, can be placed in an ActiveX component. This component can be shared among applications. As long as we maintain a backward-compatible interface, we can modify the component without changing the UI or database tier of the application. Likewise, if modifications are made to the data processing side, the UI tier will not be aware of it. This provides a flexible, object-oriented application to the user.

CHAPTER 12

Advanced Topics in Visual Basic

Threads, Processes, and Asynchronous Program Flow

With each release of Visual Basic, its power continues to grow. One important addition in the past few years has been the ability to create ActiveX servers, dynamic link libraries, and controls. This capability has greatly extended the reach of Visual Basic, turning it from a tool that could be used mainly for database front ends and standalone apps into a full-blown Windows development environment.

Up to this point, we've been talking about a single, standalone application going about its business in a single thread of execution. While many programs are still written this way, since the release of Windows 95 the use of *multithreading* has enabled programmers to get the most out of their applications by boosting performance. With the release of version 5.0 of Visual Basic, programmers had the ability to build multithreaded components without having to use a more difficult programming language like C++. However, the ability to use multithreading was limited; for one thing, you could not have any user interface in a server that used multithreading. With the release of version 6.0, this is no longer the case, making multithreading with Visual Basic a more attractive option.

In addition to multithreading, the last two releases of Visual Basic have greatly extended its power by providing the ability to build ActiveX servers. These servers come in two varieties. An *in-process* or DLL server is a Visual Basic version of the familiar Windows dynamic link library. An *out-of-process* or EXE server is an executable program that can expose its objects for use in other applications, known as clients. These types of applications help the Visual Basic programmer take full advantage of the Windows operating system, which among other things provides a powerful means for communicating between applications. Visual Basic can also develop ActiveX controls, formerly the private domain of C++ programmers.

Another new feature that extends the capabilities of Visual Basic is the ability to develop DHTML applications. We all know that the World Wide Web is becoming an integral part of everyone's lives. Microsoft has recognized this fact and is moving to make its products more Internet-aware and -capable. Visual Basic is no exception. You'll find that the same ease of use that made Visual Basic so popular for Windows development will make developing DHTML applications a breeze.

In this chapter, we'll talk about using multithreading in a Visual Basic application. Then we'll explore building a server in Visual Basic and compare the relative benefits of in-process and out-of-process servers. Next, we will see how Visual Basic can be used to create an ActiveX control. Finally we'll take a look at the use of Visual Basic to build a DHTML application.

Processes and Threads

A *process* consists of a single executing application and all of the resources that have been allocated for it by Windows. For example, a single instance of Microsoft Word is a process. A standalone executable that you created and compiled in Visual Basic is a process. Each process runs inside its own virtual computer, where the application thinks that it has the whole system to itself. It will have its own memory or address space separate from other processes. A *thread*, meanwhile, is a single path of execution in the computer. Each process has at least one thread, and in the 32-bit Windows operating system, a process can have many threads running together at the same time. Each thread, however, can only belong to a single process. When a process has many threads, this is called multithreading.

Advantages of Multithreading Applications

Each thread will get a time slice of the microprocessor, which is an allotted time for the thread to execute. Inside Windows, threads are prioritized by the operating system. When a thread's time slice is up, Windows will choose the thread with the highest priority and give it the processor. To determine thread priority, Windows considers the threads' internal priority as well as whether or not the thread is waiting for something, such as a background print job. You can see from this model that threads will not only be competing with the "outside" for processor time, but they also compete with threads in the same application.

There are a variety of circumstances when multithreading can be useful to an application. The first factor to consider is the possibility of running the application on a machine with two or more processors. If this is what you will be doing, your application is a good candidate for multithreading. In this kind of scenario, Windows will be able to allocate one thread to each processor, which can drastically improve the performance of the application. In the ideal case, the number of threads used should match the number of processors. If you are running on a single processor, multithreading may not be a good idea, and it might actually hurt the performance of the application. The next question to ask is what kinds of tasks will the application be doing? If a program has several tasks that require a lot of time to complete but could be run concurrently, it is a good candidate for multithreading. For example, let's consider a program that does some number crunching on a large chunk of data, say, calculating statistics on the data stored in a large array. If each piece of data could be considered independently and we were running on two processors, we could finish the task quite a bit faster by splitting the data into two chunks and using a thread to process each one.

Another area where number crunching might benefit from multithreading is when you have a series of operations that operate in assembly-line fashion. Let's suppose we have operations A, B, and C. The operations proceed in sequence, so A processes some data, feeds it to B, which completes its task and then feeds the data to C. As operations B and C start crunching numbers, operation A has fetched some more data, and when it's done with that data, it again feeds it to B. The process will continue until A runs out of data. If we also imagine that we happen to be working on a computer with three processors, we can imagine that this program could benefit from multithreading. By giving each operation its own thread, A, B, and C can be working simultaneously. This will work quite a bit faster than running the process in an entirely sequential fashion on a single processor.

Many tasks that need to be done in Windows suffer from a "hurry-up-and-wait" mode of operation. For example, we could consider printing or disk I/O. These types of tasks are suitable for multithreading since your application can move on to other things while such a thread is running in the background. If an application will run on at least two processors, you can put tasks like this into their own threads to improve performance. When running on a single processor, however, you should keep in mind that multithreading can actually make performance worse. This is because the operating system will be adding overhead to an operation by having to swap threads in and out of the lone processor until they are completed. As a result, if you know you'll be on a single processor, you should probably stay with a single thread.

Apartment Model Multithreading

Visual Basic uses a type of multithreading known as *apartment model* threading. In this type of threading, the objects in each thread run in a space known as an apartment. Each apartment is completely isolated from all others. This isolation includes global data; each thread will get its own copy. While this increases the safety of operation, it means that you cannot use global data to communicate between threads. Note that even when an application is not multithreaded, it is still using the apartment model with its single thread running in a single apartment.

In previous versions of Visual Basic, you had to set the project for *unattended execution*, which meant that a multithreaded application could not have any user interface. With version 6.0 however, this is no longer the case. You can still select the unattended execution option if desired, but this means that all forms of user interaction will not be allowed. This includes any message boxes or error messages.

Specifying the Threading Model

The threading model can be specified from the General tab of the Project Properties dialog (see Fig. 12-1). When specifying the thread model

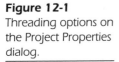

Figure 12-1
Threading options on the Project Properties dialog.

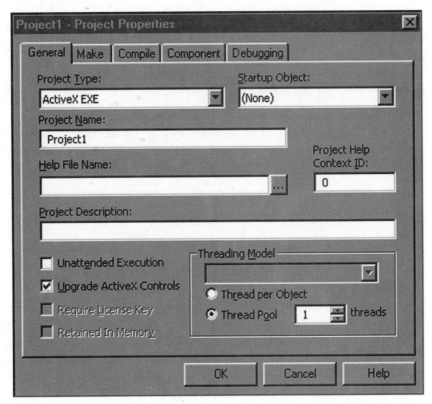

used, the available choices will be determined by what type of project you are building. For an in-process server or DLL, your choices are limited because the client program furnishes the threads and as such will determine the number used. You can, however, specify if you want the DLL to be single threaded or use apartment model threading. Again, keep in mind that if you select apartment model threading, the number of threads will be determined by the client application.

For an ActiveX EXE project, you have two choices. These are *Thread per Object* and *Thread Pool*. Thread Pool is the default selection for an ActiveX EXE project. If you select *Thread Pool*, you can specify the number of threads used by your application. As objects are created in a thread pool, Visual Basic associates each object with the next available thread. The advantage of this type of threading is that you can specify the number of threads and try to match that to the number of processors for the optimum performance.

With Thread Per Object, when a client application requests an object, a new thread is created. That means each object gets its own thread. While this sounds good at first, in practice this can cause problems. With each object getting its own thread, the operating system might get bogged down with too many threads. That means the application will actually end up worse off than if it had been single threaded. If you think a large number of objects in your server may be referenced, use a thread pool.

Identifying a Thread

A thread can be identified by its Win32 ThreadID. Visual Basic allows you to access this information from the App object. The ThreadID property is type Long, and can be returned with this line of code:

```
Dim lngThreadID As Long

lngThreadID  = App.ThreadID
```

Events

In the old days, a program typically started execution in a procedure called *main* and accomplished its task by going through a series of sequential steps. With the advent of the Windows operating system, this model has changed. Now it's the user who drives program flow, by initiating events. Events can also be generated automatically by the system, such as a form load event.

When you are building an ActiveX server, an event can also be a useful tool for communication with the client. For example, when your server completes some task such as writing a file to disk, it can raise an event to notify the client that the operation was completed. It will be up to the client application to decide how to respond to the event.

The process of using events in an ActiveX EXE server involves the following steps. First, we need to cause the event to occur, or *raise* the event. To do this in your project, you'll need to

- Add an externally creatable class to your project
- Declare the event in the general declarations section of the class
- Create a procedure in the class that will raise the event

It's up to the client application to respond to the firing of the event. In a project that has a reference to the ActiveX server, this can be done with the following steps:

- Set a reference to the ActiveX EXE server.
- Declare an object of the class type defined in the server project. This declaration must use the `WithEvents` keyword.
- Write code to use the methods and properties of the class.
- Add code for the event handler.

Let's consider a simple example that will demonstrate how to raise an event. Suppose we have an ActiveX DLL with a class called `clsCalculate`. This class has one function, called `Calculate`, that performs some time-intensive calculation. When the function is finished we want it to notify the client. We can accomplish this by adding an event to the class and then raising that event when the calculation is complete. The first step is to place an event declaration in the general declarations section of the class. If we call the event `Done`, we can declare the event like this:

```
Option Explicit
Public Event Done()
```

Next, we need to force the event to occur, which is known as raising the event. Since we want to notify the client application that we're finished doing the calculation, we can raise the event as the last line in the `Calculate` subprocedure. The `Calculate` subprocedure is a public procedure in the class, and the code looks something like this:

```
Public Sub Calculate()
```

```
' to process data goes here

  RaiseEvent Done

End Sub
```

We simply use the keyword `RaiseEvent` and provide the name of the event that we wish to occur. It's the responsibility of the client application to take care of the `Done` event. Inside the client application, the first step is to open the References dialog from the Project menu and set a reference to the `Calculate` class. Once this is done, we can declare an object variable of type `Calculate`. To be able to program the events that the class has, we must declare it by using the `WithEvents` keyword:

```
Option Explicit
Private WithEvents objDoCalculations As clsCalculate
```

We do this in the general declarations section of a form or module. Now the object is declared. However, before using it we must set a reference by using the `Set` and `As New` keywords.

```
Set objDoCalculations = New clsCalculate
```

Now we can access the methods and properties of the `clsCalculate` class. This line of code will call the Calculate method:

```
Call objDoCalculations.Calculate()
```

Once the method has been invoked, we can sit back and wait for it to finish. The method will raise the `Done` event to let us know that the calculations have been completed. By clicking on the code window where you declared the object, you'll notice that Visual Basic has added the object just like it would any other object, such as a command button or text box. By clicking open the drop-down list of objects found in the upper left corner of the code window, we can find the `objDoCalculations` object that we declared. When we select it, the events for that object will be available in the Events drop-down list to the right. It is up to the client application to fill in the code necessary to respond to an event, in the same way as you would for programming any other object, such as the mousepointer or a command button. When we click on the `Done` event for the `objDoCalculations` object, we'll see an event procedure like this one:

```
Private Sub objDoCalculations_Done()

End Sub
```

Now we can place the code necessary for responding to the Done event. For this example, we'll simply display a message box informing the user that the calculations were completed:

```
Private Sub objDoCalculations_Done()

 MsgBox "Calculations Are Complete."
End Sub
```

In the following sections, we'll discuss how to build an ActiveX server. We'll explore both in-process and out-of-process components, and in doing so we'll come across some of these procedures again.

Choosing a Server Type

An ActiveX project is one that you can use to build a COM component that exposes its objects to other applications. In Visual Basic, there are five different types of ActiveX projects. These are:

- *ActiveX* EXE: An ActiveX EXE is a standalone application that can expose its objects to other programs. The objects that are exposed by this type of server can be programmatically manipulated with properties and events, but they do not provide a user interface.

- *ActiveX DLL*: Like an ActiveX EXE, this type of server exposes objects that can be programmatically manipulated without providing a user interface. In this case, however, the project builds a dynamic link library that can be linked to other applications.

- *ActiveX Document EXE*: An ActiveX document project provides a user interface that can be used in Internet Explorer. The document loads as if it is a web page but does not use HTML. Instead, it is very much like a Visual Basic form.

- *ActiveX Document DLL*: This is similar to an ActiveX Document EXE, but this type of project builds a DLL.

- *ActiveX Control*: An ActiveX control is the familiar OCX control that developers can drop into their applications to provide a user interface element or some kind of encapsulated functionality.

All ActiveX projects can be classified as in-process or out-of-process components. If the application can run as a standalone program separate from the client application, it is known as an out-of-process server.

This is because the ActiveX server will run in its own process, completely separate from the client application. An out-of-process server is a file with an .exe extension. This type of application can function on its own apart from the clients who may use its objects. A program like Microsoft Excel is an out-of-process server.

An in-process server is a dynamic link library, or DLL. It is known as in-process because the DLL is loaded into the process space of the client application. This means that it shares the memory or address space of the client. An ActiveX control is also an in-process server. Unlike an out-of-process server, an in-process server has no existence apart from the clients that use its objects.

What Type of Server to Use: Out-of-Process or In-Process?

The decision to use an in-process server or an out-of-process server will depend on many factors. Out-of-process, or EXE, servers and in-process, or DLL, servers each have their own advantages and disadvantages. Deciding which type to use will depend on how you expect the server to be used, what the performance expectations are, and how stable the server will be, among other things.

Advantages of In-Process Servers   Since an in-process server shares the address space of the client application, it will have a distinct speed advantage over out-of-process servers. This is largely because when a client uses the objects in an out-of-process server, the operating system must provide communication across process boundaries, which can be a time-consuming affair. An in-process server functions as if it were part of the client application, so this kind of communication bottleneck does not occur. So if speed is an important factor, you should use an in-process server.

An in-process server is also an appropriate choice for building a code library. This might be a library, financial or mathematical functions, or a hardware driver. Generally, a library of related functions like these won't run as a standalone application and won't have a user interface. Such a suite of functions will probably be calculation-intensive and would benefit from the speed advantage that an in-process server can provide.

If you want to build a component that the developer can drop right into an application, then you are thinking about an ActiveX control. An

ActiveX control is an in-process component. In fact, an .ocx file is really just a special type of DLL file. While a DLL won't be used to provide a user interface, an ActiveX control can be used as a building block for the user interface. If you think of the user interface as a house, an ActiveX control might be a frame or a doorknob, which go into building the house. Many ActiveX controls only provide functionality and don't appear to the user, however. An example of this type of ActiveX control is the timer control, which is invisible at run time. Since ActiveX controls are such a large part of Windows development, we'll take them up in more detail later in this chapter.

Advantages of Out-of-Process Servers 　The most glaring advantage of building an out-of-process server stems from the fact that this type of server is an EXE, or an executable file. That means that it can run as an application in its own right, apart from the client programs that use its objects. A program that has such a dual identity is known as an *application server*. You are probably already familiar with several examples of these. All of the programs in the Microsoft Office suite can function in this way, including Word, Excel, and Access. These are powerful applications in their own right, but they expose objects that can be used in a Visual Basic application to extend its functionality. If you build an out-of-process server, you can make it perform in much the same manner.

Another advantage of an out-of-process server is that you gain a margin of safety. If your server crashes, it won't bring down the client application with it because the client is running under Windows in its own process space. This is different from an in-process server or DLL. If an in-process server crashes, it's going to bring down the whole show since it's sharing the address space of the client. So if you're concerned about bringing down client applications or stability is an overriding concern, build an out-of-process server.

An out-of-process server is also desirable if it is going to be used on a remote machine. In this case, Windows will use DCOM and remote procedure calls to provide the communication with the client. Since the out-of-process server is running in a separate process, to the client it appears to be running locally. One thing to keep in mind, however, is that an out-of-process server must use *marshalling* to communicate with another process. This is a process used by Windows for cross-process communication, which may slow down the performance.

Ultimately, however, the choice of which type of server to build will depend on the functionality that it will have. We have summarized our suggestions here:

- *Speed*: If speed is a critical factor, use an in-process server.

- *Building a code library*: If you are building a calculation-intensive library of functions and/or one that will not require a user interface, use an in-process DLL server.

- *An ActiveX component*: ActiveX controls are always in-process.

- *An application server*: If you want the component to have a dual role, functioning as an application in its own right in addition to being an ActiveX server, make it an out-of-process server.

- *Distributed computing*: Use out-of-process servers if the server will be remote from the client.

Building a Dynamic Link Library

The techniques involved in building and using an ActiveX server can be illustrated by creating a dynamic link library. We will use Visual Basic to create a simple library of statistics functions that operate on a set of data stored in an array of type Double. Our dynamic link library will contain one class that will provide the client application with the ability to perform the following set of operations on the data set:

- Mean
- Median
- Variance
- Standard deviation
- Average deviation
- Z score
- Obtain the hinge location

Creating an ActiveX DLL Project

The first step is to load a new ActiveX DLL project. When you select *New* from the File menu, the New Project dialog box will open (see Fig. 12-2). Select *ActiveX DLL* and click the *OK* button. Visual Basic will create a new project with one class and will open the code window for that class.

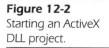

Figure 12-2
Starting an ActiveX
DLL project.

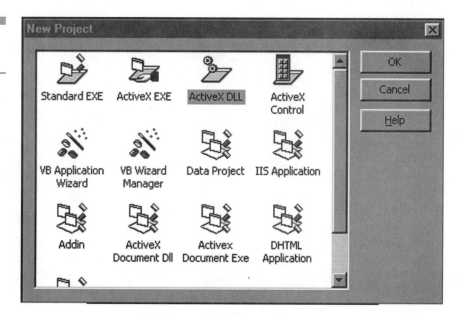

Set the Project Name of the Server for Use in the Object Browser
Once the project is open, there are two things we need to do that will
impact the way that client applications will see our objects. First, we
need to specify the *project name* for our DLL. This is important because
the project name is used by Visual Basic to represent your component in
the Project References dialog. To set the project name, open the Project
Properties dialog box. The Project Name field is found on the General tab
(see Fig. 12-3). You should enter a descriptive name that will make it
easy for clients to identify your component. For our library, we use the
name *StatisticsLib*. Note that project names cannot contain spaces.

Our next concern is the names of the classes that we will expose as
objects to client applications. You should use meaningful names for each
class because the name that you assign to the class will appear in the
Object Browser when the client sets a reference to your component. The
class name is set in the Properties window. Our project will have one
class, and we will name it *clsStats* (see Fig. 12-4).

Setting the Instancing Property ActiveX code components make
objects available to client applications by creating classes and setting
the instancing property of each class. There are five types of instancing
available for Visual Basic classes:

Figure 12-3
Setting project type,
name, and threading
model for a DLI.

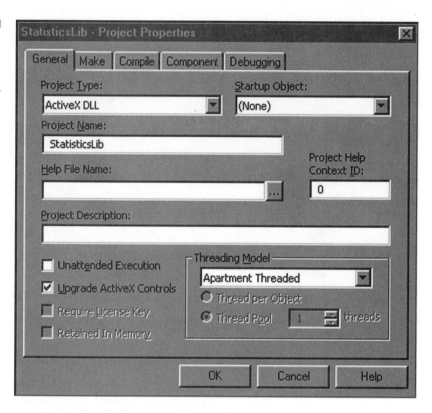

Figure 12-4
Class properties.

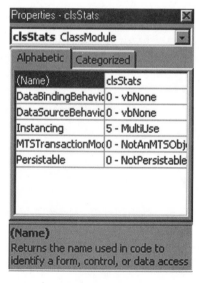

- ▪ Private: A class that has private instancing is an internal class that cannot be exposed to client applications. Private classes can be used by all types of ActiveX components, including an ActiveX control, an in-process server or DLL, and an out-of-process server or EXE.

- ▪ PublicNotCreatable: A class that is PublicNotCreatable is one that cannot be created in the client application. It can be used by the client, however, if the server creates it and then passes it on to the client. This is usually done by creating an externally creatable collection class, which itself uses the PublicNotCreatable class. The externally creatable collection class will create new instances of the PublicNotCreatable class and pass a reference to them back to the client. PublicNotCreatable classes can be used by all types of ActiveX components.

- ▪ MultiUse: A class that is MultiUse is an externally creatable class. This means that client applications can create an instance of the class by using the CreateObject method or by declaring it with the New keyword. This type of instancing is known as MultiUse because only one instance of the component is required to create all of its objects. For example, consider an ActiveX EXE that uses MultUse instancing. Only one copy of the EXE will need to be loaded even if several clients are using its objects. MultiUse instancing can be used by all types of ActiveX components.

- ▪ Global MultiUse: This is similar to MultiUse, however, in this case the client application can use the members of the class as if they were global functions and variables. The client application does not need to explicitly declare an instance of the class to use it; all it needs to do is set a reference. Global MultiUse instancing can be used with all types of ActiveX components.

- ▪ Single Use: With Single Use instancing, one instance of the component can only support one instance of the class. Returning to our example of an ActiveX EXE, if it has a class that is Single Use and if two client applications create objects of this class, two copies of the EXE will have to be loaded. Each time an instance of the class is created Windows will automatically load another instance of the component; in other words, it will launch another copy of the EXE. Each instance of the class will be running in its own thread, which can provide a safety valve for components with risky or unstable code. Single Use instancing can only be used with out-of-process, ActiveX EXE servers.

■ Global Single Use: **This works like** Single use, but the client can use the objects as if they were global variables and functions. An object of the class does not need to be explicitly declared. Since this is Single Use instancing, it can only be used with ActiveX EXE components.

It's important to remember that an ActiveX DLL or an ActiveX control cannot contain classes with Single Use instancing. The class that Visual Basic added to our DLL project is already set for MultiUse instancing, which is what we will use.

Adding a Method to an ActiveX Component

The methods of an ActiveX component work just like they do for a standard class. To add a method all we need to do is create a public sub or function procedure. For example, we can add a method called "Mean" to our statistics class that will calculate the average for a data set. The first step is to open the Add Procedure dialog box from the Tools menu (see Fig. 12-5). Mean will return a value, so we have specified *Function* as the procedure type. When Visual Basic creates the function body in the class module, we add the following code to calculate the mean:

```
Public Function mean(dblInputData() As Double, intNumItems As Integer)

'Function : Mean
'Description : Finds the mean for a set of data. Sum(X)/N

 Dim i As Integer
```

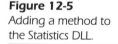

Figure 12-5
Adding a method to the Statistics DLL.

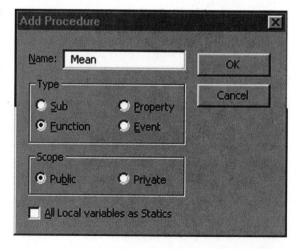

```
Dim dblSumX As Double

For i = 1 To intNumItems

  dblSumX = dblSumX + dblInputData(i)

Next i

mean = dblSumX / intNumItems

End Function
```

Adding Properties

You may recall that a class that has properties will have a set of private variables that will maintain the value of each property. Our statistics class will have two properties. One will track the standard deviation of the data set while the other will track the hinge location. Private variables that hold property values are placed in the general declarations section of the class. The variable declarations look like this:

```
Option Explicit

Private mdblStdDev As Double
Private mintHingeLocation As Integer
```

Each variable name uses Hungarian notation, with an additional prefix, m. This is used to tell us that the variables are members of the class.

Each property has a Let and a Get procedure that is used to read and set the value of the property. In this case, the properties will be read-only, so we'll leave out the Property Let procedures. The only function of the Property Get procedures will be to read the values of the private variables and return them to the client location.

```
Public Property Get HingeLocation() As Integer
  HingeLocation = mintHingeLocation
End Property

Public Property Get StandardDeviation() As Double
  StandardDeviation = mdblStdDev
End Property
```

Raising an Event

One function that our statistics DLL will provide is called the Variance. For those readers unfamiliar with statistics, it's really not that important what the variance does. However, the standard deviation depends on what the variance is; it is the square root of the variance. While this is a somewhat artificial example, we can use the dependence of the standard deviation on the variance to illustrate how an event might be used in an ActiveX component. What we'll do is use an event to tell the client that the variance has been calculated, so that the client can read the standard deviation. First we must declare the event in the general declarations section of the class:

```
Public Event VarianceCalculated()
```

We can raise this event once the variance is calculated to let the client know that it can read the standard deviation. The code for the variance method looks like this:

```
Public Function Variance(dblInputData() As Double, intNumItems As
  Integer)

' Function : Variance
' Description : Finds the sample variance for the data
'         stored in the dblInputData array,
'         and sets the standard deviation,
'         which is the square root of the variance
' Parameters: dblInputData : array of type double, contains data
'       intNumItems : total number of data points

  Dim i As Integer          'variable to function as loop counter
  Dim dblSumX As Double        'sum of the data elements
  Dim dblSumSquared As Double 'sum of data elements squared

  'loop through the array and sum the data and squares
  For i = 1 To intNumItems

    dblSumX = dblSumX + dblInputData(i)
    dblSumSquared = dblSumSquared + dblInputData(i) * dblInputData(i)

  Next i

  Variance = (dblSumSquared - (dblSumX * dblSumX / intNumItems)) / _
          (intNumItems - 1)
  'store the standard deviation
  mdblStdDev = Sqr(Variance)

  RaiseEvent VarianceCalculated 'let the client know the standard
    deviation can be read

End Function
```

When we build the client application, we'll see how to use this event. The code for the entire library is listed next. We've added methods for the average deviation, median, and z score:

```
Option Explicit

Private mdblStdDev As Double
Private mintHingeLocation As Integer

Public Event VarianceCalculated()

Public Function MeanAbsDeviation(dblInputData() As Double, intNumItems
  As Integer)

 'Function : Mean Absolute Deviation
 'Description: This function calculates the absolute value of the
  spread
 '        of values about the mean.
 'Input Parameters: dblInputData :an array of type double, contains
  the data
 '          intNumItems : total number of data points

 Dim dblSumDeviation As Double  'variable that holds the sum of x -
  xbar
 Dim dblDeviation As Double  'the deviation for each array element, x
  - xbar
 Dim dblAverage As Double      'local variable to hold the average or
  mean
 Dim i As Integer        'loop counter

 dblAverage = mean(dblInputData, intNumItems) 'find the average

 'The following loop calculates the sum of the individual deviations
 For i = 1 To intNumItems

  dblDeviation = Abs(dblInputData(i) - dblAverage)  'get absolute
   value
  dblSumDeviation = dblSumDeviation + dblDeviation

 Next i

 MeanAbsDeviation = dblSumDeviation / intNumItems

End Function

 Public Function mean(dblInputData() As Double, intNumItems As
  Integer)

 'Function : Mean
 'Description : Finds the mean for a set of data. Sum(X)/N

 Dim i As Integer
 Dim dblSumX As Double

 For i = 1 To intNumItems

  dblSumX = dblSumX + dblInputData(i)

 Next i

 mean = dblSumX / intNumItems

 End Function
```

```
Public Function Median(dblInputData() As Double, intNumItems As
  Integer)
'Function : Median
'Description: Finds the median. This function assumes that the data
  is
'        ordered.

Dim intMedianLocation As Integer

intMedianLocation = (intNumItems + 1) / 2

mintHingeLocation = (intMedianLocation + 1) / 2

'if the number of elements is even, the median is an average
If intNumItems Mod 2 = 0 Then
  Median = (dblInputData(intMedianLocation) + _
          dblInputData(intMedianLocation + 1)) / 2
Else
 Median = dblInputData(intMedianLocation)
End If

End Function
Public Function Variance(dblInputData() As Double, intNumItems As
  Integer)

' Function : Variance
' Description : Finds the sample variance for the data
'          stored in the dblInputData array,
'          and sets the standard deviation,
'          which is the square root of the variance
' Parameters: dblInputData : array of type double, contains data
'       intNumItems : total number of data points

  Dim i As Integer         'variable to function as loop counter
  Dim dblSumX As Double        'sum of the data elements
  Dim dblSumSquared As Double 'sum of data elements squared

  'loop through the array and sum the data and squares
  For i = 1 To intNumItems

  dblSumX = dblSumX + dblInputData(i)
  dblSumSquared = dblSumSquared + dblInputData(i) * dblInputData(i)
  Next i

  Variance = (dblSumSquared - (dblSumX * dblSumX / intNumItems)) _
           / (intNumItems - 1)

 'store the standard deviation
 mdblStdDev = Sqr(Variance)
  RaiseEvent VarianceCalculated 'let the client know the variance is
    calculated

End Function

Public Function Z_Score(dblInputData() As Double, intLocation As
  Integer, intNumItems As Integer)
'Function : Z_Score
'Description : Calculates the z score for the element at position
  intLocation
```

```
'Parameters : dblInputData() :  Array of data elements, type double
'       intLocation : Array index that locates the element for which to
'         find z score
'       intNumItems : total number of elements

Dim dblAverage As Double   'variable to hold the mean
Dim i As Integer    'loop counter
Dim dblStdDeviation As Double 'variable to hold the standard
  deviation

'find the mean
dblAverage = mean(dblInputData, intNumItems)

'find the standard deviation
dblStdDeviation = Sqr(Variance(dblInputData, intNumItems))
'calculate the z score

Z_Score = (dblInputData(intLocation) - dblAverage) / dblStdDeviation

End Function

Public Property Get HingeLocation() As Integer

  HingeLocation = mintHingeLocation

End Property

Public Property Get StandardDeviation() As Double

  StandardDeviation = mdblStdDev

End Property
```

Setting the Class Up for the Object Browser

Recall that the Object Browser can be used to view the properties, methods, and events that are available in a Visual Basic application. Since a client application will be programming the objects of your ActiveX server, it is a good idea to add some descriptive information that will be displayed in the Object Browser with your classes. This will make your component user friendly and in turn will keep customers happy.

The properties of each member can be set by using the Procedure Attributes dialog or by using the Properties option in the Object Browser. For this example, we will use the Procedure Attributes dialog, which can be opened from the Tools menu (see Fig. 12-6). The attributes that we set up in the Procedure Attributes dialog box will appear in the Object Browser when the client is using your objects. We can select the procedure that we want to work with by clicking open the Name drop-down list. You will see all of the properties, meth-

Figure 12-6
The Procedure
Attributes dialog.

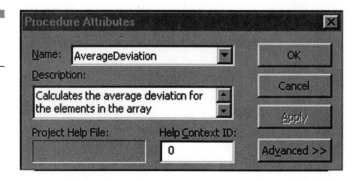

Figure 12-6
The Procedure
Attributes dialog.

ods, and events that belong to the class. In our example, since we aren't using a help file with this project, we'll simply type a description of each member in the Description field. To save the changes, click *OK*.

Compiling the DLL

An ActiveX DLL can be compiled just like an executable in Visual Basic. If you click on the File pull-down menu, you'll see an option labeled *Make ProjectName.dll*. When you select this option, Visual Basic will prompt you for the file location. Most dynamic link libraries are placed in the Windows system directory; however, you can place it in any convenient location. Just remember that the location of the .dll file is where the user of the client application will have to go in order to set a reference. We will compile our project to a file named *vbStatistics.dll*.

Creating a Client Program to Use the DLL

Now that we've built the statistics library, we are ready to create an application to use it. We'll build a standard EXE program like the one shown in Fig. 12-7. The application consists of a single form that will load an array of random values and calculate the mean, variance, standard deviation, and average deviation for the data. A single data element can also be selected and the z score for that element calculated.

Figure 12-7
The Statistics DLL test program.

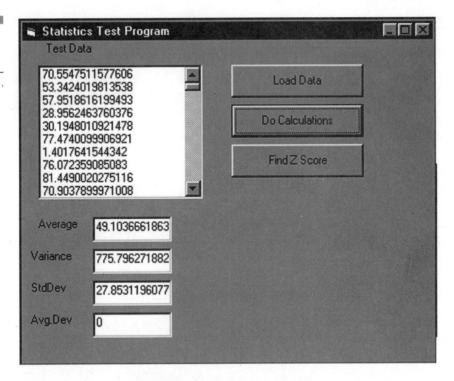

Setting a Reference to the DLL

When building the client application, the first step is to set a reference to the ActiveX server. This is done by opening the References dialog from the Project menu. If you click the Browse button, you can search for the ActiveX component you are interested in. In this case, we search for the *vbStatistics.dll* file. When you select it, you'll see the project name appear in the Available References list. This is the project name that we set in the Project Properties dialog box for the ActiveX DLL. You may recall that in this case we specified that the project name is *StatisticsLib*.

Once a reference to the server has been set, we can open the Object Browser to see the properties, methods, and events that are available (see Fig. 12-8). You'll notice that when you click open the libraries drop-down list in the upper left corner of the Object Browser, you will see the project name associated with the dynamic link library. The classes that are part of the server are listed in the left-hand pane of the browser. In this case, the only class is clsStats. By clicking on *clsStats*, we can view the members that we can use to access the statistics library.

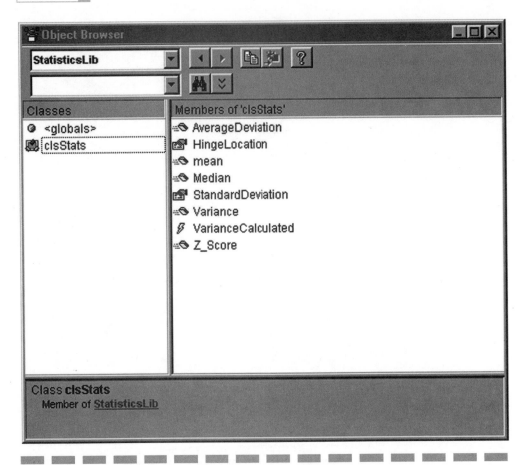

Figure 12-8 Viewing the Stats library with the Object Browser.

Creating a clsStats Object

After we have set a reference, we are ready to declare an object variable to use the library. We will declare a form-wide private variable. You will recall that the clsStats class has one event, so we'll declare our variable using the WithEvents keyword to tell Visual Basic that we want to be able to use the events of the class. The declaration looks like this:

```
Option Explicit
Private WithEvents objStatistics As clsStats
```

The variable declaration only creates the object instance. To use the object, we must also set a reference or point the variable at the object.

This is done by using the `Set... = New` construct. We can do this in the form load event:

```
Private Sub Form_Load()

  Set objStatistics = New clsStats   'set a reference to a clsStats
    object

End Sub
```

Now we're ready to use the methods and properties of the DLL.

Using the Methods and Properties of the Object

The statistics DLL works with one-dimensional arrays of type `Double`. So the first thing we need to do is declare an array to hold some data. We'll also declare variables to hold the results of various statistics functions. The number of elements in the array will be stored in a constant that we'll call `MaxItems`. With these changes in mind, the general declarations section of the form now looks like this:

```
Option Explicit

Private Const MaxItems As Integer = 1000
Private dblArrayData(1 To MaxItems) As Double

Private WithEvents objStatistics As clsStats

Private dblMean As Double
Private dblVariance As Double
Private dblStandardDeviation As Double
Private dbAbsDeviation As Double
Private dblZScore As Double
```

Before we can use the statistics library, we'll need some data to work on. This is taken care of in the Load Data command button. Since this is just a test, we'll use the built-in VB function `Rnd` to randomly generate a set of numbers. We'll then display the numbers in a list box:

```
Private Sub cmdLoadData_Click()

  Dim i As Integer

  For i = 1 To MaxItems
    dblArrayData(i) = Rnd * 100
    lstData.AddItem dblArrayData(i)
  Next i

End Sub
```

Once the data is loaded, the user can click the *Calculate* button to find the mean, variance, and average deviation of the data. In each case, we use the appropriate method of the clsStats class. This is done by simply calling the desired function from the objStatistics object that we declared earlier:

```
Private Sub cmdCalculate_Click()

 'find the mean
 dblMean = objStatistics.mean(dblArrayData, MaxItems)
 'find the variance
 dblVariance = objStatistics.Variance(dblArrayData, MaxItems)
 'find the average deviation
 dblAbsDeviation = objStatistics. MeanAbsDeviation (dblArrayData,
MaxItems)

 'display the results in the text boxes
 txtAverage.Text = CStr(dblMean)
 txtVariance.Text = CStr(dblVariance)
 txtAbsDeviation.Text = CStr(dblAbsDeviation)

End Sub
```

An additional command button allows the user to select a data point and find the z score:

```
Private Sub cmdZScore_Click()

 Dim intIndex As Integer
 Dim dblSelectedValue As Double

 intIndex = lstData.ListIndex + 1

 dblSelectedValue = dblArrayData(intIndex)
 dblZScore = objStatistics.Z_Score(dblArrayData, intIndex, MaxItems)
 MsgBox "The Z Score for " & CStr(dblSelectedValue) & " Is " &
CStr(dblZScore)

End Sub

Private Sub Form_Load()
 Set objStatistics = New clsStats
End Sub
```

Programming Events

You will recall that we built our DLL so that when the variance is calculated, an event is raised. This event tells the client application that it can read the standard deviation, which is stored in a property aptly named *StandardDeviation*. The events of an ActiveX server are avail-

Figure 12-9
Responding to an
ActiveX component's
events.

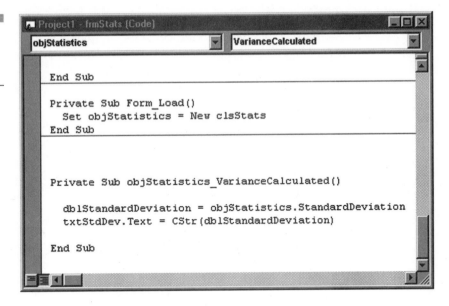

```
Project1 - frmStats (Code)

objStatistics                          VarianceCalculated

    End Sub

    Private Sub Form_Load()
      Set objStatistics = New clsStats
    End Sub


    Private Sub objStatistics_VarianceCalculated()

      dblStandardDeviation = objStatistics.StandardDeviation
      txtStdDev.Text = CStr(dblStandardDeviation)


    End Sub
```

able to the client in the code window of the form or module where an
object variable of the appropriate class type has been declared, using the
WithEvents keyword. The object will appear in the Object drop-down
list of the code window, just like any other object such as a command
button or text box. When you select the object you'll see the events that
are available in the right-hand Procedure drop-down list of the code
window. In this case, there is a single event, called Variance
Calculated (see Fig. 12-9). When this event occurs, the standard deviation can be read, so we place code in the event procedure to read the
value and display it to the user:

```
Private Sub objStatistics_VarianceCalculated()

  dblStandardDeviation = objStatistics.StandardDeviation
  txtStdDev.Text = CStr(dblStandardDeviation)

End Sub
```

ActiveX Controls

Perhaps no other factor has contributed to the popularity of Visual Basic
more than the ability to use ActiveX controls. The ActiveX control provides the developer with a simple means for creating a sophisticated

user interface, with little or no programming required. The controls that are available have a wide range of complexity and functionality. Simple controls let you add extended versions of the standard controls such as labels, command buttons, and text boxes. More sophisticated controls, such as word processor controls or communications controls, let you quickly add complex behavior to your project that would have taken months of work just a few years ago. By providing a reusable, encapsulated object, the ActiveX control has turned the idea of object-oriented programming from an abstraction into a tangible benefit to developers.

Visual Basic developers had long sought the ability to create their own controls. Until the release of version 5.0 of Visual Basic, however, this had been the private domain of the C++ programmer. This meant that you had to deal with the complexities of programming in C++ if you wanted to create your own controls. Microsoft changed all that with the release of version 5.0 of Visual Basic, which allowed developers to create ActiveX controls by using the same simple programming methods that could be applied to any application in VB.

Creating ActiveX controls is done with the `UserControl` object, which in many ways resembles a form. If you can develop an application using a form, you will be able to create your own ActiveX controls quickly and easily. You can even build an ActiveX control by using existing standard and ActiveX controls. This means that the same paradigm that makes building a user interface so easy applies to the creation of ActiveX controls as well. To develop an ActiveX control you need to understand how a user control works. In the following sections, we'll explore the user control, and then we'll see how to add our own properties, methods, and events to the control. Finally, we'll use this knowledge to create a simple ActiveX control.

Control Basics

Visual Basic has made it easy to develop an ActiveX control by using the same type of design approach that you're already used to when building forms and using modules. You begin the process of building a custom control by starting a new project in Visual Basic of type ActiveX control. Visual Basic will open a new project with a single object in the Project Explorer, which is known as a `UserControl` object. When you open a new ActiveX control project, you'll clearly see the similarities to standard Visual Basic projects you've developed in the past. The `UserControl` looks almost like a form and will be positioned in the center of the screen. If you double-click on the *UserControl* surface, Visual basic will open a code window, much as it would if you were working with a form. This familiar design approach makes it easy to develop ActiveX controls in Visual Basic.

Creating an ActiveX Control   When you create an ActiveX control in Visual Basic, you can either build your own control completely from the ground up or build it using existing controls. In either case, you will need to create the properties, methods, and events for your control. This is done in the same way as when creating VB classes. The procedure for creating your own ActiveX control generally involves the following steps:

- Create a new ActiveX control project in Visual Basic.
- If you will use any existing controls, place them on the `UserControl` object as you would when designing a form.
- Add code to handle the control's appearance. If you are using any existing controls, use the `ReSize` event. If your control has no existing controls on it, use the `Paint` event to redraw the control.
- Define the custom properties that your control will have. This will involve adding private property variables and `Property Let/Get` procedures.
- Define any custom methods and events your control will have.
- Add an About box to the control, if desired.
- Add any property pages to the control, if desired.
- Compile the control to an OCX file and test it.

Using Constituent Controls   If you use another control as part of your ActiveX control, the existing control is known as a *constituent control*. This is a powerful way to create ActiveX controls because you can bundle the functionality of an already existing component into your control without having to rewrite code. The user will have no way of knowing that your control uses other built-in controls; they are private to the `UserControl` object and can only be accessed through properties and methods that you provide. We will describe how to use constituent controls in the following sections.

Controls from Scratch   If you decide not to use any constituent controls, you will need to draw your control. This is done by using the VB drawing methods in the `Paint` event of the `UserControl` object. The drawing methods can be used to create points, lines, text, and circles.

For example, consider a hypothetical control that displays a message and paints a circle in the middle of the control. We can use the `Paint` event to draw the surface of the control:

```
Private Sub UserControl_Paint()

  Dim lngRadius As Long
  Dim lngMidWidth As Long
  Dim lngMidheight As Long
  lngMidWidth = UserControl.ScaleWidth / 2
  lngMidheight = UserControl.ScaleHeight / 2

  UserControl.FillColor = vbBlue
  UserControl.FillStyle = vbSolid

  'set the position for printing message
  'will be centered on the user control
  CurrentX = lngMidWidth - lngMidheight
  CurrentY = 0

  'set the font
  Font = "Arial"
  FontBold = True
  FontSize = 12

  'print the message
  Print strtextmessage

  'draw the circle
  lngRadius = lngMidWidth - lngMidheight
  Circle (lngMidWidth, lngMidheight), lngRadius, FillColor
End Sub
```

In this example, the built-in Visual Basic graphics methods are used to draw an image on the control's surface. When you create a control from scratch, you will use the graphics methods to draw the control's appearance. The functionality of the control will be provided by the custom properties, methods, and events that you add to the `UserControl` object. Aside from using the `Paint` event to determine the appearance of a control made from scratch, the procedures involved in creating the control are the same as those used for a control that uses constituent controls.

Using the `Resize` Event with Constituent Controls   When you build a control with constituent controls, you will have to account for the behavior of those controls as the user resizes and adjusts your control. This is because constituent controls will not resize automatically. You can account for this by adjusting the Height and Width properties in the `Resize` event of the `UserControl` object.

For example, consider a control that extends the standard list box control. This control has a single list box, which I have called *lstData* on the `UserControl`. To adjust the appearance of the list box, the following code can be placed in the `UserControl Resize` event:

```
Private Sub UserControl_Resize()
 lstData.Height = UserControl.Height
 lstData.Width = UserControl.Width

End Sub
```

This will ensure that the lstData list box will change its size appropriately as the user resizes your control.

Making a Control Invisible at Run Time   Many controls, such as the Visual Basic timer control, are only visible at design time. The user cannot see the timer control when the project is run. If you wish to have your control behave in this fashion, you can do so by setting the *InvisibleAtRunTime* property. This is a Boolean property that will make the control invisible during run time if set to True. The default value is False.

Creating Properties for an ActiveX Control

Adding a property to your ActiveX control is just like adding a property to a VB class or an ActiveX server. To create an ActiveX control property, you need two things:

- A private variable to store the value of the property
- `Property Let/Set/Get` procedures to provide the user with a means to set and read the value of the property

The private variable that stores the value of the property is declared in the General Declarations section of the `UserControl` object. `Property Let/Set/Get` procedures can be added to the `UserControl` by opening the Add Procedure dialog from the Tools menu. The `Property Get` procedure is then used to return the value of the private variable, while the `Property Let` procedure is used to set the value of the private variable. You can also use the `Property` procedures to initiate any actions or to change any properties of constituent controls that must be changed in response to the user changing the property. As an example, let's consider a custom ActiveX control that can be used to plot data. The control has a property called `NumPoints` that stores the number of points displayed on the graph. The code would look like this:

```
Option Explicit

Private mNumPoints As Integer

Public Property Get NumPoints() As Integer
  NumPoints = mNumPoints
End Property

Public Property Let NumPoints(intNewValue As Integer)
  mNumPoints = intNewValue
End Property
```

Notice that the private variable used to store the property is prefixed with an m. This is done to specify that the property is a member variable, a common notation used in object-oriented programming.

Creating Read-Only Properties   To create a read-only property, use the same method as we used for an ActiveX server or a VB class. Create the property and remove the Property Let/Set procedure. Provide only a Property Get procedure that the user can use to retrieve the value of the property.

Extender Properties   An ActiveX control has certain properties that are provided by the container where the user has situated the control. These are known as *extender properties* because they have been "extended" to the user control. These properties are accessed by using a special object, which is appropriately called the Extender object. Extender properties are the built-in properties that most controls in Visual Basic have. They include:

- Index
- Left
- Top
- TabIndex

Each of these properties is determined by the container that hosts the control. The Extender object also has built-in events, such as Got Focus and Lost Focus. Extender objects will usually not affect you, the creator of the control. They are primarily there for the user of your control.

The Ambient Object

The *Ambient object*, as its name implies, can be used to determine information about the environment of the ActiveX control. The Ambient object provides information about the state of the form where the control has been placed. This includes determining if the project is in design or run-time mode, the background color, or the foreground color of the form. A few useful properties of the ambient object are as follows:

- *Back Color*: The background color of the form.
- *Display Name*: The name the user has assigned to your control's name property.
- *User Mode*: This Boolean property can be used to determine if the control is in the design environment or in run-time mode. User Mode is False during design time, and is True during run time.

By checking the properties of the `Ambient` object, you can have your control respond appropriately. For example, you can have your control match the background color of the form or create a property that is only available at design time.

Using Constituent Control Properties The constituent controls that you add to your ActiveX control are private. This means that the user cannot access the properties, methods, and events of the constituent controls. If you want to make these members available, you will need to provide wrapper functions for them. This can be done by using the ActiveX Control Wizard or by creating your own wrapper members. Creating wrapper members is easy to do; however, you may wish to use the ActiveX Control Wizard if you have a large number of constituent members to work with.

As an example, if you want to expose the caption property of a command button that has been added to the `UserControl` object, you could do so by creating a custom property called *ButtonText*. The caption property of the command button could be exposed to the user with the `Property Let`/`Get` procedures of the ButtonText property:

```
Public Property Get ButtonText() As String

 ButtonText = cmdOK.Caption

End Property

Public Property Let ButtonText(ByVal strNewValue As String)

 cmdOK.Caption = strNewValue
End Property
```

Exposing the methods of a constituent control is done in a similar way. A public sub or function procedure is added to the user control that will function as a wrapper for the appropriate method of the constituent control. For example, to allow the user to add an item to a combo box called *cboEmployeeList*, which is part of the ActiveX control, we can write a `Sub` procedure named *AddName*, which is just a wrapper for the AddItem method of the combo box:

```
Public Sub AddName(strNewemployee As Name)

  cboEmployeeList.AddItem strNewemployee

End Sub
```

Using Property Pages with an ActiveX Control   Adding your own property pages to your ActiveX control can be done by using the Property Page Wizard. This is done by selecting *Add Property Page* from the Project pull-down menu. To use the wizard, select *VB Property Page Wizard*. After an introductory screen, the wizard uses these steps to add a property page for your control:

- The second window is the *Select the Property Pages* window. Click the *Add* button to create a new property page.
- On the *Add Properties* page, select the properties you wish to place on this property page.
- The next screen is the Finish screen. Click *Finish* so the wizard can build the page.

Like the `UserControl`, a property page is similar to a form. Once the wizard has created the property page, you can select it from the Project Explorer and modify the placement of controls on its surface. Next, open the `UserControl` object and view the Properties window. A `UserControl` has a property named *Property Pages*. Selecting this property will open a dialog box called *Connect Property Pages*, which shows a list of available property pages. Select the property pages you want to use by clicking on the appropriate check box.

The Property Page Wizard will assign a name to your property page like "Property Page1". You will want to change this name since the name used for the property page will be displayed to the user. Once a property page is completed and your control is compiled, the user can view the property pages by right-clicking your control and selecting *Properties*. We will explore the code behind a property page in the section titled "Adding a Custom Property Page to Our Control" later in this chapter.

Adding an About Box   Many ActiveX controls display an *About* box in the design environment. The About box is a dialog box that displays certain useful information to the user, such as the control name and version, copyright information, and system information. Visual Basic allows you to add an About box to your ActiveX control project by using the following steps:

- Select *Add Form* from the Project pull-down menu. Select *About Dialog* and click *OK*.

- Set the properties of the form, such as the values of the label captions that you want to be displayed to the user.

- Add a public `Sub` procedure to the `UserControl` object and name it *ShowAbout*.

- Inside the `ShowAbout` procedure, add one line of code that displays the About dialog modally.

- Open the Procedure Attributes dialog from the Tools menu.

- Click the *Advanced* button, and then click open the *Procedure ID* drop-down list and select *AboutBox*.

- Under Attributes, click the *Hide This Member* check box. This will prevent the user from using the `ShowAbout` method directly. The `ShowAbout` method will be used automatically by Visual Basic when the user clicks on the *About* property of your ActiveX control in design mode.

Saving Property Values with the Property Bag   An instance of an ActiveX control is created and destroyed by Visual Basic at several points during its lifetime, depending on whether the form it is situated on is visible. This applies to the control whether it's in the design environment or during run time. Consider a few examples of when this can happen:

- The user closes the form in design mode.

- The user presses the F5 key to leave design mode and enter run mode.

- The user selects *End* from the Run menu, returning the project to design mode.

- The user opens the form by clicking on the form in the Project Explorer.

You can see from these examples that the control instance will be created and destroyed many times while the project is open. If the user has set any property values, those changes will be lost unless you take some steps to save them. This is done by using an object called the *Property*

Bag. The property bag is an object that has two methods, ReadProperty and WriteProperty. The ReadProperty method takes two arguments:

- A string representing the name of the property
- A default value for the property

ReadProperty is a function that returns the value of the property it has read. If it can't read a value for the property, it will return the default value. Let's return to the earlier example of a graphing control with the NumPoints property. The ReadProperty method can be used in the following manner:

```
mNumPoints = PropBag.ReadProperty("NumPoints", 10)
```

The ReadProperty function is used to restore the value held by the private member variable for that property. The WriteProperty method is used to save the value of a property. WriteProperty takes three arguments:

- A string representing the name of the property
- The value to store; you will pass the private member variable for the property
- A default value

To write the NumPoints property, one line of code will do it:

```
PropBag.WriteProperty("NumPoints", mNumPoints, 10)
```

The ReadProperties and WriteProperties Events   Visual Basic has provided two events of the UserControl object that can be used to read and write the property values. These are the ReadProperties and WriteProperties events. Each procedure is passed a single parameter, the PropBag object. You place your code to read and write the property values in these two event procedures. The events will fire automatically as the instance of the control is created and destroyed. For example, the code for the NumPoints property of the graph control will look like this:

```
Private Sub UserControl_ReadProperties(PropBag As PropertyBag)

        mNumPoints = PropBag.ReadProperty("NumPoints", 10)
End Sub

Private Sub UserControl_WriteProperties(PropBag As PropertyBag)

        PropBag.WriteProperty("NumPoints", mNumPoints, 10)
End Sub
```

The `PropertyChanged` Method   You must take action to ensure that the value of a property is saved. Otherwise, Visual Basic has no way to know that the property changed and consequently won't save it. To ensure that the value of a property is saved, you use the `PropertyChanged` method each time the user changes the property. When the user changes the value of a property, the `Property Let` procedure is called, so this is where we will call the `PropertyChanged` method. `PropertyChanged` takes a single parameter, the name of the property as string. To ensure that the value of the `NumPoints` property will be saved, we can modify the `Property Let` procedure to look like this:

```
Public Property Let NumPoints(intNewValue As Integer)

  mNumPoints = intNewValue
    PropertyChanged "NumPoints"

End Property
```

Testing an ActiveX Control   An ActiveX control can be debugged by creating a *program group*. This is a collection of Visual Basic projects that can be loaded into the IDE at the same time. Each project is accessible through the Project Explorer. You need to specify a startup project by right-clicking on the project name in the Project Explorer and selecting *Set As Start Up*. If you want to test the control in an executable, as opposed to the Internet Explorer, an ActiveX control project cannot be the startup project. You will have to create a standard or ActiveX EXE project that uses the control and set that project as your startup project.

By including the ActiveX control in the same project group as an executable, you can debug the control and the EXE as if they were a single project. You need to close all of the windows in the `UserControl` project before you use it in the test project. However, you can set breakpoints in the code that is part of the user control and then execute the test program. When the control is used in the test program and a breakpoint is reached, Visual Basic will enter break mode and display the code window for the `UserControl`. You can then go through the normal debug process, as described in Chapter 13.

If you set an ActiveX control project as the startup project, Visual Basic will launch Microsoft Internet Explorer, which is the default container for an ActiveX control. The behavior of the control can be tested within Internet Explorer in this way.

Distributing ActiveX Controls

In Chapter 15 we will discuss using the Package and Deployment Wizard to distribute a Visual Basic project. You can use this wizard to distribute an ActiveX control as well. There are a few specific items to keep in mind when distributing ActiveX controls. If the control will be used in a design environment other than Visual Basic, you must include the Property Page DLL in your setup package. The wizard will let you know this and can take care of this for you. If you are distributing your component over the Internet, you will have to mark it as safe for scripting and safe for initialization. Two other issues that are of concern when distributing ActiveX controls are maintaining version compatibility and registering the control with Windows.

Version Compatibility One of the central goals of object-oriented programming and COM in particular is to make it possible for a client project to be able to continue to use an object even after it has been updated or modified. In COM, this is taken care of with *versioning*. Through versioning, a COM component can remain compatible with client applications that use it while adding new functionality. The COM component is identified through the Windows registry by using a 128-bit identification number called the *ClassID*. If the COM component maintains the old interfaces and the same ClassID, the client will be able to continue using the newest version of the component.

You can specify the versioning used for your control by opening the Component tab of the Project Properties dialog. This should be done early on in the development of your control to ensure that clients that use it will be able to continue using it each time you recompile it. There are three options available:

- *No compatibility*: This unfriendly option is the default setting. Each time the component is compiled, a new ClassID and interface is created for the component. If you use this option, the new version of your control will have no relation to any previous versions. Any client applications that use your control will have to be redesigned.

- *Project compatibility*: This option will maintain the same ClassID for your component each time it is compiled. However, the interface IDs will change. This setting should be used for debugging a control, but not for released versions.

- *Binary compatibility*: This option specifies complete version compatibility. Binary compatibility will ensure that clients that used a previous version of your control will be able to use the new one. The control will maintain the same ClassID and interface ID of older versions. This will allow you to build upon the functionality of the control through properties, methods, and events. Binary compatibility requires that you keep the existing interfaces used by the control; however, you can add additional optional parameters. If the compiler detects a change in the interface that could break compatibility, it will warn you so that you can take the appropriate action. To use binary compatibility, you must maintain the previous version of the control on your system.

Registering Components An ActiveX component must be registered with Windows before it can be used. The Windows registry has an entry for each component that specifies where the component is and what its unique ClassID is. Each component has a unique ClassID. The client application uses the ClassID to look up the location of the compiled version of the component in the registry. A control can be registered by using the Regsvr32 program. From the command line, the following will register the control:

```
Regsvr32  ControlName.ocx
```

Controls can be unregistered by using the line:

```
Regsvr32 /u ControlName.ocx
```

If you create a setup program with the Package and Deployment Wizard for your control, it will take care of registering the control for you.

ACTIVEX CONTROL EXAMPLE: CREATING AN ALARM CLOCK

This example uses VB standard controls to build a simple alarm clock. The clock will display the current time and an alarm time to the user. The user can turn the alarm on and off and set the alarm time. If the alarm is on it will beep when the current time reaches the time set for the alarm.

The first step is to create a new Visual Basic project of type ActiveX Control. Visual Basic will create the project with a single UserControl object. The control will be identified by the Name property of the user control; so the first thing we do is set the name property to *AlarmBox*. Next, we set the *Toolbox Bitmap* property, which allows us to select a bitmap to represent the control in the user's tool box.

Adding the Constituent Controls

We will build our control by using existing VB controls. To display the alarm setting and the current time, we will use two text boxes. Two label controls will identify each text box. The alarm can be turned on or off with a check box control. A timer control will be used to retrieve the current system time on a periodic basis and compare it to the alarm setting. If it's time for the alarm to go off, we'll sound the alarm by using the Beep function. The following controls are placed on the UserControl object:

Control	Name	Left	Top	Caption	Text
Label	lblAlarm	120	240	Alarm	N/A
Label	lblTime	120	960	Time	N/A
TextBox	txtAlarmClock	960	240	N/A	12:00
TextBox	txtTime	960	840	N/A	12:00
CheckBox	chkSetAlarm	1080	1440	Set Alarm	N/A
Timer	Timer1	2640	1560	N/A	N/A

We set the interval property of the timer control to 100. So that our control will have a nice border like a Picture Box, we set the Border Style property of the user control to *Fixed Single*. After these controls are added, the user control will appear as shown in Fig. 12-10.

Adding Custom Properties

To run the alarm clock, we'll need to track the following information:

- The current time
- The time for the alarm setting
- Whether or not the alarm is set

For illustration purposes, we will also permit the user to set the foreground color of the alarm setting. The first step is to define private variables to hold each property value. This is done by declaring the variables in the general declarations section of the UserControl:

```
Option Explicit
Private mAlarmTime As Date
Private mAlarmForeColor As OLE_COLOR
Private mCurrentTime As Date
Private mAlarmSet As Boolean
```

Figure 12-10

The Alarm Box user control object.

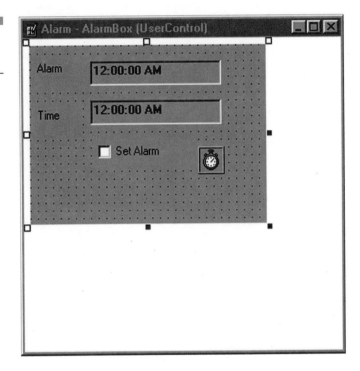

Notice that the `mAlarmForeColor` variable is a special type, `OLE_COLOR`. This will allow us to use a Property Page dialog to represent the property. Once private variables to hold the property values have been declared, we can create `Property Let/Get` procedures to provide an interface to allow the user to access the properties. The code looks like this:

```
Public Property Get AlarmTime() As Date

 AlarmTime = mAlarmTime

End Property

Public Property Let AlarmTime(ByVal dtmNewValue As Date)

 mAlarmTime = dtmNewValue
 txtAlarmClock.Text = CStr(mAlarmTime)
 PropertyChanged "AlarmTime"
 End Property

 Public Property Get CurrentTime() As Date
  CurrentTime = mCurrentTime

End Property

Public Property Let CurrentTime(ByVal dtmNewValue As Date)
```

```
    mCurrentTime = dtmNewValue
    txtTime.Text = CStr(mCurrentTime)
    PropertyChanged "CurrentTime"

End Property

  Public Property Get AlarmForeColor() As OLE_COLOR

   AlarmForeColor = mAlarmForeColor

End Property

Public Property Let AlarmForeColor(ByVal bytNewValue As OLE_COLOR)

    mAlarmForeColor = bytNewValue
    txtAlarmClock.ForeColor = mAlarmForeColor
    PropertyChanged "AlarmForeColor"

End Property

Public Property Get AlarmSet() As Boolean

  AlarmSet = mAlarmSet

End Property

Public Property Let AlarmSet(ByVal blnNewValue As Boolean)

  mAlarmSet = blnNewValue
  chkSetAlarm.Value = mAlarmSet
  PropertyChanged "AlarmSet"

End Property
```

Notice that the `Property Let` procedure of each property calls the
`PropertyChanged` method to tell Visual Basic that the user has
changed the value of the property. This will ensure that the new property value will be saved if the current instance of the control is
destroyed. We also include code to manipulate the constituent controls
based on changes the user makes to the property values. For example,
we are using the `chkSetAlarm` check box to tell the user if the alarm is
set or not. In the `AlarmSet Property Let` procedure, we change the
Value property of the check box to reflect the new property setting.

Adding Custom Methods

Custom methods are added to the control by adding a public sub or function procedure to the `UserControl` object. Our control will have one
method, *Snooze*, which allows the user to "hit the snooze button" and
delay the alarm for a five-minute period. The code looks like this:

```
Public Sub Snooze()

  mAlarmTime = DateAdd("n", 5, mAlarmTime)
  txtAlarmClock.Text = CStr(mAlarmTime)

End Sub
```

The alarm time is adjusted by five minutes, and the new alarm time is set in the `mAlarmTime` property.

Initializing Property Values

The first time that a user places your control on a form, you must provide a set of default or initial values for each property. This is done in the `InitProperties` event of the user control. The `InitProperties` event fires only once in the lifetime of the control; that's when the user selects your control from the tool box and places it on a form. The `InitProperties` event for our control looks like this:

```
Private Sub UserControl_InitProperties()

  mAlarmTime = Now
  mCurrentTime = Now
  mAlarmForeColor = vbBlack
  txtAlarmClock.Text = CStr(mAlarmTime)
  txtTime.Text = CStr(mCurrentTime)

End Sub
```

Here we set the alarm and clock times to the current system time. The color used to display the alarm time is set to black. We also use the `InitProperties` event to display the current time in the AlarmClock and Time text boxes.

Saving and Retrieving Property Values

Earlier, we indicated that you must save and retrieve the property values of your control by using the `WriteProperties` and `Read Properties` events. The code for our control looks like the following:

```
Private Sub UserControl_WriteProperties(PropBag As PropertyBag)
  PropBag.WriteProperty "AlarmTime", mAlarmTime, Now
  PropBag.WriteProperty "CurrentTime", mCurrentTime, Now
  PropBag.WriteProperty "AlarmForeColor", mAlarmForeColor, vbBlack
```

```
End Sub

Private Sub UserControl_ReadProperties(PropBag As PropertyBag)

 'read the saved property values
 mAlarmTime = PropBag.ReadProperty("AlarmTime", Now)
 mCurrentTime = PropBag.ReadProperty("CurrentTime", Now)
 mAlarmForeColor = PropBag.ReadProperty("AlarmForeColor", vbBlack)

 'display property values in text boxes
 txtAlarmClock.ForeColor = mAlarmForeColor
 txtAlarmClock.Text = CStr(mAlarmTime)

End Sub
```

Notice that we use the `ReadProperties` event to load the property values into the text boxes, which are visible to the user.

Sounding the Alarm

We have placed a timer onto the user control. When the control is in run-time mode, we want to periodically update the current time and then compare it to the time set for the alarm. If the current time is greater than or equal to that time, we want to sound the alarm, which we will do by calling the Visual Basic `Beep` function. We set the Interval property of the timer control to 100 ms so that the time is checked on a reasonably frequent basis. The code to sound the alarm is placed in the timer event:

```
Private Sub Timer1_Timer()

 If Ambient.UserMode = True Then
 'update the current time
 mCurrentTime = Now
 txtTime.Text = CStr(mCurrentTime)

 'check to see if the current time
 'is the time set for the alarm
 If mCurrentTime > mAlarmTime Then
 'if it is, turn on the alarm
 Do While chkSetAlarm.Value = Checked
  Beep
  DoEvents
 Loop

 End If  'current time greater than alarm time

 End If  'Ambient user mode is true

End Sub
```

The first statement of this procedure uses the `Ambient` object to make sure we are in run-time mode. If we don't do this, the timer event will fire even in design mode, which is not a desirable behavior. User Mode is True if the control is in run-time mode. If so, we update the current time and then compare it to the alarm setting. If the time has passed the alarm setting, we use a `Do` loop to sound the alarm if the set alarm check box has been checked by the user. The user can shut the alarm off by unchecking the box.

One final item to notice about the procedure is that we have included a call to `DoEvents`. This allows Windows to process all pending events on the event cue before going through the next iteration of the loop. When the user clicks off the *Set Alarm* check box, this event is pushed onto the event cue where it will wait until our control gives up execution to the operating system. If we didn't call `DoEvents`, our program would get stuck in the loop and hang.

Using the Procedure Attributes Dialog

The Procedure Attributes dialog can be used to specify important behavior of the control. Properties can be made data bound, they can be hidden, and they can be set to use standard behavior, such as displaying a font dialog box. For our control, we will use the Procedure Attributes dialog box to display a color dialog box for the Alarm ForeColor property.

When we open the Procedure Attributes dialog for the AlarmForeColor property, we click open the *Advanced* button to specify the manner in which the user will be able to set the property in design mode (see Fig. 12-11). First, we set the *Procedure ID* property to *ForeColor*. Next, we set the *Use this Page in Property Browser* attribute to *Standard Color*. With this setting, Visual Basic will display a standard color dialog box whenever the user clicks on this property in the VB Properties window. The final setting is *Property Category*, which we set to *Appearance*. If the user clicks the *Categories* tab of the Properties window for our control, the AlarmForeColor property will be displayed under the Appearance category.

Adding an About Box

We will design our control so that an About dialog box is displayed to the user when he or she clicks on the *About* property in the Properties window. This is done in four easy steps:

■ We select *Add Form* from the Project pull-down menu. Select *About Dialog* and click *Open*.

Figure 12-11
Setting Procedure
Attributes for an
ActiveX control.

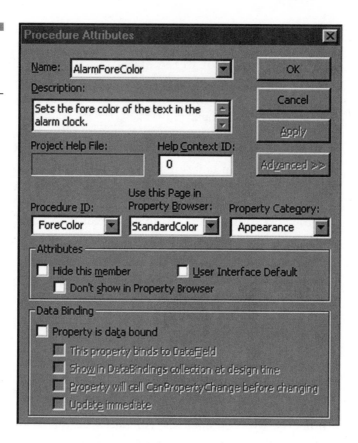

- Set the properties for the label and picture controls on the About dialog to display the information you want the user to see. You can include copyright, version, and licensing information for the control.

- Add a public Sub procedure to show the About dialog box. Call this procedure *ShowAbout*.

- Open the Procedure Attributes dialog for this procedure. Open the Advanced settings. Set ProcedureID to *About Box*. Under Attributes, select *Hide this member*. This will prevent the user from being able to call the ShowAbout method. Visual Basic will automatically call the method when the user clicks the *About* property in the Properties window for the control.

The About box must be shown modally. The code to show the form will look like this:

```
Public Sub ShowAbout()

 frmAbout.Show vbModal
End Sub
```

Adding a Custom Property Page to Our Control

We can use the Property Page Wizard to create a custom property page for this control. To do so, we use the steps described earlier for creating a property page. In this section, we will talk about the code behind the property page. The wizard created a page that has this code:

```
Private Sub txtCurrentTime_Change()
  Changed = True
End Sub

Private Sub txtAlarmTime_Change()
  Changed = True
End Sub

Private Sub chkAlarmSet_Click()
  Changed = True
End Sub

Private Sub PropertyPage_ApplyChanges()
  SelectedControls(0).AlarmSet = (chkAlarmSet.Value = vbChecked)
  SelectedControls(0).CurrentTime = txtCurrentTime.Text
  SelectedControls(0).AlarmTime = txtAlarmTime.Text
End Sub

Private Sub PropertyPage_SelectionChanged()
  chkAlarmSet.Value = (SelectedControls(0).AlarmSet And vbChecked)
  txtCurrentTime.Text = SelectedControls(0).CurrentTime
  txtAlarmTime.Text = SelectedControls(0).AlarmTime
End Sub
```

The property page has a check box representing the `AlarmSet` property and two text boxes for the `AlarmTime` and `CurrentTime` properties. The text box change events and the check box `Click` event are used to call the Changed method of the property page object. This causes the Apply button of the property page to activate. A property page has a collection called *Selected Controls*. Selected Controls represents the property values for your control. A property page has two events:

■ `SelectionChanged`: When this event fires, you populate the property page with the current values of the control properties. In `SelectionChanged`, the controls on the property page are set to the values of each property.

■ ApplyChanges: This event will fire if the user has clicked the *Apply* button. You place code in this event procedure to change the values of the properties the user has indicated.

When the user right-clicks on the control and selects *Properties*, the custom property page will be shown along with any standard property pages we have selected for the project.

Compiling the Control

Compiling an ActiveX control is done just like it is for any other project. We select *Make alarmbox.ocx* from the File pull-down menu. Once the control is compiled for the first time, we set the version compatibility for the control on the Components tab of the Project Properties dialog to *Binary*. This will ensure that projects that use our control will be able to continue using it as the control is updated.

Testing the Control

To test the control, we create a new standard EXE project (see Fig. 12-12). The first step is to open the Project Components dialog box and add the control to our project. We do this by clicking the *Browse* button and selecting the *AlarmBox.ocx* file. Once this is done, we can add the control to a form and set its properties. A command button on the form will set the alarm time:

```
Private Sub cmdSetAlarm_Click()
 Dim dtmTemp As Date
 dtmTemp = DateAdd("s", 10, Now)
 AlarmBox1.AlarmTime = dtmTemp

End Sub
```

The alarm can be turned on either at design time by using the Properties window or during run time by clicking on the check box, which is part of the control. While the user can interact with the constituent controls on the form, the controls cannot be manipulated directly in code or during design time because they are private to the user control.

In design mode, we can see how the settings in the Procedure Attributes dialog that we used for the control are realized. In Fig. 12-13, we see the Properties window for the control, which shows the AlarmForeColor property, categorized under *Appearance* as planned.

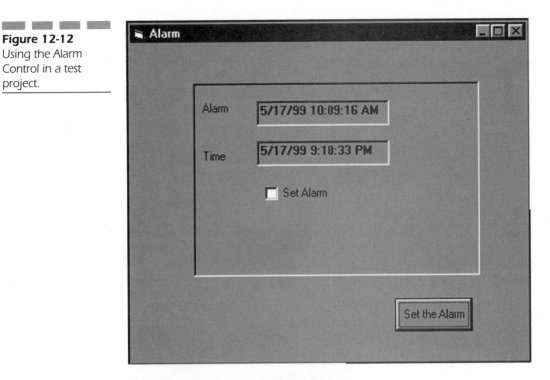

Figure 12-12
Using the Alarm
Control in a test
project.

Figure 12-13
Categorized proper-
ties of the Alarm
Control.

Figure 12-14
The Alarm Control
About box.

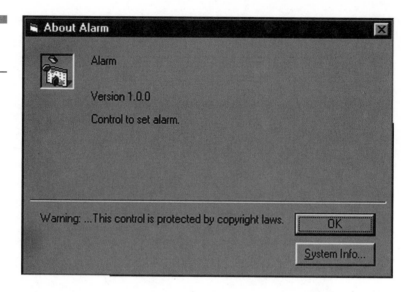

If the user clicks the *About* property, the About box shown in Figure 12-14 opens on the screen.

Internet Applications

Microsoft has continued to enhance the Internet capabilities of Visual Basic with version 6.0. There are two main areas of interest: developing DHTML applications and developing IIS applications. There is not sufficient space in this book to cover Internet development in detail, so in this section we will just provide a brief description. For a good introduction to building Internet applications with Visual Basic, check out *Visual Basic 6: The Complete Reference* by Noel Jerke (Osborne/McGraw Hill, 1999).

DHTML Applications

DHTML is the dynamic HTML object model. A DHTML application provides a way to use Visual Basic to build an Internet application that uses HTML rather than forms. The DHTML application combines DHTML with Visual Basic code to provide a client-side application that runs in the Internet browser. Using Visual Basic for a DHTML application lets you create a very dynamic and interactive web page since you have the ease and power of Visual Basic behind it.

In Visual Basic, DHTML applications are built using the DHTML page designer. The first step is to create a new Visual Basic project and select *DHTML application* as your project type. Visual Basic will create an application with one DHTML page and one module, which it will call *modDHTML*. You will notice that once again Visual Basic is using the same development model it has used all along, thus maintaining a similarity with the forms and modules that you are used to.

If you open the DHTML page in the Project Explorer, Visual Basic will open the DHTML page designer (see Fig. 12-15). The page designer can be used to build the pages that will run in the user's Internet browser. You do this almost like you would using a form. A set of HTML controls are available in the tool box (see Fig. 12-16). These controls can be placed in the right-hand pane of the page designer. You can click on the controls and place code behind them in much the same way that you would when editing a form. The DHTML pages in your project can be saved as part of the project or externally. This is done by opening the page designer's Save Mode settings dialog.

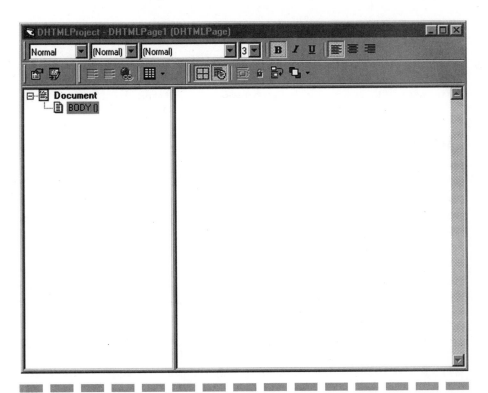

Figure 12-15   DHTML project.

Figure 12-16
Controls in a DHTML
project.

You build the DHTML application by placing controls and text onto the DHTML page designer. You can then put code behind each element. The page will then run in a web browser like Internet Explorer.

IIS Applications

An IIS application is an Internet information server application. This is an application that will run on a server that is running IIS 3/4. IIS applications are built on web classes. To build an IIS application, you will need to have Internet Information Server or Peer Web Services 3.0 on your computer to run web classes. Peer Web Server is used on a machine running Windows NT 4.0 Workstation. If you are running Windows 95/98, you will need to have the Personal Web Server 3.0 or later with Active Server Pages.

A web class runs on the server and responds to input from the user's web browser. A web class has two important components: HTML pages and custom web items. HTML pages can be built to receive user input. The functionality of the application is built in Visual Basic by using the web class designer. The application can be tested by running it in a web browser.

ActiveX Documents

An ActiveX document is a COM object that can be hosted by Internet Explorer, Microsoft Office Binder, or a Visual Basic Tool Window. You can create an ActiveX document project as either an executable file (*.exe*) or as a dynamic link library (*.dll*). Like an ActiveX server, an ActiveX document that is an EXE is an out-of-process server and thus runs in its own address space. An ActiveX document that is a DLL is an in-process server. As with ActiveX DLL servers, an ActiveX document DLL will probably provide better performance than an out-of-process component. ActiveX documents created in Visual Basic are "Visual Basic Documents." When you compile your project, a Visual Basic Document, which is a file with a *.vbd* extension, will be created along with the server program, which will be either an *.exe* or *.dll*. The VBD file is the actual document, and it works much like a DOC file in relation to *WinWord.exe*.

The `UserDocument` Object

The core of the ActiveX document project is the *UserDocument object*. Like the `UserControl`, the `UserDocument` object resembles a form during design time. You can add user interface elements to its surface, and you can place code behind several events. Unlike a form, however, a `UserDocument` object cannot run independently as a standalone application. Instead, Visual Basic creates a web page built around your user document and shows this page in a host program, such as Internet Explorer. There are a few events of the `UserDocument` object that you should know about. We discuss them in the following sections.

The `InitProperties` Event   The first time the `UserDocument` object is loaded into a browser, the `InitProperties` event will fire. In other words, it functions in the same way that the form load event does with a Visual Basic form. This means that the `InitProperties` event will fire whenever your ActiveX document project gets loaded into memory. Internet Explorer maintains a list of the most recent web pages in memory. If the web page representing your ActiveX document is contained in this list, the `InitProperties` event does not fire when your document is loaded. However, if the web page falls off this list and it must be reloaded into memory, the `InitProperties` event will fire again. This works just like a form; if a form is hidden the form load event does not fire when you show the form again. However, if the form is unloaded from memory, the next time you show the form the form load event will fire. `InitProperties` takes no parameters. You can use the `InitProperties` event to perform the same type of initialization that you might when loading a form, such as filling the values in a list box. For example, suppose we had a combo box on our ActiveX document that tracked tax filing status. We could use the `InitProperties` event to load the combo box:

```
Private Sub UserDocument_InitProperties()
 cboTaxStatus.AddItem "Single"
 cboTaxStatus.AddItem "Married-Filing Jointly"
 cboTaxStatus.AddItem "Married-Filing Separately"
End Sub
```

The `WriteProperties` Event   The `WriteProperties` event will fire when the user navigates to another web page. This lets the `User Document` object know that it needs to save any data that it wishes to keep persistent between sessions. If you read the section on ActiveX controls, you're already familiar with the `WriteProperties` event since it works just like the `WriteProperties` event of the `UserControl` object. `WriteProperties` takes a single parameter, `PropBag`, of type property bag. You can use the `WriteProperty` method of `PropBag` to save property values in the same way that you would with a user control object. As an example, say we wanted to save a property named "MyData." We could do so with the following line of code:

```
Private Sub UserDocument_WriteProperties(PropBag As PropertyBag)
 PropBag.WriteProperty "My Data", mData, 5
End Sub
```

`WriteProperty` takes the name of the property as a string, the variable that holds the property value, and a default value to use if there is any problem writing the data.

The `ReadProperties` Event   Again, this event is similar to the `ReadProperties` event of the user control. This event will fire whenever the user navigates back to your document. `ReadProperties` takes a single parameter, `PropBag`, of type property bag. You can use the `ReadProperty` event of the `PropBag` object to retrieve saved property values. For example, the following code reads a property value into the private property variable `mData`:

```
mData = PropBag.ReadProperty("MyData",5)
```

Note that the `ReadProperties` method takes two parameters. The first is a string that identifies the name of the property that you wish to read. The second parameter, which is optional, is a default value you can specify if the property value cannot be read.

The `HyperLink` Object

An ActiveX document has a `HyperLink` object that can be used to navigate web pages. It has three methods:

- GoBack
- GoForward
- NavigateTo

For example, suppose our ActiveX document had a command button on its surface that allowed the user to visit Microsoft's web site. We can use the `NavigateTo` method of the `HyperLink` object to do this. `NavigateTo` takes a single parameter, a string representing the URL of the desired web page. In this example, our code would look like this:

```
Private Sub cmdOpenMicrosoft_Click()
 UserDocument.Hyperlink.NavigateTo "http://www.microsoft.com"

End Sub
```

Using the `Viewport` of an ActiveX Document

The `Viewport` represents the area that the container application, such as Microsoft Internet Explorer, has given our ActiveX document. There are four properties of the `Viewport` that you can use:

- ViewportHeight
- ViewportLeft
- ViewportTo
- ViewportWidth

For example, we can use the `Resize` event of the `UserDocument` object to right-justify a label control:

```
Private Sub UserDocument_Resize()

 lblCompanyName.Left = UserDocument.ViewPortWidth - lblCompany.Width
End Sub
```

Asynchronous Downloads

ActiveX Documents use *asynchronous downloading* as a way to reduce the impact of downloading large files over the Internet. An asynchronous download will allow your application to continue to function while the download progresses. To use an asynchronous download, the ActiveX document must be completely loaded in the browser. When this happens, the Show event will fire. Once the Show event fires, asynchronous downloading is available for use.

The AsyncRead Method   The UserDocument object has a method called AsyncRead that can be used to initialize an asynchronous download. AsyncRead takes the following parameters:

- ▪ Target: This is a string that represents the URL of the file to download.

- ▪ AsyncType: A long parameter that specifies the type of file. This can be one of the following constants: vbAsyncTypeByteArray, vbAsyncTypeFile, and vbAsyncTypePicture. Use the appropriate constant depending on what type of object you are downloading.

- ▪ PropertyName: Optional. This is the property name to identify the data. This will be useful if you perform more than one download.

- ▪ AsyncReadOptions: This is an optional long parameter. One of the AsyncRead constants can be used to specify the asynchronous download behavior.

The AsyncReadComplete Event   This event will fire when the download is completed. For example, suppose that we wanted to read a bitmap file from a web site and place it in an image control. We use the Show event to initiate the file download. Suppose that the variable strURL contains the URL for the desired file. The code would look like this:

```
UserDocument.AsyncRead strURL, vbAsyncTypeFile, "MyPicture"
```

We can use the AsyncReadComplete event to load the bitmap into the image control. This is done by using the AsyncProp object, which is a parameter passed to the AsyncReadComplete event. The Value property of AsyncProp contains the downloaded file. We can test PropertyName to determine which download is being completed (this is helpful if you initiated multiple downloads in the Show event):

```
If AsyncProp.PropertyName = "MyPicture" Then
   imgPhoto.Picture = LoadPicture(AsyncProp.Value)
End If
```

Testing an ActiveX Document Project

When testing an ActiveX document project, the first step is to open the Project Properties dialog box. Select the *Debugging* tab. Select *Start Component* and choose an ActiveX document from your project to use. Next, make sure that the Use Existing Browser check box is selected. This will ensure that the user document will load in Internet Explorer. To test the DLL, select *Make ProjectName.dll* from the File menu.

You can then test your project by selecting *Start* from the Run pulldown menu. You can add breakpoints and do any debugging and testing required for your project. When testing your project, you should unload Internet Explorer before stopping your project. This will prevent several errors from occurring.

The ActiveX Document Migration Wizard

The ActiveX Document Migration Wizard is a tool in Visual Basic that you can use to convert forms in a project into ActiveX documents. The first step to using the wizard is to open the Add-In Manager. Select *VB 6 ActiveX Doc Migration Wizard* to open the wizard.

The first screen of the ActiveX Document Migration Wizard is an introductory screen. This window simply tells you what the wizard will do. It notes that it will convert forms into ActiveX documents but that it does not convert the project into an ActiveX document project. Select the *Next* button to continue.

The second screen of the Wizard allows you to select which forms you want to convert to ActiveX documents. This is done by checking off each form name in the list. Click *Next* to continue.

The next screen is the Options screen. First, you can specify that the wizard comment out all invalid code. This will comment out code that is not valid in an ActiveX document. The next option allows you to remove the forms that have been converted to ActiveX documents. If you don't select this option, those forms will remain in the project.

At the bottom of the screen you will see a frame titled *Your Project Type is Invalid.* This frame will be visible if you are converting a standard EXE or other non-ActiveX document type project. You must convert the project to an ActiveX EXE or ActiveX DLL to proceed.

The next screen is a summary screen that informs you that the ActiveX Document Wizard is finished collecting information. You have the option of printing a summary report once the conversion is completed. To perform the conversion, click the *Finish* command button.

Building Your Own Web Browser

Visual Basic has all the tools you need to build a simple web browser. The first step is to add the Microsoft Internet Controls to your project. To do this:

- Open the Components dialog box from the Project pull-down menu.
- Select *Microsoft Internet Controls*.

This will add the following controls to your project:

- Web Browser
- Shell Folder View

In this section, we will focus on the Web Browser control. To see how to use the control, we'll create a new standard EXE project with a single form that we'll use as our web browser.

Adding Controls to the Web Browser

Our web browser will have the following controls:

- *cmdYahoo*: A command button to visit the Yahoo! web site.
- *cmdMicrosoft*: A command button the user can use to visit the Microsoft web site.
- *cmdBack*: A command button that can be used to return to the previous web page.
- *cmdForward*: A command button that can be used to return to the next web page.
- *cmdStop*: A command button to stop the download of a web page.
- *cmdGo*: A command button that can be used to navigate to a specified web site.

- *txtURL*: A text box that will display the current web site URL or where the user can enter a desired web site.
- *WebBrowser1*: A web browser control to navigate the web and display web pages.

Displaying Web Pages

The Web Browser control will be used to display web pages. We will need to size it on our form to display the web pages in an attractive manner. We will also need to resize the Web Browser control as the user resizes the form. This is done in the Form Resize event:

```
Private Sub Form_Resize()

  WebBrowser1.Height = Me.Height - MAXHEIGHT
  WebBrowser1.Width = Me.Width - MAXWIDTH

End Sub
```

MAXHEIGHT and MAXWIDTH are two constants that we have defined to size the web browser appropriately in relation to the form.

Navigating to a Web Page

To view a particular web page, we can use the *Navigate* method of the web browser control. All we need to do is pass a string representing the URL of the desired web page. For example, to visit the Microsoft web page, the code would look like this:

```
Private Sub cmdMicrosoft_Click()

  WebBrowser1.Navigate "http://www.microsoft.com"
End Sub
```

The code to open the Yahoo! web page looks like this:

```
Private Sub cmdYahoo_Click()

  WebBrowser1.Navigate "http://www.yahoo.com"

End Sub
```

In the cmdGo Click event, we want to allow the user to enter a specific web page for viewing. We can use the txtURL text box to retrieve the URL that the user wishes to view. We can then visit the web page by passing this value to the Navigate method of the web browser:

```
Private Sub cmdGo_Click()

  Dim strURL As String
  strURL = txtURL.Text
  WebBrowser1.Navigate strURL

End Sub
```

Moving Forward, Moving Back, and Stopping a Web Page Download

In any web browser you're likely to see Forward, Back, and Stop buttons. The Web Browser control has methods to perform these actions. For example, to stop a web page download, we use the Stop method:

```
Private Sub cmdStop_Click()

  WebBrowser1.Stop

End Sub
```

To go back or move forward we use the GoBack and GoForward methods, respectively:

```
Private Sub cmdBack_Click()

  WebBrowser1.GoBack

End Sub

Private Sub cmdForward_Click()

  WebBrowser1.GoForward

End Sub
```

To display the URL of the web page that just loaded, we can use the DocumentComplete event, which fires when the web page is loaded:

```
Private Sub WebBrowser1_DocumentComplete(ByVal pDisp As Object, URL As
Variant)

  txtURL.Text = WebBrowser1.LocationURL
  Me.Caption = WebBrowser1.LocationName

End Sub
```

The LocationName property can be used to display the location name for the web site. For example, Microsoft's web site sets the LocationName to *Welcome to Microsoft's Home Page*. We display this value in the caption property of the form.

With this simple code, we have a functional web browser. In Fig. 12-17, we are using it to visit the Microsoft home page.

Figure 12-17 Microsoft home page accessed by web browser.

Reviewing, Testing, and Distributing Software

CHAPTER 13

Debugging

Introduction

When a new software project is completed, even the most carefully written program will contain errors that keep it from running properly. These errors are known as *bugs*, and the process of locating and correcting these errors is known as *debugging*. Debugging even a moderately sized software project can be quite time consuming. In the past, a programmer would have to compile a program and run it several times, perhaps printing out error messages along the way in attempts to locate the bug. Visual Basic, however, provides an extensive set of tools that not only make the debugging process easier but let you debug your software without leaving the design environment. Visual Basic also provides a standardized way to catch run-time errors known as an *error handler*.

In the world of software development, there are three general classes of errors:

■ *Syntax Errors:* A syntax error is an invalid statement in your program that won't compile. A syntax error is often a typing mistake. Examples of syntax errors include misspelling the name of a keyword, using an If statement without an End If, declaring a variable with an unknown data type, or failing to declare a variable before it is used in code (when you have used the `Option Explicit` keyword). When you compile your program or select *Run with Full Compile* in the design environment, Visual Basic will alert you to these errors so they can be corrected. You can also have Visual Basic try to detect syntax errors as you type by setting the Auto Syntax Check option from the Tools Options dialog.

■ *Run-Time Errors*: A run-time error occurs after a program is successfully compiled and is up and running. While the program contains the correct language syntax and all variables are declared correctly, it may perform some action that could cause the software to crash, such as reading in bad data. For example, your program might have the wrong path to a database file and not be able to open it. One of the most common examples of a run-time error is division by zero. Run-time errors are generally taken care of, or *trapped*, with an error handler. If you are in the design environment, an untrapped run-time error will cause Visual Basic to enter break mode. An untrapped run-time error in a compiled program will cause it to crash.

■ *Logic Errors*: A logic error or *bug* is a problem that arises from bad program logic. This is a flaw in the way your program was designed. Bugs can be difficult to track down because the software will compile and may even run without crashing. The end result of a bug will often appear far from where the actual problem occurred. This may be far in terms of program code or far in time; bugs are often not discovered until months later when users run into problems. As a result, a great deal of effort will be needed to step through the program code to make sure it is really working as the design intended. As mentioned, the process of tracking down the bug is known as debugging. To track down and correct bugs in Visual Basic you will use the integrated debugger.

When debugging, fixing logic errors will be your primary focus, although you may spend some time trying to correct run-time errors as well. In this chapter, we'll focus on how to use the debugging tools provided by Visual Basic to help you do this. The following topics will be discussed:

■ Setting breakpoints

■ Using watches to track the value of a variable

■ Stepping through code

■ Using the debug object

■ Assertions

■ Tracking down and killing bugs

■ Using error messages to trap run-time errors

Each of the debugging tools can be found on the Debug pull-down menu or on the Debug toolbar.

Debugging Tools and Windows

The Visual Basic development environment has several useful windows that you should be aware of during the debug process. These are:

■ *Call Stack*: The Call Stack can be viewed in break mode by selecting *Call Stack* from the View menu (see Fig. 13-1). The Call Stack dialog box will show all of the procedures that are loaded into memory. The top listing in the call stack is the current procedure. You can click the *Show* button to view the code of a selected procedure.

Figure 13-1
The Call Stack.

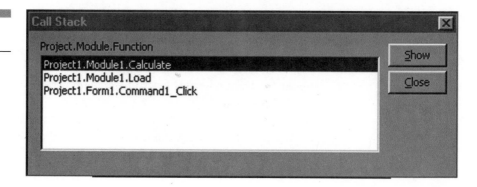

- *Immediate window*: The Immediate window can be used to execute lines of code or to query the values of variables while the application is in break mode. The Immediate window can be opened from the View menu.

- *Locals window*: The Locals window displays the value of local variables for the procedure that is currently executing. You can open the Locals window from the View menu.

- *Quick Watch*: A Quick Watch lists the current value of a variable or expression while in break mode (see Fig. 13-2). The Quick Watch dialog can be opened from the Debug menu. By clicking the *Add* button, you can add the expression to the Watch window.

- *Watch window*: The Watch window displays the values of watch expressions.

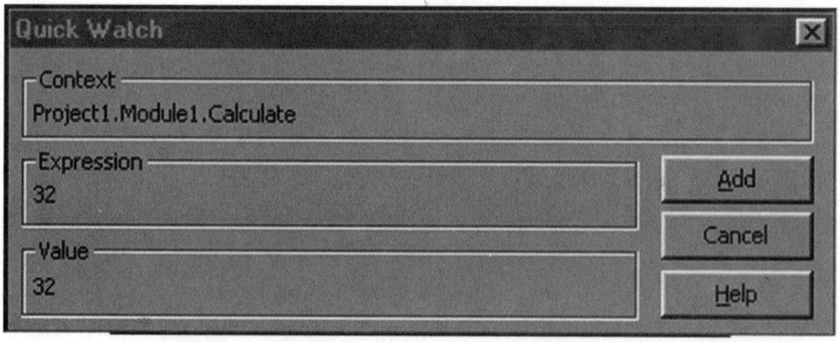

Figure 13-2
Quick Watch dialog.

Setting Breakpoints

When you run a program with the debugger, you have the ability to step through code one line at a time. While Visual Basic allows you to single-step through a program from the start, if it is even of modest length this can be quite tedious and time consuming. It makes more sense to run the program normally until execution nears the point where it is believed a problem is located. For this reason, Visual Basic provides the ability to set *breakpoints*. A breakpoint is a specified line of code that tells Visual Basic to pause execution when you are in the development environment. When Visual basic reaches a breakpoint line, execution is paused, and the debugger displays the line containing the breakpoint. Note that Visual Basic pauses before it executes the line of code that represents the breakpoint. You can then use the debugging tools to examine the contents of variables or to single-step through the code. You can set as many breakpoints as you want in your program, as long as they are on executable lines. You cannot set a breakpoint on variable declarations or on a line that uses `Option Explicit` **or** `Option Base`. Breakpoints are not saved with your project and will have to be set every time the project is loaded. Remember that when Visual Basic suspends execution because it encountered a breakpoint, the next line of code to be executed is the breakpoint line. To set a breakpoint, place the cursor on the line of code where you want execution to pause. You can then set the breakpoint by pressing the F9 key or by selecting *Toggle Breakpoint* from the Debug menu.

When you set a breakpoint, that line of code will be highlighted in a different color and will have a circle on the left side of the line (see Fig. 13-3). You can set the color used for breakpoint lines from the Editor Format tab of the Options dialog, which is found on the Tools menu. Once Visual Basic enters break mode, you can use one of the step methods to execute one line of code at a time.

Stepping through Code

Visual Basic provides you with several methods you can use to single-step through the code in your project. Single-stepping through code will allow you to see the flow of execution of the program. This will aid you

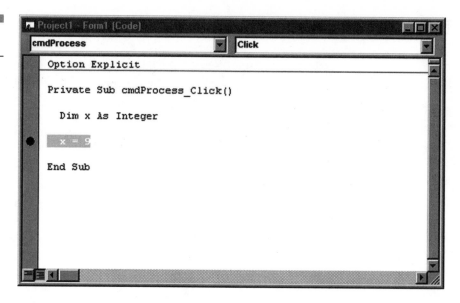

in determining which code the program will run through and where it will pause, so you can examine the contents of variables or see where a crash occurs. The debugger lets you control the flow of your program with the following methods:

- Step Into
- Step Over
- Step Out
- Run to Cursor

The first two methods, Step Into and Step Over, can be used to enter run-time mode. The application will pause on the first line of code that is run. Note that at any time during break mode you can use the F5 key to return to normal execution.

Step Into

During break mode, using Step Into allows you to execute a single line of code. You can single-step through the code by repeatedly using Step Into. To use Step Into, press the F8 key or select *Step Into* from the Debug menu.

Step Over

Using Step Over will also execute code one line at a time. However, Step Over treats procedure calls as a single line of code. If a call to a sub or function procedure is encountered, it will run that procedure in one step. It will then continue stepping through code one line at a time in the current procedure. This is different than Step Into, which will continue single-stepping through a called procedure. To use Step Over, press the Shift and F8 keys simultaneously or select *Step Over* from the Debug menu.

Step Out

Step Out lets you get out of the currently executing procedure. Using Step Out will execute every line of code in the current procedure at once and suspend execution on the line of code immediately after the point where the procedure was called. You can then use one of the other stepping methods to continue single-stepping through code. To use Step Out, press the Ctrl, Shift, and F8 keys simultaneously or select *Step Out* from the Debug menu.

Run to Cursor

If you are stepping through code and you want to skip over a number of statements and select another line of code on which to pause, you can use Run to Cursor. To use Run to Cursor, place the cursor on the line where you want execution to pause and then select *Run to Cursor* from the Debug menu.

Using Watch Expressions

A *Watch* expression can be used to display the value of a variable or expression in your program while it is executing in the development environment. While the program is running in the development environment, you can use the Watch window to view the value of the expression. The Watch window displays each Watch expression, its value, the type of expression, and the context. You can add a watch by opening the Add Watch dialog box from the Debug menu (see Fig. 13-4).

Figure 13-4
The Add Watch
dialog.

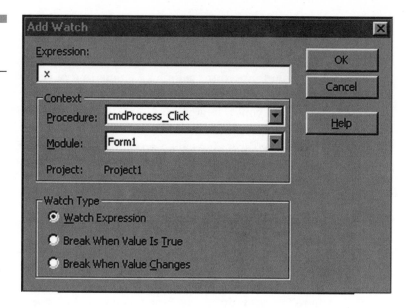

There are three types of watches you can create:

- *Watch Expression*: A Watch expression displays the current value of a variable or expression while the program is being run in the development environment. You can check the value of Watch expressions by selecting *Watch Window* from the View menu.

- *Break When Value Is True*: With this setting, Visual Basic will monitor the Watch expression to see when it becomes True. When it does, Visual Basic will enter break mode. For example, suppose a program that reads in a list of customers from a file crashes when it reaches the fiftieth customer. If we were tracking the count in a variable called NumCustomers, we could set the Watch expression to the following:

```
NumCustomers  = 49
```

When the program reaches the forty-ninth customer, execution will be suspended and you can single-step through the code and find out what's causing the error.

- *Break When Value Changes*: This type of Watch can be used to enter break mode whenever the value of a variable or expression changes. The Watch window will appear on your screen, and execution will be suspended on the line immediately after the point where the expression changed. For example, suppose we had a watch expression of type `Break When Value Changes` to monitor the value of `NumCustomers`, and the following code is executed:

```
NumCustomers = NumCustomers + 1

If (x > 7) then
```

In that case, Visual Basic will enter break mode, with the cursor suspended on the line containing the `If` statement.

A Watch can be added at design time or at run time. To add a Watch expression, do the following:

- Select *Add Watch* from the Debug menu or highlight the expression you want to monitor, right-click, and select *Add Watch*. This will bring up the Add Watch dialog box.

- In the Expression text box, type in the variable name or expression that you want to monitor. If you had previously highlighted an expression or variable to monitor, this value will show up in the Expression box automatically.

- Under *Context*, specify the scope for the watch expression. You can specify the procedure and module name in which to evaluate the variable.

- Select *Watch Type* as *Watch Expression, Break When Value Is True*, or *Break When Value Changes*.

The Debug Object

Visual Basic has an object that can be used during the debug process called the `Debug` *object*. The `Debug` object can be used to send output to the immediate window or to suspend execution during run time. The `Debug` object has two methods you can use, *Assert* and *Print*.

Using the Print Method of the Debug Object

By using the Print method, you can send the value of a variable or expression to the immediate window. For example, suppose we wanted to check the value of an integer variable called x. We could do so by using the Debug object's Print method. Print will send the value of x to the immediate window. The code would look like this:

```
x = y + z
debug.print x
```

Remember, setting breakpoints or adding watches is temporary. If you close down Visual Basic, the next time you open your project all of these settings will be gone. Using the Debug object effectively allows you to save breakpoints and watches between Visual Basic sessions. The methods of the Debug object only work in the design environment. When you compile your project, all references to the Debug object will be ignored.

Assertions and Defensive Programming

The second method of the Debug object is the Assert method. The Assert method can be used to enter break mode. This means that you can use the Assert method to save breakpoints between Visual Basic sessions. To use the Assert method, you must provide a condition that when evaluated to False will cause execution to pause. Using the Assert method is like setting a breakpoint or a Watch expression that would be of type Break When Value Is False. Execution will be suspended on the statement that contains the Assert method. For example, consider the following code:

```
Private Sub cmdLoadTemps_Click()

Dim intInitialTemp As Integer

intInitialTemp = StartTemp
intNumitems = intNumitems + 1
Debug.Assert intNumitems < 0
If intInitialTemp > Min Then
```

The Debug Assert method is used to monitor the value of the public variable intNumitems. The condition being evaluated tests to see if this variable is less than zero. Since the Assert method causes a break when the test condition evaluates to False, this means that Visual Basic will enter break mode if intNumitems is greater than or equal to zero.

The Assert method has two helpful characteristics. First, it allows you to evaluate conditions that might lead to problems in your code. Second, it allows you to save breakpoints in between VB sessions. This is important because chances are you will have to leave your project in the middle of the debug process. Having to reopen the project and remember every place where you inserted a breakpoint or a watch is not conducive to effective debugging. By using the Print and Assert methods, you will be able to debug your code more efficiently.

Tracking Down and Killing Bugs

Since not many people (if any) can write perfect code the first time, chances are you will have to spend a great deal of effort tracking down bugs. To get the most out of the debugging process, planning is essential. Planning ahead will save you time and many headaches later on. We can increase the efficiency of the debug process by tracking variable and object lifetimes and by creating debugging and error logs that can be analyzed.

Tracking Object Lifetimes

Object and variable lifetimes can be tracked during the debug process if you have set a watch. In Fig. 13-5, we see two Watch variables, the

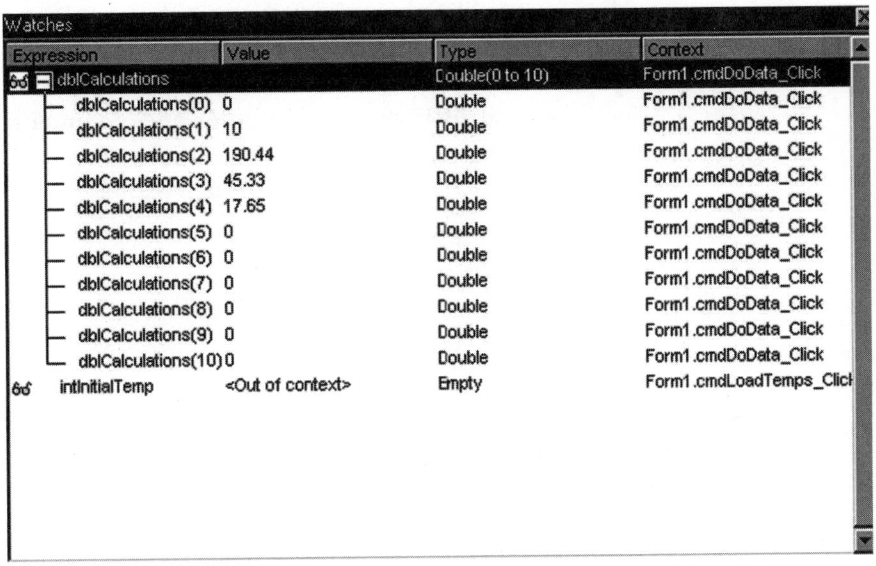

Figure 13-5
The Watches window.

Expression	Value	Type	Context
dblCalculations		Double(0 to 10)	Form1.cmdDoData_Click
dblCalculations(0)	0	Double	Form1.cmdDoData_Click
dblCalculations(1)	10	Double	Form1.cmdDoData_Click
dblCalculations(2)	190.44	Double	Form1.cmdDoData_Click
dblCalculations(3)	45.33	Double	Form1.cmdDoData_Click
dblCalculations(4)	17.65	Double	Form1.cmdDoData_Click
dblCalculations(5)	0	Double	Form1.cmdDoData_Click
dblCalculations(6)	0	Double	Form1.cmdDoData_Click
dblCalculations(7)	0	Double	Form1.cmdDoData_Click
dblCalculations(8)	0	Double	Form1.cmdDoData_Click
dblCalculations(9)	0	Double	Form1.cmdDoData_Click
dblCalculations(10)	0	Double	Form1.cmdDoData_Click
intInitialTemp	<Out of context>	Empty	Form1.cmdLoadTemps_Click

array `dblCalculations` and an integer variable called `intInitialTemp`. The watch window is shown at a breakpoint that was set in a procedure that manipulates the array. The `intInitialTemp` variable is a local variable that is declared in an `Event` procedure. At the time of the break, the event procedure is not executing, and the lifetime of the `intInitialTemp` variable has expired. This is indicated by the `Out of context` entry in the Value column. The `dblCalculations` array is in scope, so the contents of the array are displayed.

Debugging and Error Logs

You can create log files to track the debugging process. You can create a text file and use the file system objects to write the values of variables and expressions to disk for analysis. The type of information that can be tracked includes:

- The procedure that is currently running, along with the form or module that contains that procedure.
- The value of each variable. This can include local variables as well as variables with module-wide or public scope.
- The date and time that the program is executing.

Debug logs provide the programmer with another way to track down bugs by providing a useful tool for analysis. If large chunks of code need to be executed, you can simply run the code and then print out and examine the Debug log to see where the problem lies. This may be preferable to sitting at the computer and stepping through code one line at a time, say, if a large `For...Next` loop is executing. In the following hypothetical example, we create a debugging log for this procedure:

```
Public Function Compute(intData() As Integer, intNumItems As Integer)
  As Double

  Dim dblValue As Double, dblTemp As Double
  Dim intLoopCounter As Integer
  'debug log code
  Dim fsoFile As FileSystemObject
  Dim MyTextStream As TextStream
  Dim MyFile As File
  Dim strTemp As String

  Call fsoFile.CreateTextFile("C:\Debug.log")
  Set MyFile = fsoFile.GetFile("C:\Debug.log")
  Set MyTextStream = MyFile.OpenAsTextStream
```

```
          dblValue = 0

      For intLoopCounter = 1 To intNumItems

        'write values to the debug log
        strTemp = CStr(Now) & " Loop Counter : " & intLoopCounter & "  Array
          Data: " & intData(intLoopCounter)
      MyTextStream.WriteLine (strTemp)

        dblTemp = CDbl(intMax / intData(intLoopCounter))
        If dblTemp < dblValue Then

          dblValue = dblTemp

        End If

        Next intLoopCounter

        MyTextStream.Close

    End Function
```

The log will list the date and time, the value of the loop counter, and the contents of the array. This data can then be analyzed to track down and correct the bug.

Handling Run-Time Errors

In this section, we consider the problem of dealing with run-time errors. There are many conditions that will cause run-time errors: division by zero, attempting to open a nonexistent file, assigning an out-of-range value to a variable, just to name a few. The fact is, no matter how carefully you design your software, it's just impossible to account for every situation. In Visual Basic, run-time errors can be dealt with by using an error handler in conjunction with the `Err` object. This approach allows the programmer to identify which error occurred, determine a path of action in response to the error, and most importantly, avoid crashing the program and losing data.

An error handler should be provided for every procedure in your project. The process of dealing with run-time errors involves the following steps:

■ Enabling error handling in the current procedure.

■ Determining which error occurred.

■ Displaying a message to the user.

■ Recovering from the error. This may involve asking the user to take corrective action, such as placing a floppy disk in the drive, or programmatically correcting the situation. There may be times when no action is necessary, so the program may recover from the error simply by skipping to the next line.

Turning on Error Handling

Error handling must be turned on or enabled in each procedure for error trapping to occur. This is done with the following line:

```
On Error Goto Label
```

where *label* is a programmer-defined label that tells Visual Basic where to transfer program control when an error occurs. As a simple example, let's say we had a procedure called "doubleIt" that doubled the value of an integer:

```
Public Sub doubleIt(inputvalue as integer)

 Dim result As Integer

 result = 2 * inputvalue

 MsgBox "Doubled Value is : " & CStr(result)
End Sub
```

If we don't put an error handler in this procedure, overflow errors can arise that will cause the program to crash. For example, imagine that the user calls the procedure and passes the value 30,000. The program will crash since the variable `result` does not have enough memory to hold twice this value. Running this program will cause the error `number 6: Overflow`.

To keep the program from crashing, we can add an error handler. The first step is to enable error handling with the `On Error` statement. Let's change the procedure to look like the following:

```
Public Sub doubleIt(inputvalue as integer)
On Error Goto  errDoubleIt
 Dim result As Integer

 result = 2 * inputvalue
```

```
MsgBox "Doubled Value is: " & CStr(result)

Exit Sub

errDoubleIt:
 MsgBox "Error: Cannot Double Input Value"
End Sub
```

The label `errDoubleIt` now identifies an error handler for this procedure. In the first line of the procedure, we've added the `On Error Goto` statement, which enables error handling and provides a label that tells Visual Basic where to transfer control in the event of an error.

If an error occurs, Visual Basic will transfer control to the label we defined in the `On Error Goto` statement. This label must be followed by a colon, and this is where you put the code for the error handler. In this example, all the error handler does is display a message to the user indicating that the operation cannot be performed:

```
errDoubleIt:
 MsgBox "Error: Cannot Double Input Value"
```

You will notice that we've added the line `Exit Sub` before the label that identifies our error-handling routine. This prevents the error-handling code from being executed if no error occurs. Note that you can turn off or disable error handling with the line `On Error GoTo 0`.

The `Err` Object

The `Err` object is a globally accessible object that can be used to obtain information about run-time errors. For example, you can use the `Err` object to display important information to the user when an error occurs, such as the Visual Basic error number and a descriptive message that tells the user what happened. Every Visual Basic project can automatically access the `Err` object: you do not need to set a reference.

Properties of the `Err` Object   The following table shows the important properties of the `Err` object.

Property	Description
Description	A string that provides a description of the error
HelpContext	Help file context ID for this error
HelpFile	Path and file name for the appropriate help file
LastDLLError	System error code produced when a call to a DLL fails
Number	An integer code indicating which error occurred
Source	Name of the object that generated the error

The `Err` object also has two methods, Clear and Raise. Clear resets the properties of the `Err` object. Raise can be used to generate an error. This can be done to generate your own error codes, say in a class module, or to pass an error up the call stack. Generally, the most useful properties of the `Err` object are the Number and Description properties. These can be used to display a meaningful message to the user. If the problem is something simple, such as not having a floppy disk in the drive, the user can correct the situation. If the problem is more complex, he or she can relay the error information to tech support to resolve the problem. As we mentioned earlier, the `Err` object is an intrinsic object with global scope, so you can refer to it anywhere in your code.

Using the `Err` object, we can display the error number and description to the user. For example, we can modify the error handler for the `DoubleIt` function to look like the following:

```
Public Sub doubleIt(inputvalue as integer)

 On Error Goto  errDoubleIt

  Dim result As Integer

  Rresult = 2 * inputvalue

  MsgBox "Doubled Value is: " & CStr(result)

  Exit Sub

errDoubleIt:

  Msgbox "ERROR  " & Err.Number & "  " & Err.Description "Occurred in
    DoubleIt"
End Sub
```

Resuming Execution after an Error Occurs   Once an error is handled, you must decide how to respond to the error. There are three options:

- ■ Resume: A Resume statement returns execution to the line of code that raised the error. This can be used to complete an operation if the error handler takes some action to resolve the error condition or if the user can take some corrective action, such as placing a floppy disk in the drive.

- ■ Resume Next: This statement will cause execution to begin on the line of code that comes immediately after the line that caused the error. This type of Resume can be used if the error that occurred will not affect the rest of the code in the procedure.

- ■ Resume Label *or* GoTo Label: This is one place where the dreaded GoTo statement of yesteryear is useful. If some initialization code is required before reexecuting the offending line of code, you can use a Resume Label or GoTo Label statement to retry the initialization before the offending line of code executes.

In Fig. 13-6, we show a form that will display the directories and files on the user's computer. The form uses a drive list box, directory list box, and file list box to display the information to the user. If the user attempts to open the floppy drive or CD-ROM drive when a disk is not in the drive, this will generate an error. In the drive list box change event, we assign the drive and path to each object. We can handle the error with the following code:

```
Private Sub Drive1_Change()
On Error GoTo ReadDriveErr
```

Figure 13-6
The View Files
program.

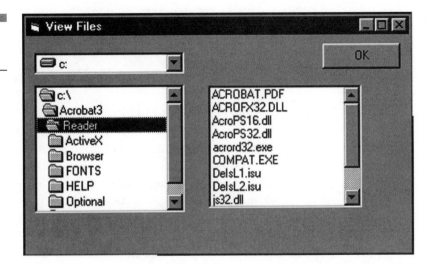

```
   Dir1.Path = Drive1.Drive
   File1.Path = Dir1.Path

   Exit Sub

ReadDriveErr:

 If Err.Number = 68 Then

  Dim resp As Integer
  resp = MsgBox("Please Place a Disk in the Drive",
   vbAbortRetryIgnore)
  If resp = vbRetry Then
   Resume
  Else
   Exit Sub
  End If
 Else

  MsgBox Err.Number & " " & Err.Description
  Resume Next

 End If

 Resume
End Sub
```

In the error handler we check to see if the error that occurred was error number 68, which occurs when the user does not have a disk in the drive. If so, we ask the user if he or she wants to place a disk in the drive. If the user clicks the Retry button, we use a Resume statement to reexecute the line of code that caused the error. If he or she clicks the Abort or Ignore button, we simply exit the procedure. For all other errors we display an error message to the user and then use a Resume Next statement to resume execution on the line of code following the line that caused the error.

Creating an Error Handler Add-In

Visual Basic has several add-ins that extend the functionality of the IDE. Some of the add-ins you may be familiar with include the API Viewer, the Class Builder utility, and the many wizards that can help you build your projects. From the perspective of the creator of an add-in, it is an in-process ActiveX component (DLL). This means that you can build your own add-ins for Visual Basic. In this section, we will create a simple add-in that will add error-handling routines to the open code windows of a project. First, let's take a slight detour to learn about the steps necessary to create an add-in.

Add-In Basics The first step to creating an add-in is to start a new project in Visual Basic. Select *Add-In* from the New Project dialog. Visual Basic will create a new project with a single form, named "frmAddIn," and an object (class) called *Connect*. The frmAddIn form will function as the user interface for your add-in. When the user selects Your Add-In from the Visual Basic Add-Ins pull-down menu, this form will load. Connect is used to specify how the add-in connects to the Visual Basic IDE, such as load behavior and display name. You will use the Visual Basic object model to interact with the object in the Visual Basic environment.

The Visual Basic Object Model Visual Basic provides several objects that can be used to interact with the IDE. There are objects that represent a project, menus, windows, forms, code modules, and procedures. You can add menu or toolbar items to the IDE or view or edit the code in a code window, among other things.

The Visual Basic object model is a hierarchy. The top of the hierarchy is an object called VBE (Visual Basic Environment). VBE represents the current copy of Visual Basic that is running. An add-in can access the elements of the IDE by setting a reference to VBE. The VBE object has several useful methods and properties. Some of these are as follows:

- *ActiveCodePane*: This property can be used to set or return the currently active code pane. A code pane is a window in which code is displayed.

- *ActiveVBProject*: This returns the active Visual Basic project.

- *CodePanes*: This is a collection that represents the currently visible code windows. The actual code is accessed through a Code Module object.

- *CommandBars*: This collection represents buttons, menus, and toolbars. You can use the CommandBars collection to add new menus for your add-in, for example.

- *Events*: The Events collection can be used to detect events inside the VB IDE. For example, you can detect when the user saves a file or sets a new reference with the References dialog.

- *Quit*: The Quit method can be used to shut down Visual Basic.

- *SelectedVBComponent*: This returns the component that is currently selected.

- *VBProjects*: This is a collection of the projects that are currently open inside Visual Basic.

■ *Windows*: The Windows collection represents all open windows in the IDE. This includes dockable windows. You can use this collection to open and close windows in the IDE.

When you create an add-in with Visual Basic 6.0, the VBE object model will be referenced automatically. If you need to set a reference manually, this can be done from the References dialog by selecting *Microsoft Visual Basic 6.0 Extensibility*. To work with toolbars and menus, you use the Office object model. This is referenced through the Microsoft Office 8.0 Object Library. Each of these object models can be examined in the Object Browser.

Setting Connect Properties   When you create an add-in, you will see a `Connect` object displayed in the Project Explorer along with the frmAddIn form (see Fig. 13-7). The `Connect` object is a Visual Basic class interface known as IAddinDesigner. This object will manage the loading and connection behavior of your add-in. If you open the `Connect` object, a dialog box will open on your screen that allows you to set several properties.

Starting a New Add-In Project

To illustrate how the VBE object model can be accessed to manipulate the objects in the Visual Basic environment, we will create an add-in. This add-in will insert error-handling routines into the open code windows of a Visual Basic project. When the add-in completes writing the error handler to a procedure, the procedure name will be added to a list box and displayed to the user. This add-in will work on all types of modules.

The first step is to create a new VB project of type Add-In. Visual Basic will create a new add-in project with a frmAddIn form and a `Connect` object. The first step is to set the properties of our project, which will determine how the add-in is known to the user. First, we open the `Connect` object from the Project Explorer. The Addin Display Name is changed to *Error Handler Add-in* and the Addin Description is set to *Adds Error Handlers to the open code windows of a VB project*. These settings determine how your add-in is displayed in the Visual Basic Add-In Manager. The display name is shown under the heading *Available Add-Ins* while the description is displayed when the user selects your add-in.

Figure 13-7
The Connect object

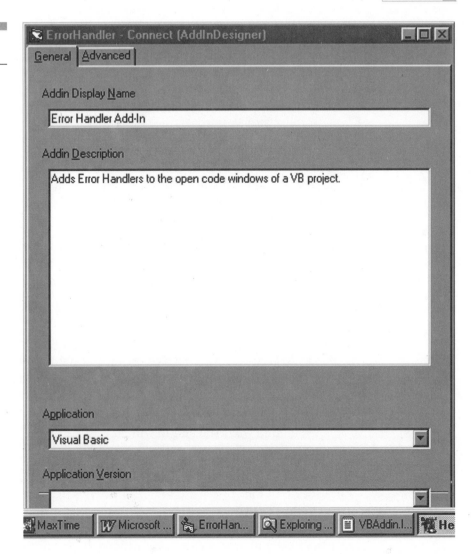

Next, we want to open the code window of the `Connect` object and view the `AddinInstance_OnConnection` event procedure. This procedure sets the display name of the menu that will represent your add-in in the VB IDE. Visual Basic has already placed the appropriate code in this event for you. However, we are interested in customizing the AddToAddInCommandBar method. This call is what determines what the menu item for your add-in will display to the user. The default setting is `My AddIn`, which is not very descriptive. We will change it to reflect the purpose of our add-in. The code then looks like this:

```
If ConnectMode = ext_cm_External Then
    'Used by the wizard toolbar to start this wizard
    Me.Show
Else
    Set mcbMenuCommandBar = AddToAddInCommandBar("Error Handler
      Builder")
    'sink the event
    Set Me.MenuHandler = VBInstance.Events.CommandBarEvents
      (mcbMenuCommandBar)
End If
```

Customizing the Add-In Form   Now we are ready to fix up the add-in form. When you open the frmAddIn form, it is a blank form with two command buttons, OK and Cancel. We will fix up our add-in by including the following controls:

- *lstProcedures*: This is a list box that will show the user the procedures in which our add-in was able to insert error-handling routines.

- *optResumeNext*: This is the first of two option buttons. If the user selects this option, the add-in will insert inline error handlers into each procedure. The error handlers will simply read *On Error Resume Next*.

- *optHandlers*: If the user selects this option, our add-in will create an error handler that displays the description property of the Err object to the user.

- *cmdHelp*: This command button will display a message to the user explaining what the add-in will do.

The user will initiate the action of the add-in by clicking the *OK* button. He or she can abort by clicking the *Cancel* button. The fromAddIn form is shown in Fig. 13-8.

Adding Code to the Error Handler Add-In   For our add-in to work, it will have to access each code window in the project. It will then have to determine which procedures are in the project, locate those procedures, and then insert the error-handling code into each procedure. The code is placed in the Click event of the cmdOK command button and looks like this:

```
Private Sub OKButton_Click()

    Dim c As CodePane
    Dim m As Member

    Dim strProcedureName As String
    Dim strOnError As String
    Dim lngProcedureLocation As Long
    Dim lngProcLines As Long
```

Figure 13-8
The frmAddIn form.

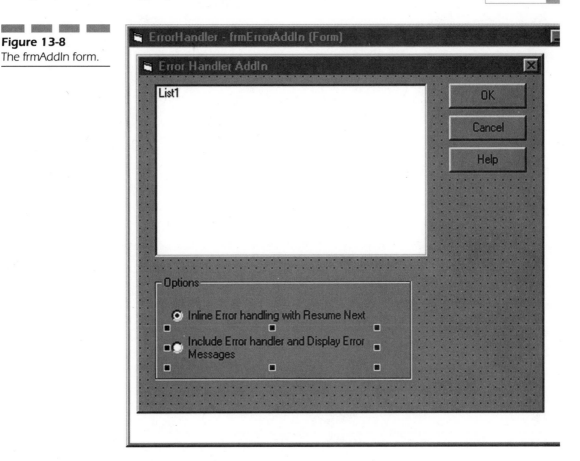

```
Dim lngEndPos As Long
Dim strErrorCode As String
Dim blnAddHandler As Boolean
Dim strDisplayError As String
Dim strResume As String
Dim intLocated As Integer
Dim strExit As String
Dim strHeader As String

'check which option button the user has selected
If optResumeNext.Value = True Then
    strOnError = "On Error Resume Next"
    blnAddHandler = False
Else
    blnAddHandler = True
End If

For Each c In VBInstance.CodePanes

  For Each m In c.CodeModule.Members
    'if this member is a procedure then add error handling
    If m.Type = vbext_mt_Event Or m.Type = vbext_mt_Method Then
      'get the name of this procedure
```

```
      strProcedureName = m.Name
      lngProcedureLocation = m.CodeLocation
      'get header
      strHeader = c.CodeModule.Lines(lngProcedureLocation, 1)
      intLocated = InStr(strHeader, "Sub")
      If intLocated > 0 Then
        strExit = "Exit Sub"
      Else
        strExit = "Exit Function"
      End If

      'add the On Error Statement as the first line of the
        procedure
      Call c.CodeModule.InsertLines(lngProcedureLocation + 1,
        strOnError)

      If blnAddHandler = True Then

          'build the on error string and error handler label for
            this procedure
          strOnError = "On Error GoTo err" & strProcedureName
          strDisplayError = "    MsgBox Err.Description"
          strErrorCode = "err" & strProcedureName & ":"

          'find out how many lines of code are in this procedure
          lngProcLines =
    c.CodeModule.ProcCountLines(strProcedureName, vbext_pk_Proc)

          'get the last line in the procedure where we can insert
            code
          lngEndPos = lngProcedureLocation + lngProcLines - 2

          'add the Exit string
          Call c.CodeModule.InsertLines(lngEndPos, strExit)
          'insert the error handler
          Call c.CodeModule.InsertLines(lngEndPos + 1, strErrorCode)
          Call c.CodeModule.InsertLines(lngEndPos + 2,
    strDisplayError)
          Call c.CodeModule.InsertLines(lngEndPos + 3, "    Resume
            Next")

      End If

      'completed, add the procedure name to the list box
      lstProcedures.AddItem m.Name

    End If

  Next m

  Next c

End Sub
```

Declaring Variables   At the top of the routine we have declared several variables that we will use to access VB IDE objects, determine the location of procedures, and insert code. The first object we need is a

Code Pane object. A code pane is a window in the VB IDE that contains code. We will use the code pane variable c to loop through the CodePanes collection of the current VB instance. Each code pane contains a Code Module object, which is the actual VB code that we are interested in.

The next variable to note is the Member variable. A member is an event, method, property, or variable that is part of a code module. The members of each code module in a VB project are represented by the Members collection of the Code Module object. We can check each member to get important information, such as what type of member it is (event, method, property, or variable); the location of that member, that is, the line number of the code module where we can find the member; as well as the name of the member. The remaining variables that we have declared are strings and longs that will hold the information we need and build the error-handling code for each procedure.

The first code fragment in this procedure tests to see which option button the user has selected. Recall that we will permit the user to simply add inline error handling or build an error handler that displays the description property of the Err object. Our code sets a Boolean value that we can test later to see which choice the user made. In addition, if the user has selected inline error handling, we build the line of code that we will insert in each procedure:

```
If optResumeNext.Value = True Then
    strOnError = "On Error Resume Next"
    blnAddHandler = False
Else
    blnAddHandler = True
End If
```

Looping through the Code Modules   The next piece of code is used to loop through the open code modules in the project. Since we are using collections of objects, we can use the For Each...Next construct to do this. First, we use the VBInstance object to get each code pane. VBInstance is a public variable that VB inserts in the frmAddIn form when you create an add-in project. It is type VBE, which means that we can use it to access the Visual Basic object model. We will use the CodePanes collection of the VBE object variable VBInstance to loop through the open code windows in the IDE. This is done with the statement:

```
For Each c In VBInstance.CodePanes
```

Each code pane has a CodeModule object. This is used to actually get at the Visual Basic code for each window. The CodeModule object has a

`Members` collection, which contains the members for each module in the project. The next line of code is a `For Each…Next` loop that loops through the members of each code module:

```
For Each m In c.CodeModule.Members
```

Using the `Members` Collection   Each element of the `Members` collection has important properties that we can use to determine what kind of member it is, its location, and its name. Our add-in will only insert an error handler if we encounter a `Sub` or `Function` procedure (which is a method) or an event procedure. The `m` variable is used to loop through the `Members` collection. We test each element of the collection with an `If` statement at the top of the loop:

```
If m.Type = vbext_mt_Event Or m.Type = vbext_mt_Method Then
```

Visual Basic has defined an enumerated type called *vbext_MemberType*. The enumerated values are as follows:

- *vbext_mt_Const*: This tells us that the member is a constant.
- *vbext_mt_Event*: This tells us that it is an event procedure.
- *vbext_mt_Method*: This tells us that the member is a method, that is, a sub or function procedure.
- *vbext_mt_Property*: This tells us that this is a property procedure.
- *vbext_mt_Variable*: This tells us that this member is a variable.

In our case, we are only interested in Event procedures or methods, so our `If` statement tests for this case. If we don't have an Event procedure or a method, the loop will go on to the next element in the `Members` collection.

Getting Information about Each Procedure   If the current member is an Event procedure or method, we need to find out some information about that procedure before we can move on. First, we need to know the name of the procedure. Then we need to find out the location of that procedure. This is given by the line number of the procedure, which is type `Long`. Finally, we also need to know if this is a `Sub` or `Function`. Our routine uses the following code to find out this information:

```
'et the name of this procedure
strProcedureName = m.Name
lngProcedureLocation = m.CodeLocation

'get header
```

```
strHeader = c.CodeModule.Lines(lngProcedureLocation, 1)

intLocated = InStr(strHeader, "Sub")

If intLocated > 0 Then
  strExit = "Exit Sub"
Else
  strExit = "Exit Function"
End If
```

The name property of the member object variable contains the name of the procedure. We can then use the CodeLocation property to determine the line number where this procedure is located.

The next line of code uses the Lines method of the Code Module object to get the first line of the procedure. We will use this to build an exit string for the procedure, that is, Exit Sub or Exit Function, which must be placed before the error handler. The Lines method returns a string that contains a fragment of code. You supply two parameters: the starting line and the number of lines to retrieve. To get the first line of the procedure, we pass the line number where the procedure is located and tell the Lines method to return one line.

The first line of the procedure can be used to tell us if we have a function or a sub. We use the InStr function to test if the substring Sub is located in the procedure declaration. We then use this information to build the appropriate exit string.

Enabling Error Handling You will recall that we must "turn on" error handling in each procedure where we want to use it. This is done with an On Error statement. We will insert the On Error statement at the beginning of each procedure, immediately below the procedure header. This is done by using the InsertLines method of the Code Module object. InsertLines takes two parameters: the line number where we want to add text and the text string to insert. We add the On Error statement to each procedure with this line:

```
'add the On Error Statement as the first line of the procedure
Call c.CodeModule.InsertLines(lngProcedureLocation + 1, strOnError)
```

You will recall that if the user has opted for inline error handling, the strOnError variable will contain the text On Error Resume Next. If this is the case, we're done for this procedure. If not, we need to place the Exit Sub and Function Exit line, a label to identify the error handler, and the error handler code at the end of the procedure. This is done with the following block of code:

```
If blnAddHandler = True Then

        'build the on error string and error handler label for this
          procedure
        strOnError = "On Error GoTo err" & strProcedureName
        strDisplayError = "    MsgBox Err.Description"
        strErrorCode = "err" & strProcedureName & ":"

        'find out how many lines of code are in this procedure
        lngProcLines = c.CodeModule.ProcCountLines(strProcedureName,
          vbext_pk_Proc)

        'get the last line in the procedure where we can insert code
        lngEndPos = lngProcedureLocation + lngProcLines - 2
        'add the Exit string
        Call c.CodeModule.InsertLines(lngEndPos, strExit)

        'insert the error handler
        Call c.CodeModule.InsertLines(lngEndPos + 1, strErrorCode)
        Call c.CodeModule.InsertLines(lngEndPos + 2, strDisplayError)
        Call c.CodeModule.InsertLines(lngEndPos + 3, "    Resume
          Next")
    End If
```

At the top of the `If` statement we test the `blnAddHandler` variable, which was set at the beginning of the procedure to tell us which option button the user checked. If this variable is set to True, the user wants the complete error handler added to each procedure.

The first line uses the ProcCountLines method of the Code Module object to retrieve the number of lines in the current procedure. We pass it the name of the procedure, which we obtained from the `Members` collection. We also pass the enumerated constant vbext_pk_proc, which tells the method that the object we are interested in is a procedure. This value is used for all procedures that are not property procedures.

We can then calculate the line number of the last line of the procedure and use this value to insert the exit command, the label for the error handler, and the error handler itself. For our add-in, the error handler will simply display a message box containing the description property of the `Err` object and issue a `Resume Next` statement. The code includes these three lines:

```
Call c.CodeModule.InsertLines(lngEndPos + 1, strErrorCode)
Call c.CodeModule.InsertLines(lngEndPos + 2, strDisplayError)
Call c.CodeModule.InsertLines(lngEndPos + 3, "    Resume Next")
```

The last line of the loop adds the procedure name to the list box.

Testing, Compiling, and Distributing the Add-In   To test an add-in, select *Start* from the Run pull-down menu. Start another copy of VB and load a project. Your add-in will be automatically loaded for use in the second project. You can then test the add-in and debug it by setting breakpoints.

Once the add-in code is completed, it can be compiled just like any other in-process component. This is done by selecting *Make Addin.dll* from the File pull-down menu. Once compiled, the add-in can be used with any project in the VB IDE. It will be available in the Add-In Manager dialog box. The add-in can also be distributed to other users in the same manner you would use for other in-process components. Simply use the Package and Deployment Wizard to build your setup program.

CHAPTER 14

Testing VB Applications

There comes a time in the life of a software project when the coding is completed and we are sure that the code corresponds well to the specified design requirements. It is at this point that formal testing can begin. Testing, just like any other aspect of RAD, is a phase that requires careful planning. In the real world, I've seen too many programmers get seduced by the illusion that a RAD environment is capable of producing: if an application looks good, it must be working correctly. Testing the project seems like an afterthought. With this assumption in mind the product gets shipped out the door before it's really ready to go. Just like any other aspect of the RAD design process, it's important to avoid falling victim to this kind of behavior. You do so by maintaining a rigorous testing protocol.

Before beginning a testing program, you should ask yourself what the goal of testing is. Most developers would probably agree that the goal of testing is to show that the software is free of defects. However, writers such as Pressman have suggested that successful testing involves uncovering errors in the software. Pressman states: "Testing cannot show the absence of defects, it can only show software defects are present" [Roger S. Pressman, *A Manager's Guide to Software Engineering*, McGraw-Hill, 1993].

With this in mind, we can approach the subject of testing software more realistically. Bugs and errors are inevitable in the design of software that's of any substantial complexity. If a testing process is uncovering those errors, this isn't necessarily an indication of bad software design; it just means that the testing process is an effective one. Testing can be broken down into two distinct areas:

- Testing the internal operations of the various components to ensure that they perform according to specifications. This is known as *white box* testing.

- Higher level or interface testing. Here we test to ensure that the software behaves as expected. Does it accept data input correctly and produce the correct output? This is known as *black box* testing.

Testing a Visual Basic project will involve both types of testing. Your project will use many built-in Windows components as well as several ActiveX controls. We aren't worried about the internal functioning of these objects; we want to make sure that they have been integrated correctly so the program produces the expected output. This means we will do a lot of black box testing. However, a VB program is made up of many individual units, forms, code modules, or classes. You will write the code that makes these units function. In this case, you will do white box testing to make sure that the internal operations of each component work as specified in the design requirements. The functioning of each of these elements will then be tested in the larger context of the entire project, meaning that we will do more black box testing. In any programming language, testing should proceed through the following phases:

- Testing for proof of concept
- Unit testing
- Integration testing
- System testing
- Beta testing
- Regression testing

As testing proceeds, it tends to move in an inside-out fashion. We start our testing process at the lowest levels, the level of the code inside each function and subroutine. Testing then moves to the level of the module to see if all modules are integrated correctly. Only then do we test the system as a whole under different configurations of hardware and software. Once the testing process by the developer is complete, we expand the testing to include the end user. The testing process must be repeated as code is maintained and modified. We will explore each testing phase in the following sections.

The Importance of Documenting the Testing Process

The testing process should be formalized. This means developing a standard series of testing phases and documenting each step. Documentation should include a list of what tests were done, what data was used, the expected results, and the actual results. Standardizing the testing process will make it easier to implement it in the future and save time. By maintaining good documentation we can ensure that we will be able to go back and repeat the *exact* same tests if necessary.

Testing for Proof of Concept

Above all, a software product must be tested to ensure that it meets any architectural and design specifications. This is known as testing for *proof of concept.* In other words, does the software do what it's supposed to do? Testing for proof of concept will involve examining the following areas:

■ Does the software accept the data the customer expects it to?

■ Does the software produce the proper output and reports?

■ Are the correct algorithms and data formats used? Sometimes developers don't understand exactly what the customer wants, so it's important to make sure that the problem solved is on target. As a simple example, a customer might expect data to be output in square meters while the program uses square feet.

■ Is the user interface what the customer expects? Does each form display the data fields expected?

Testing for proof of concept is not something that begins when the program is finished; rather, it will go on throughout the entire development life cycle. When we are sure the program does what the design requirements specify, we are ready to begin the testing of each component.

Unit Testing

The start of any effective testing program begins with *unit testing*. This is a testing process that focuses on testing individual units of code. In the past, this would probably involve testing a suite of subroutines or functions. In Visual Basic, this type of testing is facilitated by the way the language is structured. Consider the fact that a Visual Basic project is made up of zero, one, or more of the following elements:

■ Forms

■ Standard code modules

■ Class modules

■ User Control objects

■ User Document objects

This means that we can approach unit testing by testing the behavior of each form, module, or object on an individual basis. This makes possible a robust testing process because we can ensure that each form or module is in good working order before testing the project as a whole. When we are testing the individual units of the program, we are engaging in white box testing. Testing can proceed in an orderly fashion, ensuring that forms or modules work as expected one by one. When it comes time to test the entire project, the testing process is reduced to making sure that each element interacts with the others correctly.

The object-oriented nature of Windows programming also helps to speed the unit testing process. If a form has several controls on it, such as a calendar, an ADO data control, some text boxes, and command buttons, we don't have to worry about whether or not these objects work—that was already done by the manufacturer. Since we know that these black box elements already function properly, our focus shifts to worrying about whether they are configured and integrated correctly. This means we can add a great deal of functionality to our programs without adding an additional cost to the testing process.

Integration Testing

After we test each individual unit or component in the project, we need to see how these units work together. This brings us to the concept of *integration testing*. In integration testing, the focus starts to shift from the individual units to the software architecture as a whole. Integration testing is a form of black box testing. Each unit in the project has already been tested to ensure that the internal "parts" are working. Now we are testing to see how each unit interfaces with the other units it must interact with. Black box techniques are used that focus on the required output. For example, suppose we know from unit testing that a form gets the user input correctly, and a procedure in a module crunches numbers and produces the right output. In the integration phase, we will see what happens when the form passes the data to the procedure, and then the procedure returns the output for display to the user. Many errors are uncovered during this phase of testing because such data interchanges were not planned correctly.

System Testing

After the integration process is complete, the next stage is *system testing*, which involves testing at a higher level that may involve more than the components of the software. This means testing with different hardware configurations, operating systems, and databases. System testing will involve one or more of the following activities:

- Testing the software on single-user machines.
- Testing the software on a network as well as on various network configurations.
- Trying different memory and hard disk configurations.
- If the software uses multithreading, it should be tested on single- as well as multiple-processor machines to ensure that performance is not compromised.
- Testing on different processors, such as Pentium, Pentium II, or AMD chips.
- Testing with different operating systems. For example, the code may perform differently under Windows 95/98 than it will under Windows NT 4.0.
- If this is an Internet application, it will have to be tested with different browsers.

Some aspects of system testing may be beyond the reach of small companies. In that case, the system and beta testing phases can overlap. For example, if your company does not have a network, arrangements can be made with a customer to test the product under network conditions.

Beta Testing

Once the software team has pushed a product through its own round of testing, it's time for real-world customers to have a chance at it. When customers are given the opportunity to use the product under real-world conditions, they will inevitably uncover several faults in the software. This process is known as *beta testing*. During beta testing, a "prerelease" version of the software is provided to a subset of customers. The understanding is that they will use the product and attempt to discover remaining bugs or errors. This puts the product through the paces of day-to-day use, giving the developer an opportunity to correct many problems before the product actually hits the market. This is an important phase of the testing process. No matter how careful the software team is during testing, a developer simply can't anticipate every action the end user will take or what kind of data might be encountered. The only way to push the software to the limit is to have real users get a chance to break the product.

The size of the beta testing pool will vary widely depending on the kind of market you are developing for. If you're designing customized software as a consultant, beta testing will only involve one customer. In this case, beta testing follows naturally as the feedback between the client and developer continues throughout the testing process.

In a vertical or widespread software market, where the number of customers can range from a few hundred to millions, beta testing can be done by selecting clients that represent a cross section of users. A free version of the software can be provided in exchange for the knowledge gained by the customer using the software under real-world conditions. As updates or new versions of the software are released, beta testers can provide feedback on user interface changes or performance.

An effective beta testing program should involve the following steps:

- Choose a representative subset of customers. They should reflect a cross section of your market, including both large and small clients and different levels of usage. If possible, the beta testers should be spread out among rural and urban clients as well as government and commercial users. The goal is to maximize the variety of conditions under which the software will be used.

- Customers should receive the complete product, including documentation such as user's manuals. Don't forget that the user's manual and online help system are part of the beta testing process as well. If users find the help confusing or don't like the manual, this is the time to find out.

- Provide a reasonable time period for evaluation. This will vary according to factors such as market size or pressure to get the product out. However, don't rush the beta process; it's better to take your time and release a software product that works well than to simply get to market as quickly as possible.

- Beta testers should maintain a "bug" or error log, where they make a detailed entry every time they run into a problem. The information recorded should include a detailed description of the error. What data was being entered or what user action was taking place when the error occurred? Did the program crash? If the program reported an error message, what was the error number and description?

- Beta testers should report their overall impressions of the product. Did they like the user interface? Was it difficult to use? Did they approve of the manual?

Many companies cringe at the thought of giving away their software. If we imagined a vertical software product that we only expected to sell a few hundred copies of per year, we might be taken aback by the lost revenue. However, the payback from letting 15 or 20 real customers test the software over a reasonable amount of time will be enormous. They will unearth many bugs and discover problems the developer never thought of. Feedback on the user interface and overall flow of the software will be invaluable. By cleaning up the product after the beta process is complete, we've ensured that the software is as ready for market as it can be. Happy beta testers will push the product to their friends in the industry, and in exchange for the free software, positive customer comments can be used in marketing materials.

Many smaller companies try to avoid beta testing. They figure they can "wing it," fixing problems as they go along and simply shipping out a "patch" to the client. However, failure to use an effective beta testing program will result in higher costs later on. This means more technical support calls, more time spent fixing bugs *after* the product has been released, and more customer complaints. If you're continually shipping "patches" to your customers, after a while they'll start to question your abilities and judgment. The time and resources that will have to be directed toward continual fixing of undertested software will mean fewer resources are available to develop new products. For these reasons, a highly structured and carefully planned beta testing program is recommended. Beta testing will likely involve many successive iterations as the software gets closer and closer to an acceptable level of performance. When the beta testers can no longer find errors, the software is ready to be released.

Regression Testing

During the life cycle of a software product, it will undergo many modifications as customers demand new features or the software team dreams up innovations. Another factor that needs to be considered is that despite our best testing efforts, users will continue to discover new bugs during the course of product use. As a result, continued coding and testing will be required.

Whenever such modifications are made to a software product, previous testing procedures must be repeated. This process is known as *regression testing*. The purpose of regression testing is to ensure that any code maintenance or modification has not introduced new errors into previously functioning software. To engage in regression testing, you must maintain a detailed record of testing procedures. By documenting the testing procedures used, you can repeat the same tests to make sure that the software still behaves as expected. Regression testing is also important when using an incremental software development model. It can be applied at each increment or release of the software. In this way, old tests are repeated to maintain the integrity of the software as new features are added. At each stage or increment, the battery of tests used will have to be expanded. Since most software products follow the incremental model, they will need to use regression testing.

CHAPTER 15

Distributing the
Software

Once the application has been developed, debugged, and thoroughly tested, it's time to distribute it to the end user. There are many ways this can be done, including disk media, over the Internet, or on a network. In this chapter, we will explore the issues involved in deploying an application, such as the choice of media and method of distribution. We'll also explore the use of the VB Package and Deployment Wizard to create professional setup applications. Finally, we'll discuss the issues involved in providing patches or updates to existing users.

Identifying the Target Audience

Being aware of the needs of your target audience is an important factor when you are distributing an application. One concern is the level of technology available to the user. For example, a few years ago it would have been important to ask if the average user had access to a CD-ROM drive or if distribution on 3.5-inch disk would be necessary. Today, that focus is more likely to shift to issues involving the Internet. There are several issues to keep in mind:

- What is the level of technological sophistication of the end user?
- What level of hardware technology will the average user have; for example, will they have CD-ROM drives?
- Does the average end user frequently browse the Internet?
- If so, is Internet distribution feasible?
- Will the program be used on a network?

Answering questions like these will help you develop an effective deployment strategy. For example, what if most users browse the Internet, but they tend to have 33K modems? If your program is large and would take a long time to download, Internet deployment may not be the ideal method to use.

Creating a Setup Program for the Application

The development of the setup program is the final stage of rapid application development. Just like every other phase, it needs to be taken seriously. The ease with which setup wizards can be used to build a setup program can give the developer a smug feeling that he or she can simply speed through the steps of the wizard without adequate testing and planning.

Once the setup program is complete, it is important to test it in a wide variety of scenarios that might be encountered by users. A system should be used that does not have Visual Basic or a previous version of your program installed. This is necessary because Windows programs have a large number of dependencies. By testing the installation on a clean system, you can make sure that you've included every .dll, .ocx, or database file that your program requires for operation. If a computer that has not been exposed to VB or your application is not available, you may consider renting one to test the setup program. In any case, careful planning and documentation must be done to develop a listing of dependencies for your program. You can't completely trust a setup wizard program to automatically detect every .dll file that you need. The Package and Deployment Wizard can determine dependencies by reading a *dependency file*. A dependency file is a text file that is set up like an INI file. For example, an OCX control may have a dependency file that provides information about DLLs the OCX requires as well as CAB file information, and the CAB file URL. Incomplete, missing, or incorrect dependency files can lead to errors in the DLL, OCX, or other files that are loaded by a setup wizard for your project. Therefore, it's always a good idea to sit down and work out the dependencies before running the setup wizard. Most ActiveX controls will have some documentation to help you do this. Another important point to keep in mind is the licensing requirements for any ActiveX controls your project uses. Make sure that you have the right to distribute the control before including it in your setup program.

Don't forget that the setup program will be the first impression customers have of your program. First impressions often leave the deepest impact, so it's important to make sure your setup program is professional and runs smoothly.

Package and Deployment Wizard

The Package and Deployment Wizard is Microsoft's latest incarnation of the Setup Wizard of the past. The wizard has been extended with many new features to make it a more powerful tool. It can be opened by browsing the Visual Basic 6 folder and selecting *Microsoft Visual Basic 6.0 Tools*.

Figure 15-1
The Package and
Deployment Wizard.

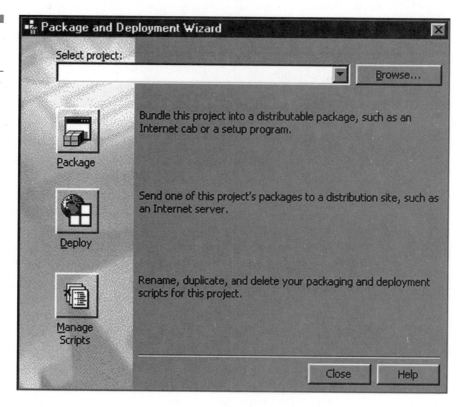

When you open the Package and Deployment Wizard, the first screen
provides three options (see Fig. 15-1):

- *Package*: Selecting the *Package* option will load a wizard that steps
  you through the process of creating a self-extracting executable or a
  CAB file.
- *Deploy*: Selecting the *Deploy* button steps you through the deployment phase, where you can choose the media of distribution.
- *Manage Scripts*: This button allows you to manage the scripts used in
  the packaging and deployment phases.

At the top of the wizard's first screen, you'll see a drop-down list and
Browse button, which allow you to select a project to work with. Projects
that have already gone through the Package and Deployment Wizard
will be available in the drop-down list. Use the Browse button if this is
the first time for your project.

Before you use the Package and Deployment Wizard, it is a good idea to compile the project. If you have not compiled the project, or if source code files are newer than the latest compile, the wizard will ask you if you wish to compile. If you select *Yes*, it will compile the program before moving to the next step.

Package If you select the Package button, the second step is to select the type of setup program that you want to create (see Fig. 15-2). Options include:

- *Standard Setup Package*: This creates a standard setup.exe program that can be used to install your program on end user's machines.

- *Internet Package*: This type of package is used for CAB files. A CAB file contains INF files, OCX files, and any dependencies for the application.

- *Dependency File*: This option will create a dependency file for your application.

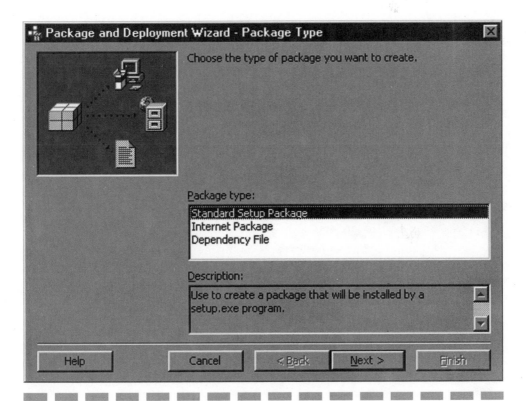

Figure 15-2 The Package Type screen.

Creating a Standard Setup Program   If you select *Standard Setup Package*, the wizard will ask you where you want the setup package assembled (see Fig. 15-3). You can select an existing folder, create a new folder, or select a location over the network.

If you are packaging an application that uses Data Access Objects, the Package and Deployment Wizard will open a screen that allows you to include the relevant database drivers with your setup program. The screen is divided into two panels. On the left, you will see the drivers that are on your system. This will include drivers for Access, ODBC, and others. Select the drivers that you wish to include in the setup program with the arrow buttons. The selected drivers will be displayed in the right-hand window pane.

The next step is to review the Included Files screen, shown in Fig. 15-4. This screen displays a listing of files that the Package and

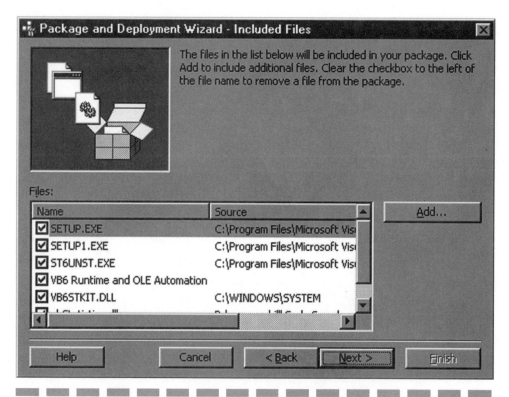

Figure 15-3   *Selecting a folder for your package.*

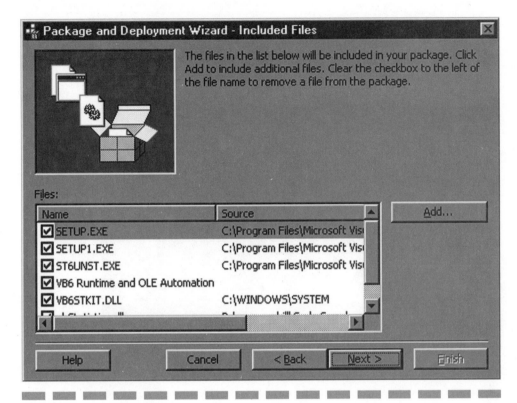

Figure 15-4 Included Files.

Deployment Wizard has determined should be included with your setup program. These files are shown in the *Files:* list in the lower half of the window. If you carefully documented the files your program needs before loading the wizard, you can compare your list to the list shown here to make sure nothing is missing. Additional files can be included by selecting the Add button on the right side of the screen. Files that don't need to be included can be removed by deselecting the appropriate check box in the *Files:* list.

In Fig. 15-5, you'll see the CAB Options screen. Here you can decide whether or not your setup program should use a single CAB file or use multiple CABs. Recall that a CAB file will contain any INF files, OCX files, or other dependencies used by your application. The type of deployment that you plan to use will determine which option you select here. The only time that you will use multiple CAB files is if you will distrib-

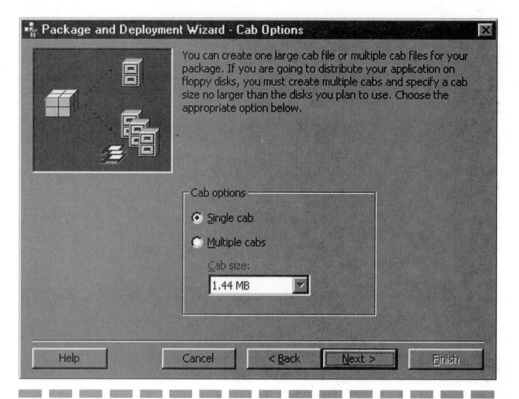

Figure 15-5   Setting Cab Options.

ute the application on floppy disk. If you select *Multiple cabs*, the *Cab size:* drop-down list will be enabled. Here you can select a CAB size to match the capacity of the floppy disks you will be using. Your choices include 1.44 MB, 2.88 MB, 1.2 MB, and 720 KB. If you will use a CD-ROM, the Internet, a network location, or a folder on your local machine, use a single CAB file.

The next screen is the Installation Title screen, shown in Fig. 15-6. Here you can specify the installation title that is displayed when the setup program is run. The project name you specified on the General tab of the Project Properties dialog box of Visual Basic will be inserted here. You can accept this default or type in a new value. The installation title can be up to 256 characters in length and can include spaces. While you probably don't want a 256-character installation title, you should take advantage of the allowed size and give your application a meaningful name.

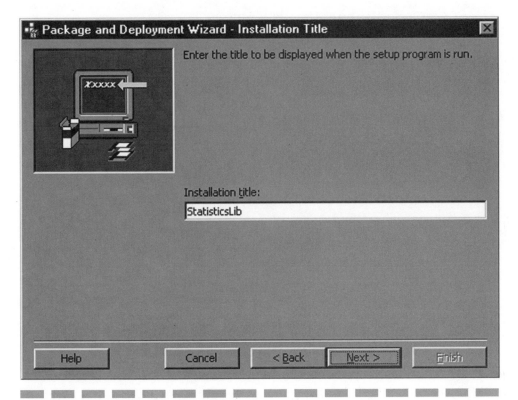

Figure 15-6 *Selecting an Installation title.*

The next step is the Start Menu Items screen (see Fig. 15-7). This allows you to specify how your application will be displayed in the Windows Start menu. You can add additional groups or menu items by clicking the New Group and New Item buttons, respectively. You should give the Start menu items meaningful, descriptive names. If an executable file has a cryptic name, you can change the name displayed by clicking on the *Properties* button. If you add a new item or select the *Properties* button, the Start Menu Item Properties dialog box will open (see Fig. 15-8). Use the *Name:* field to specify the text displayed in the Start menu. The *Target:* drop-down list can be used to select the application or help file that the menu item will represent, and the *Start in:* drop-down list specifies the location where the item can be loaded.

The Install Locations screen allows you to specify where the files in the installation package will be deployed. Each file that can be modified is displayed in the Files grid. You can change where the file will be

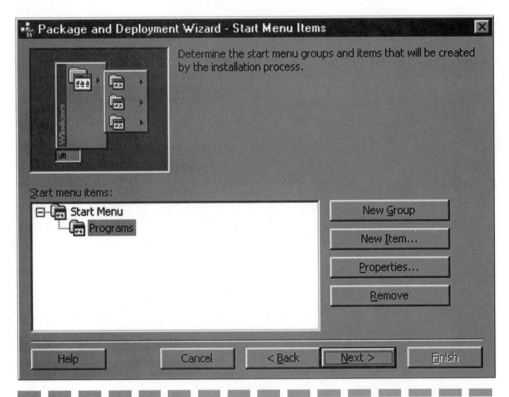

Figure 15-7   Building the Start Menu for your project.

Figure 15-8
Setting the properties
of a Start Menu item.

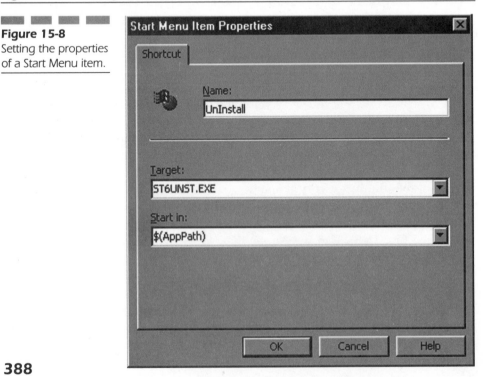

388

installed by clicking open the *Install Location* drop-down list, which is the third column for each file. Options will include Application Path, Common Files, Program Files, and Windows System Path, among others. If you are including DLLs with your application, you may want to place them in the Windows System directory, for example.

The Shared Files screen allows you to specify that a file will be used by multiple applications. This means that if the user decides to run an uninstall program to remove your application, the shared files will remain on the hard disk. This ensures that uninstalling your program does not cause any disruptions of other computer activities. If all applications that use the file have been removed, then the shared file will be deleted by the uninstall program.

The final screen for the standard setup option is the Finished! screen. The Package and Deployment Wizard gives you the option of specifying a script name. A script allows you to reuse the setup configuration that you specified for the project. When you click *Finish*, the wizard will create the setup files. When the process is complete, the wizard will display a packaging report. This report will provide information about the location of CAB files and batch files that can be used to re-create the CAB files after any modifications have been made. The report can be saved if desired.

Internet Packaging   If you select *Internet Package*, the first two screens will be the same ones used in standard setup. The wizard will prompt you to specify a package folder and will then display a listing of included files. The next step is the File Source screen shown in Fig. 15-9. The Package and Deployment Wizard will create a run-time CAB file for each component in your project. These CAB files can be linked to a web site so the user can receive the latest download. Microsoft components will be linked to the Microsoft web site. For other CAB files, you can either provide another URL or select *Include in this cab*.

The next window is the Safety Setting screen. Each component of the project will be listed. You can specify if the component is safe for scripting and safe for initialization. Once all settings are specified, you can click the Next button to complete the creation of the CAB file.

Creating a Dependency File   You can create a dependency file for your project from the Package Type screen. The dependency file will list all the OCX, DLL, and other files that your project requires for operation. If the Package and Deployment Wizard finds a component in your project without dependency information, it will open the Missing Dependency Information dialog box. You can proceed to build a depend-

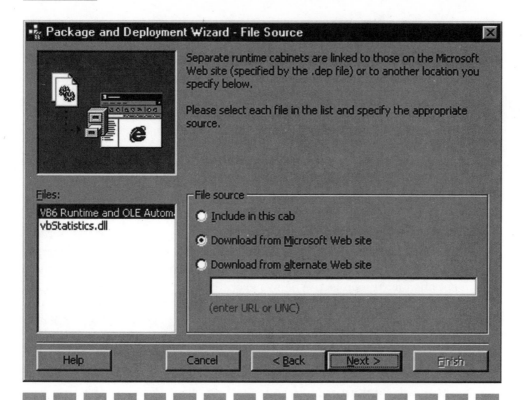

Figure 15-9   CAB File Source for a component.

ency file for your project by clicking the *OK* button. You will also be notified if there are any out-of-date dependency files.

The Included Files screen will show you a list of the files on which your project is dependent. You can click the *Add* button to add additional files. The next step is the CAB Information Screen. If you wish to create dependency information for use on the Web, you can do so by packaging the dependency information into a CAB file. To do this, enter the name of the CAB file, the URL where the CAB file can be downloaded, and the default file to execute when the CAB is downloaded. This must be a file with an *.inf* or *.exe* extension.

The next screen is the Install Locations screen. This lists the name of each component, the source location on your computer, and the install location. Once this information is complete, the Finished! screen will appear, on which you can create the dependency file. The following is a simple dependency file for a VB project for a project named *Vending_Manager*:

```
[Version]
Version=2.1.0.0

[Vending_Manager.exe <0009>]
Dest=$(AppPath)
Date=5/16/99
Time=12:00
Version=2.1.0.0
CABFilename=Vending_Manager.CAB
CABINFFile=Vending_Manager.INF
Uses1=MSVBVM60.DLL
Uses2=OLEAUT32.DLL
Uses3=OLEPRO32.DLL
Uses4=ASYCFILT.DLL
Uses5=STDOLE2.TLB
Uses6=COMCAT.DLL
Uses7=MSADO15.DLL
Uses8=MSDBRPT.DLL
Uses9=SCRRUN.DLL
Uses10=vbStatistics.dll
Uses11=COMDLG32.OCX
Uses12=DBGRID32.OCX
Uses13=DBLIST32.OCX
Uses14=MSCAL.OCX
Uses15=THREED32.OCX
Uses16=MSCOMCTL.OCX
Uses17=MSADODC.OCX
Uses18=MSCOMCT2.OCX
Uses19=MSCHRT20.OCX
Uses20=COMCT332.OCX

[MSDBRPT.DLL <0009>]
Dest=$(WinSysPath)
Date=6/18/98
Time=00:00
Version=6.0.81.69
```

Notice that each section is delimited by a title in brackets. Version information is available, along with the date and time at which the executable was compiled. File destination information is provided along with a list of the DLL and OCX files the project depends on.

Using Third-Party Utilities

The Package and Deployment Wizard is a significant improvement over previous versions of the VB Setup Wizard. However, many developers continue to find that other third-party setup tools are useful for their needs. Many third-party tools provide professional setup programs for your application and include many options, such as the ability to add password protection; customize setup screens, such as by using different colors and fonts; create a single executable file to use for installation;

display licensing agreements; and add typical, custom, and minimum setup options. If you work with multiple programming languages, you may find that owning a third-party setup tool is useful. Some of the most popular setup programs include Setup 98 from Sax Software, PC-Install from 20/20 Software, InstallShield Express from Install Shield Software, and Setup Factory from Indigo Rose Design Corporation.

Distribution of the Software

In today's world, there are several methods that can be used to distribute a software product. The days of the 5-inch diskette have been replaced by a wide range of choices. This includes 3.5-inch disk, CD-ROM, the Internet, and network distribution. The choice that you make for distribution will depend on the users of your product and may involve one or more of these options. Distribution methods should be as flexible as possible, so that the end user can select the most convenient option.

CD-ROM or Disk

The CD-ROM is currently the most popular means for deploying an application. CD-ROMs are low in cost while providing ample storage space for most projects. The availability of low-cost CD writing devices makes the option of distribution on CD-ROM available to software companies of all sizes, all the way down to a single consultant. A CD-ROM is also easier to ship. If you need to distribute a large number of CDs, low-cost duplication services are available. Distribution on CD-ROM also makes life easier for the end user. Instead of having to sit there and pop disks in and out during installation, he or she can just pop in the CD-ROM and let it run. Even the smallest application in 32-bit Windows is likely to take at least 10 floppy disks to install, so it's clear that a CD-ROM provides a more convenient means of distribution. If you plan to use CD-ROM deployment, you should use the Package and Deployment Wizard to create a folder deployment on your machine and then burn the folder to a CD-ROM. This means that you will create a single CAB file from the Cab Options screen.

Despite the advantages and popularity of CD-ROM deployment, you are likely to come across some users who do not have a CD-ROM drive on their computer. As a result, it is a good idea to have installation using 3.5-inch disks available for these users. If you are using floppy-based distribution you must specify a *Multiple cabs* option for the setup package.

Internet Distribution

Internet distribution is becoming an increasingly attractive option for software companies, especially small ones. The user can be given a password that allows the software to be downloaded from a secure web site. Another option that can be used is to have a "demo" version of the software. This demo can be downloaded by users free of charge, and if they like it they can call for a password or ID to activate the software. Internet distribution can save time and money by avoiding shipping costs and time spent packaging and duplicating disks. This option also has appeal for the end user since he or she can enjoy the feeling of instant gratification rather than having to wait for the product to arrive by mail. However, this option still remains limited. If your program is even of moderate size, the long download time may be unattractive. Users may also demand a printed manual, and they might prefer to have something "solid" to represent their purchase, such as the CD-ROM. Some users may not even have access to the Internet, although this is becoming less of a factor.

Workstation Duplication and Distribution

If you are developing applications for internal use by a large organization, you will probably use some form of network-based deployment. Arrangements can be made with the network administrator to provide a folder where the deployment will be stored and accessed. You can then use the Package and Deployment Wizard to create the setup program. When using network-based deployment, you will specify a single CAB file from the Cab Options screen.

When packaging is complete, click the *Deploy* button. The first screen will allow you to select a script to use for the deployment. The next screen is the Deployment Method screen, shown in Fig. 15-10. The Deployment Method list box provides a list of deployment options. You will select *Folder* for most options, including CD-ROM, floppy disk, and network-based deployment. If you are using CD-ROM or floppy disk, you can copy from the folder to the distribution media later on.

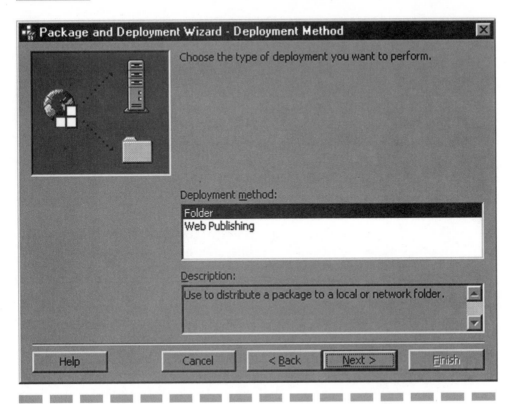

Figure 15-10   *Selecting a Deployment Method.*

The next screen is the Folder screen, which allows you to select the folder used for deployment. If you are using network-based deployment, click on the *Network* button to select the appropriate folder. Once this is done, the Wizard loads the Finished! screen, which allows you to specify a script name where you can save the settings in a file known by the script name. If you click the *Finish* button, the wizard will create the deployment package.

Managing Scripts

Once a setup program has been created for your project, you can save the selections you made in a script file. Scripts can be managed later by clicking the *Manage Scripts* button of the Package and Deployment Wizard. Scripts are divided into packaging scripts and deployment

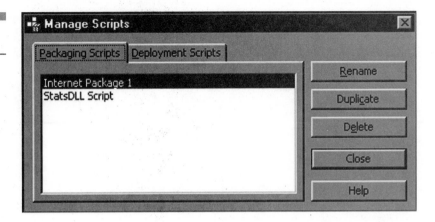

Figure 15-11
Managing Scripts.

scripts, which can be accessed by clicking the appropriate tab on the Manage Scripts dialog (see Fig. 15-11). Options are available to rename, duplicate, or delete a script.

Patches and Updating Applications

Throughout the lifetime of an application, chances are it will be updated as bugs are corrected and new features are added. To handle these situations you will need to create new setup packages. The nature of these packages will be determined on a case-by-case basis. Patches can be divided into two cases: fixing bugs and adding updated components. For example, if you are correcting a bug in the application, you might only need to ship a new executable file. Rather than mailing it to your customers on CD, it may be more attractive to provide the file for download off the Web.

If your application uses any third-party ActiveX controls, new versions of these controls will be released from time to time. If they provide extended functionality, you may be interested in including the new controls in your application. This will require shipping a new executable, the OCX file, and any new DLL dependencies for the ActiveX control. Another scenario, when a patch will be used to update a component, can include an update to a DLL file that your application uses directly.

Software products typically go through several iterations or versions. As each version is released, it will be provided to existing customers in the form of an update. An update will require a different setup package than a full version provided to a new customer. The update might include a subset of project files, including new ActiveX controls and other dependencies. Data files and initialization files associated with the application will probably be left out of an update setup package.

APPENDIX

Code Samples

Bank Simulation Program

```vb
'Customer Class
Option Explicit
Private mName As String
Private mCustomerID As String * 12
Private mAddress As String
Private mInBank As Boolean
Public Property Get Name() As String
 Name = mName
End Property
Public Property Let Name(ByVal strNewValue As String)
 mName = strNewValue
End Property
Public Property Get InBank() As Boolean
 InBank = mInBank
End Property
Public Property Let InBank(ByVal blnNewValue As Boolean)
 mInBank = blnNewValue
End Property
Public Property Get Address() As String
 Address = mAddress
End Property

Public Property Let Address(ByVal strNewValue As String)
 mAddress = strNewValue
End Property
Public Property Get CustomerID() As String
 CustomerID = mCustomerID
End Property

Public Property Let CustomerID(ByVal strNewValue As String)

 If Len(strNewValue) = 12 Then
   mCustomerID = strNewValue
 Else
   MsgBox "Cannot Set Customer ID"
 End If

End Property

'Account Class
Option Explicit
Private mCustomerID As String * 12
```

```
Private mType As String
Private mBalance As Currency

Public Property Get CustomerID() As String
 CustomerID = mCustomerID
End Property

Public Property Let CustomerID(ByVal strNewValue As String)
 mCustomerID = strNewValue
End Property

Public Property Get AccountType() As String
  AccountType = mType
End Property

Public Property Let AccountType(ByVal strNewValue As String)
 mType = strNewValue
End Property

Public Property Get Balance() As Currency
 Balance = mBalance
End Property

Public Property Let Balance(ByVal curNewValue As Currency)
 mBalance = curNewValue
End Property

Public Function WITHDRAWAL(Amount As Currency) As Boolean

 If Amount < mBalance Then
   mBalance = mBalance - Amount
   WITHDRAWAL = True
 Else
   WITHDRAWAL = False
 End If

End Function

Public Sub Deposit(Amount As Currency)
 mBalance = mBalance + Amount
End Sub

 'Customers and Accounts Collection Classes
 Option Explicit
 Public colAccounts As New Collection
 Public colCustomers As New Collection

 'Subroutine to run the Simulation

 Public Sub RunSimulation()
  'enable timer to allow customers to enter bank
  frmBank.tmrAddCustomer.Enabled = True

  'set time to 9:00 a.m.
  datTime = TimeSerial(9, 0, 0)

  'update time display for user
  frmBank.lblTime = CStr(datTime)
```

```
'get the current hour
intHour = Hour(datTime)

'run the simulation until 3:00 p.m.
Do While intHour < 15
'Process the customer line
Call ProcessCustomer
'increment the clock and update user display
datTime = DateAdd("n", 1, datTime)
intHour = Hour(datTime)
frmBank.lblTime = CStr(datTime)
'process events so timer event can fire
DoEvents

Loop

frmBank.tmrAddCustomer.Enabled = False

End Sub
```

TmrAddCustomer Timer Event:
```
Private Sub tmrAddCustomer_Timer()
 Dim dblRandom As Double
 Dim intHour As Integer
 Dim objPerson As New clsCustomer
 Dim blnAddCustomer As Boolean
 Dim temp

 Static MaxCustomers As Integer

 intHour = Hour(datTime)
 dblRandom = Rnd * 100

 blnAddCustomer = False

 If (intHour > 11) And (intHour < 13) Then

    If dblRandom > 50 Then

      blnAddCustomer = True

    End If

  ElseIf dblRandom > 75 Then

    blnAddCustomer = True

  End If

  If blnAddCustomer Then

    Set objPerson = ReturnCustomer
    lstCustomerLine.ListItems.Add
    temp = lstCustomerLine.ListItems.Count
    lstCustomerLine.ListItems.Item(temp).Text = objPerson.
      CustomerID
    lstCustomerLine.ListItems.Item(temp).SubItems(1) =
objPerson.Name
```

```
      End If
   End Sub
   Public Function ReturnCustomer() As clsCustomer

   Dim objPerson As New clsCustomer
   Dim intKey As Integer

   Do

     intKey = Int(MAX) * Rnd + 1
     Set objPerson = colCustomers.Item(CStr(intKey))
     If objPerson.InBank = False Then
        objPerson.InBank = True
        Set ReturnCustomer = objPerson
        Set objPerson = Nothing
        Exit Function
     End If

   Loop

 End Function
```

EXAMPLE: OPENING A SEQUENTIAL FILE WITH FILE SYSTEM OBJECTS

```
Option Explicit

Private strFileName As String
Private fsoFile As New FileSystemObject
Private MyFile As File
Private MyTextStream As TextStream

Private Sub cmdOpenFile_Click()
On Error Resume Next
 CommonDialog1.ShowOpen
 strFileName = CommonDialog1.FileName
 If (Trim(strFileName) = "") Then Exit Sub  'if user hits cancel,
   file name is blank string
 If (fsoFile.FileExists(strFileName) = False) Then
     'file not there, ask the user if he or she wants to create it
     Dim resp As Integer
     resp = MsgBox("File Does Not Exist. Create?", vbYesNo)
     If resp = vbYes Then
        'create the file
        Call fsoFile.CreateTextFile(strFileName)
     Else
        Exit Sub
     End If
 End If

 'get a reference to the file
 Set MyFile = fsoFile.GetFile(strFileName)

 'test to make sure file is not too big
 If MyFile.Size > 32768 Then
   MsgBox "Error: File is too large to open. Max file size is 64k."
```

```
    Exit Sub
End If
Set MyTextStream = MyFile.OpenAsTextStream(ForReading)
'read it in
Text1.Text = MyTextStream.ReadAll
MyTextStream.Close

txtFileName.Text = strFileName
txtLastModified = MyFile.DateLastModified
txtSize = MyFile.Size
txtFileType = MyFile.Type

End Sub

Private Sub cmdWriteFile_Click()
On Error Resume Next

Set MyTextStream = MyFile.OpenAsTextStream(ForWriting)
MyTextStream.Write (Text1.Text)
MyTextStream.Close
MsgBox "File" & strFileName & "has been saved."
End Sub
```

Reading Random Access Files

```
Option Explicit

Type Employee
 Last As String * 20
 First As String * 10
 Phone As String * 13
 Title As String * 20
 Date_Hired As Date
End Type

Private Sub cmdRead_Click()

Dim intFileNum As Integer
Dim lngRecLength As Long
Dim i As Integer
Dim MyEmployees(1 To 100) As Employee
Dim NumRecs As Integer
Dim itmEmployee As ListItem

intFileNum = FreeFile
lngRecLength = LenB(MyEmployees(1))

Open "C:\Employees.Dat" For Random Access Read As #intFileNum Len =
  lngRecLength

For i = 1 To 100

 Get #intFileNum, , MyEmployees(i)
 Set itmEmployee = lstEmployees.ListItems.Add(, ,
   MyEmployees(i).Last)
```

```
  itmEmployee.SubItems(1) = MyEmployees(i).First
  itmEmployee.SubItems(2) = MyEmployees(i).Title

Next i

Close #intFileNum

End Sub
```

Reading/Writing Binary Files

```
Option Explicit
Dim NumRows As Integer
Dim NumCols As Integer

Private Sub cmdWriteFile_Click()

 Dim strFileName As String
 Dim intFileNum As Integer
 Dim i As Integer, j As Integer
 Dim intVal As Integer

 strFileName = InputBox("Enter File Name", "Binary Files")

 If Trim(strFileName) = "" Then
   MsgBox "No File Name Entered"
   Exit Sub
 End If

 intFileNum = FreeFile

 Open strFileName For Binary As intFileNum
 For i = 1 To NumRows - 1
  flxData.Row = i
  For j = 1 To NumCols - 1
   flxData.Col = j
   intVal = CInt(flxData.Text)
   Put intFileNum, , intVal
  Next j
 Next i

 Close intFileNum

 MsgBox "File Written"

End Sub

Private Sub cmdReadFile_Click()

 Dim strFileName As String
 Dim intFileNum As Integer
 Dim i As Integer, j As Integer
 Dim intVal As Integer
 strFileName = InputBox("Enter File Name", "Binary Files")
 If Trim(strFileName) = "" Then
```

```
   MsgBox "No File Name Entered"
   Exit Sub
 End If

 intFileNum = FreeFile

 Open strFileName For Binary As intFileNum

 For i = 1 To NumRows - 1
  flxData.Row = i
  For j = 1 To NumCols - 1
   flxData.Col = j
   Get intFileNum, , intVal
   flxData.Text = CStr(intVal)
  Next j
 Next i

 Close intFileNum
 MsgBox "File Read."
End Sub
```

Complaints Program: Illustrating SQL

```
Private Sub cmdAll_Click()

On Error GoTo Err_cmdAll

 strQuery = "Select * from Complaints"
 datComplaints.RecordSource = strQuery
 datComplaints.Refresh
 optDate.Value = False
 optBuilding.Value = False
 Exit Sub

Err_cmdAll:
  MsgBox Err.Description & "  Occurred in cmdAll Click."
  Resume Next
End Sub

Private Sub optDate_Click()
On Error GoTo Err_optDate

 strQuery = "Select * from Complaints Order By Date"
 datComplaints.RecordSource = strQuery
 datComplaints.Refresh
 Exit Sub

Err_optDate:
  MsgBox Err.Number & "Occurred in optDate Click"
  Resume Next

End Sub
Private Sub optBuilding_Click()
```

```
On Error GoTo Err_optBuilding

 strQuery = "Select * from Complaints Order By Building"
 datComplaints.RecordSource = strQuery
 datComplaints.Refresh
 Exit Sub

Err_optBuilding:
 MsgBox Err.Number & "Occurred in optBuilding Click"
 Resume Next

End Sub

Private Sub cmdRunQuery_Click()
On Error GoTo Err_cmdRunQuery

 strQuery = "Select * from Complaints "

 If chkDate.Value Then

     strQuery = strQuery & "where Date Between #" & txtStartDate.
       Text _
        & "# And #" & txtEndDate.Text & "#"

 End If

 If chkBuilding.Value Then
 If chkDate.Value Then
   strQuery = strQuery & " AND "
  Else
   strQuery = strQuery & " WHERE "
  End If
  strQuery = strQuery & " Building = '" & dbBuildings.Text & "'"

 End If

 If chkEmployee.Value Then

   If chkDate.Value Or chkBuilding.Value Then
    strQuery = strQuery & " AND "
   Else
    strQuery = strQuery & "  WHERE "
   End If
   strQuery = strQuery & " Employee = '" & dbEmployees.Text & "'"

 End If

 strQuery = strQuery & " ORDER BY Date"
 datComplaints.RecordSource = strQuery
 datComplaints.Refresh

 Exit Sub

Err_cmdRunQuery:

 MsgBox Err.Description & " Occurred in cmdRunQuery Click"
 Resume Next

End Sub
```

Statistics Library: clsStatistics Class

```
Public Event VarianceCalculated()

'We can raise this event once the variance is calculated to let the
  client know that they 'can read the standard deviation.

Public Function Variance(dblInputData() As Double, intNumItems As
  Integer)
' Function : Variance
' Description : Finds the sample variance for the data
'            stored in the dblInputData array,
'            and sets the standard deviation,
'            which is the square root of the variance
' Parameters: dblInputData : array of type Double, contains data
'            intNumItems : total number of data points

  Dim i As Integer          'variable to function as loop counter
  Dim dblSumX As Double          'sum of the data elements
  Dim dblSumSquared As Double 'sum of data elements squared

  'loop through the array and sum the data and squares
  For i = 1 To intNumItems

    dblSumX = dblSumX + dblInputData(i)
    dblSumSquared = dblSumSquared + dblInputData(i) * dblInputData(i)

  Next i
  Variance = (dblSumSquared - (dblSumX * dblSumX / intNumItems)) /  _
          (intNumItems - 1)

  'store the standard deviation
  mdblStdDev = Sqr(Variance)

  RaiseEvent VarianceCalculated 'let the client know the standard
    deviation can be read

End Function

Public Function MeanAbsDeviation(dblInputData() As Double,
intNumItems As Integer)

 'Function : Mean Absolute Deviation
 'Description: This function calculates the absolute value of the
   spread
 '          of values about the mean.
 'Input Parameters: dblInputData :an array of type Double, contains
   the data
 '            intNumItems : total number of data points

  Dim dblSumDeviation As Double 'variable that holds the sum of x -
    xbar
  Dim dblDeviation As Double  'the deviation for each array element,
    x - xbar
  Dim dblAverage As Double        'local variable to hold the average
    or mean
  Dim i As Integer        'loop counter
```

```
    dblAverage = mean(dblInputData, intNumItems) 'find the average

    'The following loop calculates the sum of the individual deviations
    For i = 1 To intNumItems

    dblDeviation = Abs(dblInputData(i) - dblAverage)    'get absolute value
    dblSumDeviation = dblSumDeviation + dblDeviation

    Next i

    MeanAbsDeviation = dblSumDeviation / intNumItems

End Function

Public Function mean(dblInputData() As Double, intNumItems As Integer)

' Function : Mean
' Description : Finds the mean for a set of data. Sum(X)/N

    Dim i As Integer
    Dim dblSumX As Double

    For i = 1 To intNumItems

     dblSumX = dblSumX + dblInputData(i)

    Next i

    mean = dblSumX / intNumItems

End Function

Public Function Median(dblInputData() As Double, intNumItems As
    Integer)
' Function : Median
' Description: Finds the median. This function assumes that the data
    is
'           ordered.

    Dim intMedianLocation As Integer

    intMedianLocation = (intNumItems + 1) / 2

    mintHingeLocation = (intMedianLocation + 1) / 2

    'if the number of elements is even, the median is an average
    If intNumItems Mod 2 = 0 Then
      Median = (dblInputData(intMedianLocation) + _
              dblInputData(intMedianLocation + 1)) / 2
    Else
     Median = dblInputData(intMedianLocation)
    End If

End Function

Public Function Z_Score(dblInputData() As Double, intLocation As
    Integer, intNumItems As Integer)

'Function : Z_Score
```

```
'Description : Calculates the z score for the element at position
  intLocation
'Parameters : dblInputData() :  Array of data elements, type Double
'        intLocation : Array index that locates the element for which
            to find z score
'        intNumItems : total number of elements

Dim dblAverage As Double 'variable to hold the mean
Dim i As Integer     'loop counter
Dim dblStdDeviation As Double 'variable to hold the standard
  deviation

'find the mean
dblAverage = mean(dblInputData, intNumItems)

'find the standard deviation
dblStdDeviation = Sqr(Variance(dblInputData, intNumItems))

'calculate the z score

Z_Score = (dblInputData(intLocation) - dblAverage) / dblStdDeviation

End Function

Public Property Get HingeLocation() As Integer

 HingeLocation = mintHingeLocation

End Property

Public Property Get StandardDeviation() As Double

 StandardDeviation = mdblStdDev
End Property
```

Using the clsStatistics Object in Code

```
Option Explicit

Private Const MaxItems As Integer = 1000
Private dblArrayData(1 To MaxItems) As Double

Private WithEvents objStatistics As clsStats

Private dblMean As Double
Private dblVariance As Double
Private dblStandardDeviation As Double
Private dbAbsDeviation As Double
Private dblZScore As Double

'load test data
Private Sub cmdLoadData_Click()
 Dim i As Integer
```

```
 For i = 1 To MaxItems
  dblArrayData(i) = Rnd * 100
  lstData.AddItem dblArrayData(i)
 Next i

End Sub

Private Sub cmdCalculate_Click()

  'find the mean
  dblMean = objStatistics.mean(dblArrayData, MaxItems)
  'find the variance
  dblVariance = objStatistics.Variance(dblArrayData, MaxItems)
  'find the average deviation
  dblAbsDeviation = objStatistics. MeanAbsDeviation (dblArrayData,
    MaxItems)

  'display the results in the text boxes
  txtAverage.Text = CStr(dblMean)
  txtVariance.Text = CStr(dblVariance)
  txtAbsDeviation.Text = CStr(dblAbsDeviation)

End Sub

Private Sub cmdZScore_Click()

 Dim intIndex As Integer
 Dim dblSelectedValue As Double

 intIndex = lstData.ListIndex + 1

 dblSelectedValue = dblArrayData(intIndex)

 dblZScore = objStatistics.Z_Score(dblArrayData, intIndex, MaxItems)
 MsgBox "The Z Score for " & CStr(dblSelectedValue) & " Is " &
   CStr(dblZScore)

End Sub

'use the form load event to instantiate a new clsStatistics object
Private Sub Form_Load()
 Set objStatistics = New clsStats
End Sub

'when the stats library raises the variance calculated event, report
  the standard deviation
Private Sub objStatistics_VarianceCalculated()

 dblStandardDeviation = objStatistics.StandardDeviation
 txtStdDev.Text = CStr(dblStandardDeviation)

End Sub
```

EXAMPLE: ACTIVEX CONTROL

```
'This ActiveX control uses constituent timer and text box controls to
  'function as an alarm clock.
Option Explicit
```

```
Private mAlarmTime As Date
Private mAlarmForeColor As OLE_COLOR
Private mCurrentTime As Date
Private mAlarmSet As Boolean

Public Property Get AlarmTime() As Date
 AlarmTime = mAlarmTime

End Property

Public Property Let AlarmTime(ByVal dtmNewValue As Date)

 mAlarmTime = dtmNewValue
 txtAlarmClock.Text = CStr(mAlarmTime)
 PropertyChanged "AlarmTime"

End Property

Public Property Get CurrentTime() As Date

 CurrentTime = mCurrentTime

End Property

Public Property Let CurrentTime(ByVal dtmNewValue As Date)

 mCurrentTime = dtmNewValue
 txtTime.Text = CStr(mCurrentTime)
 PropertyChanged "CurrentTime"

End Property

Public Property Get AlarmForeColor() As OLE_COLOR

 AlarmForeColor = mAlarmForeColor

End Property

Public Property Let AlarmForeColor(ByVal bytNewValue As OLE_COLOR)

 mAlarmForeColor = bytNewValue
 txtAlarmClock.ForeColor = mAlarmForeColor
 PropertyChanged "AlarmForeColor"

End Property

Public Property Get AlarmSet() As Boolean

 AlarmSet = mAlarmSet

End Property

Public Property Let AlarmSet(ByVal blnNewValue As Boolean)
 mAlarmSet = blnNewValue
 chkSetAlarm.Value = mAlarmSet
 PropertyChanged "AlarmSet"

End Property

'the snooze method allows the user to reset the alarm with a
  five-minute delay
```

```
Public Sub Snooze()

 mAlarmTime = DateAdd("n", 5, mAlarmTime)
 txtAlarmClock.Text = CStr(mAlarmTime)

End Sub

Private Sub UserControl_InitProperties()

 mAlarmTime = Now
 mCurrentTime = Now
 mAlarmForeColor = vbBlack
 txtAlarmClock.Text = CStr(mAlarmTime)
 txtTime.Text = CStr(mCurrentTime)

End Sub

Private Sub UserControl_WriteProperties(PropBag As PropertyBag)

 PropBag.WriteProperty "AlarmTime", mAlarmTime, Now
 PropBag.WriteProperty "CurrentTime", mCurrentTime, Now
 PropBag.WriteProperty "AlarmForeColor", mAlarmForeColor, vbBlack

End Sub

Private Sub UserControl_ReadProperties(PropBag As PropertyBag)

 'read the saved property values
 mAlarmTime = PropBag.ReadProperty("AlarmTime", Now)
 mCurrentTime = PropBag.ReadProperty("CurrentTime", Now)
 mAlarmForeColor = PropBag.ReadProperty("AlarmForeColor", vbBlack)
 'display property values in text boxes
 txtAlarmClock.ForeColor = mAlarmForeColor
 txtAlarmClock.Text = CStr(mAlarmTime)

End Sub

Private Sub Timer1_Timer()

 If Ambient.UserMode = True Then
  'update the current time
  mCurrentTime = Now
  txtTime.Text = CStr(mCurrentTime)

  'check to see if the current time
  'is the time set for the alarm
  If mCurrentTime > mAlarmTime Then

  'if it is, turn on the alarm
  Do While chkSetAlarm.Value = Checked
   Beep
   DoEvents
  Loop
   End If     'current time greater than alarm time

   End If      'Ambient user mode is true

End Sub
```

```
Public Sub ShowAbout()

 frmAbout.Show vbModal

End Sub

Private Sub txtCurrentTime_Change()
  Changed = True
End Sub

Private Sub txtAlarmTime_Change()
  Changed = True
End Sub

Private Sub chkAlarmSet_Click()
  Changed = True
End Sub

Private Sub PropertyPage_ApplyChanges()
  SelectedControls(0).AlarmSet = (chkAlarmSet.Value = vbChecked)
  SelectedControls(0).CurrentTime = txtCurrentTime.Text
  SelectedControls(0).AlarmTime = txtAlarmTime.Text
End Sub

Private Sub PropertyPage_SelectionChanged()
  chkAlarmSet.Value = (SelectedControls(0).AlarmSet And vbChecked)
  txtCurrentTime.Text = SelectedControls(0).CurrentTime
  txtAlarmTime.Text = SelectedControls(0).AlarmTime
End Sub
```

Using the Web Browser Control

```
Private Sub Form_Resize()

 WebBrowser1.Height = Me.Height - MAXHEIGHT
 WebBrowser1.Width = Me.Width - MAXWIDTH

End Sub

Private Sub cmdMicrosoft_Click()

  WebBrowser1.Navigate "http://www.microsoft.com"

End Sub

Private Sub cmdYahoo_Click()

  WebBrowser1.Navigate "http://www.yahoo.com"

End Sub

Private Sub cmdGo_Click()
```

```
    Dim strURL As String
    strURL = txtURL.Text
    WebBrowser1.Navigate strURL

End Sub

Private Sub cmdStop_Click()

  WebBrowser1.Stop

End Sub

Private Sub cmdBack_Click()

  WebBrowser1.GoBack

End Sub

Private Sub cmdForward_Click()

  WebBrowser1.GoForward

End Sub

Private Sub WebBrowser1_DocumentComplete(ByVal pDisp As Object, URL
  As Variant)
  txtURL.Text = WebBrowser1.LocationURL
  Me.Caption = WebBrowser1.LocationName

End Sub
```

An Error-Handling Add-In

```
Private Sub OKButton_Click()

  Dim c As CodePane
  Dim m As Member

  Dim strProcedureName As String
  Dim strOnError As String
  Dim lngProcedureLocation As Long
  Dim lngProcLines As Long
  Dim lngEndPos As Long
  Dim strErrorCode As String
  Dim blnAddHandler As Boolean
  Dim strDisplayError As String
  Dim strResume As String
  Dim intLocated As Integer
  Dim strExit As String
  Dim strHeader As String

'check which option button the user has selected
If optResumeNext.Value = True Then
    strOnError = "On Error Resume Next"
    blnAddHandler = False
  Else
```

```
      blnAddHandler = True
  End If

  For Each c In VBInstance.CodePanes

   For Each m In c.CodeModule.Members
     'if this member is a procedure then add error handling
     If m.Type = vbext_mt_Event Or m.Type = vbext_mt_Method Then
       'get the name of this procedure
       strProcedureName = m.Name
       lngProcedureLocation = m.CodeLocation
       'get header
       strHeader = c.CodeModule.Lines(lngProcedureLocation, 1)
       intLocated = InStr(strHeader, "Sub")
       If intLocated > 0 Then
        strExit = "Exit Sub"
       Else
        strExit = "Exit Function"
       End If
       'add the On Error Statement as the first line of the procedure
       Call c.CodeModule.InsertLines(lngProcedureLocation + 1, _
         strOnError)

       If blnAddHandler = True Then

          'build the on error string and error handler label for this
            procedure
          strOnError = "On Error GoTo err" & strProcedureName
          strDisplayError = "    MsgBox Err.Description"
          strErrorCode = "err" & strProcedureName & ":"

          'find out how many lines of code are in this procedure
          lngProcLines = c.CodeModule.ProcCountLines(strProcedureName, _
            vbext_pk_Proc)
          'get the last line in the procedure where we can insert code
          lngEndPos = lngProcedureLocation + lngProcLines - 2

          'add the Exit string
          Call c.CodeModule.InsertLines(lngEndPos, strExit)

          'insert the error handler
          Call c.CodeModule.InsertLines(lngEndPos + 1, strErrorCode)
          Call c.CodeModule.InsertLines(lngEndPos + 2, _
            strDisplayError)
          Call c.CodeModule.InsertLines(lngEndPos + 3, "    Resume _
            Next")

       End If

       'completed, add the procedure name to the list box
       lstProcedures.AddItem m.Name

     End If

   Next m

  Next c

End Sub
```

INDEX

About the Author

David McMahon is a Microsoft Certified Visual Basic developer. He writes object-oriented software and hardware drivers for Windows NT and 95/98 using Visual Basic and Visual C++. He is also a Microsoft Certification Instructor for Visual Basic and Microsoft Access.